LEARN
New Testament
GREEK

JOHN H. DOBSON

M.A.(Oxon)   B.D.(London)

Bible Society

BIBLE SOCIETY
Stonehill Green, Westlea, Swindon SN5 7DG, England

First published 1988. Reprinted 1988, 1989, 1990.

British Library Cataloguing in Publication Data

Dobson, John H.
  Learn New Testament Greek.
  1. Greek language, Biblical
  I. Title
  478'.4   PA810

ISBN 0–564–07872–7

Printed in Great Britain by BPCC Wheatons Ltd, Exeter

Τοις μαθηταις μου
To my students

ἱνα μαθητε μετα χαρας
so that you may learn joyfully

Contents

Abbreviations

AV	Authorized Version (King James' Version)
GNB	Good News Bible (Today's English Version)
NJB	New Jerusalem Bible
NEB	New English Bible
NIV	New International Version
RSV	Revised Standard Version
RV	Revised Version

Introduction

The New Testament is a remarkable collection of writings. No book has had a more profound influence on the world's history.

If you wish to study the New Testament, it helps greatly if you are able to read it in the original language. With this course it is possible to learn New Testament Greek quickly, even if you have never attempted to learn a language before. After seventeen short lessons you will start reading selected passages from the New Testament, and by the end of the course you will be able to read much of the New Testament without constant reference to a dictionary. You will also have a grasp of the structure of the Greek language and its grammar, an ability to use commentaries that refer to the Greek text, and a growing skill as a translator.

The principles and methods used in *Learn New Testament Greek* ensure that you will make rapid progress with your studies. New information is introduced in small bits, which makes it easy to take in. It is frequently repeated, which makes it easy to remember. You learn words and forms before grammatical descriptions, which is the natural sequence – a child learns "mouse" and "mice" before it learns that "mouse" is a noun and that "mice" is plural. But because you can work through the course quickly, you can also learn the main grammatical forms and terms quickly.

In *Learn New Testament Greek* you will not be asked to memorize long lists of words, or grammatical forms. You will rather learn the principles and pointers which enable you to recognize the meaning and function of words which are new to you. This will equip you to tackle even unfamiliar passages of the New Testament with confidence.

Learning New Testament Greek

You can use these lessons for study *on your own* or *with a teacher*. Most of the Greek sentences and passages are printed with an English translation on the right-hand side of the page. This means that you can start without any fear of making serious mistakes. And, when you read the Greek without looking at the English, you can then immediately check whether you have understood it.

If you have a cassette player you will find the *Learn New Testament Greek* tape a useful aid. You can hear the Greek sentences from the first fourteen chapters read aloud: follow the relevant text as you listen, and your ears and eyes will work together to fix ideas in your mind.

Instructions and suggestions

1. When you begin a new lesson, first read it quickly through, looking at the English and the Greek. Then work through it carefully, reading and translating the passages given.

2. The "Translate" section has a line down the middle. Cover the right-hand column, using a plain piece of card or paper.

3. When you have read a line or a group of lines in Greek, move your piece of card a little way down the page and check that you have understood what the Greek means. If you made a mistake, mark that line and learn from it.

    If you do not know, and cannot guess, the meaning of a word, do not spend a long time looking at it. Use the check-column to find out what it means. Underline it, or highlight it.

4. If you find a lesson difficult you should:
    (a) continue to the end of the lesson
    (b) revise earlier lessons
    (c) go over the difficult lesson again, underlining or highlighting anything you have found to be a problem.

5. Work at your own speed, but go as fast as you can. At the end of each short section, pause for a moment of relaxation: take a few deep breaths, stretch your body, stand up, then start the next section refreshed.

    If you do two lessons a day six days a week, you will complete the course in one month. If you do only one lesson a week, you will still finish in a year. Before you start each new session of study, read through the list of contents up to that point It is a way to revise rapidly the major forms you have learned.

6. **From lesson 17 onwards you will need a copy of the** *Greek New Testament* (see lesson 52.2 for more details).

7. If you are learning Greek because you wish to read the New Testament, you need not worry about how you pronounce it. The Greek language has changed as time has passed, and there is no single way that can be called the "right" way to pronounce Greek words. Lessons 1 and 2 give guidelines, but they are not rules.

8. Copy out key forms, for example ὁ, ἡ, το in lesson 12.7. Write them in clear lettering and put them up where you can see them. Write new words on pieces of thin card, with the Greek on one side and the English on the other. Carry them with you for a few days, and revise them when you have spare moments.

9. Grammatical terms: when you go through the course for the first time, do not spend time and effort trying to learn them. To do so might hinder your efforts to learn Greek. Leave them for more careful study when you have read more of the New Testament. They will make more sense when you revise them later on.

10. As you master the lessons, take any opportunity you can to teach them to someone else. This will increase your own understanding, and your confidence.

11. Enjoy your studies and take pleasure in your progress.

LESSON 1

αβγ – learning the letters

1.1 The Greek alphabet

The first step in learning New Testament Greek is to recognize the letters of the Greek alphabet. Several are similar to English letters, although this can sometimes be misleading (ρ looks like "p" but sounds like "r").

In the first column below, you will find the Greek letters with their closest English equivalents. The second column has groups of Greek letters and tells you how they are pronounced. When you have studied these carefully, try to read the groups of letters in the third column. Cover the fourth column while you read, then use it to check that you have recognized the letters correctly.

Greek letters	Read the groups of letters	Greek groups of letters	English equivalents
α – a			
β – b	αβ – ab	βα αββα	ba abba
γ – g	γαβ – gab	βαγ	bag
δ – d	βαδ – bad	δαβ γαδ δαδ	dab gad dad
ε – e	βεδ – bed	βεγ δεδ αβεδ	beg ded abed
ζ – dz or ds, as in "cords"	βεζ – bedz	βεζ βεδ γαζ δαζ ζεδ βαδ	bedz bed gadz dadz dzed bad
η – ē ("ai", as in "air", or "ay", as in "say")	γη – gē	βη δη ηδ ηζ	bē dē ēd ēdz
θ – th	δεθ – deth	βαθ γαθ βεθ	bath gath beth
ι – i	βιδ – bid	βιγ βιζ διδ ηδιδ	big bids did ēdid
κ – k	κιθ – kith	κιδ κιζ κηκ	kid kidz kēk

Greek letters	Read the groups of letters	Greek groups of letters	English equivalents
λ – l	λιδ – lid	λαδ λεγ βελλ βεθελ	lad leg bell bethel
μ – m	μη – mē	μαθ μηκ καμελ	math mēk camel
ν – n	μαν – man	μεν νημ θιν κιν	men nēm thin kin
ξ – x	αξ – ax	εξ μιξ νιξ νικ λαξ λαζ βιξ βιζ	ex mix nix nik lax ladz bix bidz
ο – o	οξ – ox	νοδ ναγ μοθ ον	nod nag moth on
π – p	ποπ – pop	πιπ ποξ ποζ πηδ	pip pox podz pēd
ρ – r	ραν – ran	ριπ ριγ πη μαρκ	rip rig pē mark
σ, ς – s (ς is used only at the end of words)	σιπ – sip	σαπ σκιλλ γοσπελ ριβς ναγς σαγς	sap skill gospel ribs nags sags
τ – t	σετ – set	σατ σιτς τηκ τοτ	sat sits tēk tot
υ – "u" as in French "lune", or "oo" as in "book"; "w" when it starts a word	βυκ – book	λυκ κυκ τυκ υιθ υιν	look kook took with win
φ – ph, f	φυτ – foot	φιτ φατ φιστ φοξ	fit fat fist fox
χ – kh	χακι – khaki	χριστος χριστοφερ	khristos khristopher
ψ – ps	λιψ – lips	τιψ ταψ ταπ ριψ	tips taps tap rips

Greek letters	Read the groups of letters	Greek groups of letters	English equivalents
ω – ō "o", as in "phone"	φων – phōn	φωτω σωπ σοπ	phōtō sōp sop
' – h (Written over an initial vowel)	ἁτ – hat	ἱτ ἁμ ὁτ ὡπ ἱψ	hit ham hot hōp hips
' (Written over initial vowel when there is no "h" sound)	ἀτ – at	ἀμ ἰτ ὀν ἠτ ἰλλ ἰλλ ὀψ	am it on ēt ill hill hops

1.2 Writing the letters

The arrows show you the easiest place to begin when writing a Greek letter.

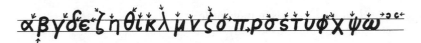

Notes
1. Do not put a dot over ι.
2. Be careful to make n pointed: ν, and u round: υ.

LESSON 2

ἐν ἀρχῃ – in the beginning

2.1 The Greek alphabet – small letters

Look again at the alphabet:

α – a	η – ē	ν – n	τ – t
β – b	θ – th	ξ – x	υ – oo, w
γ – g	ι – i	ο – o	φ – ph
δ – d	κ – k	π – p	χ – kh
ε – e	λ – l	ρ – r	ψ – ps
ζ – dz	μ – m	σ, ς – s	ω – ō

2.2

When two vowels come together, they give the following sounds:

αι – i, ai	(as in mile, aisle)
ει – ei	(as in veil)
οι – oi	(as in boil)
αυ – au, ou	(as in out)
ευ – eu, yew	(as in feud)
ου – oo	(as in root)
υι – ui, wi	(as in quick)
ιη – yē	(as in Yale)

So αἱ is pronounced like "high", εὐ is pronounced like "you", and Ἰησους is pronounced "Yē-soos".

Note that when two vowels make a single sound at the beginning of a word, ʼ or ʽ is written over the second vowel.

2.3

When γ occurs before κ, χ, or another γ, it is pronounced as "n" rather than "g".

γγ – ng   γκ – nk   γχ – nkh

So ἀγγελος is pronounced rather like "angle-os".

4

2.4

Read the following lines carefully. Cover the right-hand column. Check each line after you have read it by uncovering that part of the right-hand column. See that you know the sound the letters make. You will learn the meaning of the words in 2.5.

	Cover this column
ἐν ἀρχῃ ἠν ὁ λογος	en arkhē ēn ho logos
και ὁ λογος ἠν προς τον θεον	kai ho logos ēn pros ton theon
και θεος ἠν ὁ λογος.	kai theos ēn ho logos.

Note that ι can be written underneath α, η and ω: ᾳ ῃ ῳ. It is not pronounced, or is pronounced very lightly. You see it in this lesson in the word ἀρχῃ.

2.5 Words

ἀρχη – beginning   ἠν – he was, it was   και – and
λογος – word   ἐν – in   ὁ – the
θεος – God   προς – towards, with τον – the

2.6 Read and then translate

Cover up the right-hand column and translate the passage, uncovering the right-hand column to check each line. Do not read the notes below until you have translated the whole passage.

ἐν ἀρχῃ	In (the) beginning[1]
ἠν ὁ λογος,	was the word,
και ὁ λογος ἠν	and the word was
προς τον θεον	with (the) God[2]
και θεος ἠν ὁ λογος.	and the word was God.[3]

Notes
[1] ἐν ἀρχῃ – in beginning. "In beginning" is not good English. We translate as "In the beginning".
[2] προς τον θεον – with the God. In English we do not usually use "the" when referring to God, so we translate as "with God".
[3] θεος ἠν ὁ λογος – and the word was God. Notice that the order of words is different in English.

2.7 Translation

You have read and translated John 1.1. You have noticed that ideas in Greek and in English may be expressed in different words. To translate is not to put the *words* of one language into another: it is to express the *meaning* of the words in another language.

LESSON 3

ἐστιν – is   ἠν – was

3.1

ἐστιν means "he is", "she is", or "it is".
ἠν means "he was", "she was", or "it was".

When we translate ἐστιν and ἠν we can only tell whether to use "he", "she", or "it", by reading the passage as a whole.

Compare:

(a) Ἰησους ἠν προς τον θεον. ἀληθης ἠν
   Jesus was with God. He was true

(b) Μαρια ἠν προς τον θεον. ἀληθης ἠν
   Mary was with God. She was true

(c) ὁ λογος ἀληθης ἠν και ἀληθης ἐστιν
   The word was true and it is true.

Note that the word order is often not the same in English as it is in Greek. For ἀληθης ἠν in (a) we do not say "True he was", but "He was true". Compare θεος ἠν ὁ λογος in 2.6. In this sentence ὁ (the) indicates that the subject is λογος, so we translate it, "The word was God".

3.2 Translate

1. Ἰησους ἐστιν.	Jesus is.
2. Ἰησους ἠν.	Jesus was.
3. ὁ λογος ἠν.	The word was.

4. ὁ λογος ἐστιν.	The word is.
5. θεος ἐστιν ὁ λογος.	The word is God.
6. ἀληθης ἐστιν ὁ λογος και ἀληθης ἠν.	The word is true and it was true.
7. ἐν ἀρχῃ ἠν ὁ λογος, και ἐν ἀρχῃ ἀληθης ἠν.	In the beginning the word was, and in the beginning it was true.

3.3 Words

ὁ λογος – the word
  οἱ λογοι – the words
ὁ Μαρκος – Mark
ὁ Ἰησους – Jesus
του – of the
οὑτος – this, he
  οὑτος ὁ λογος – this word
  οὑτοι – these
ἀληθης – true

ἐστιν – he is, she is, it is
εἰσιν – they are
ἠν – he was, she was, it was
γραφει – he writes, she writes
γραφει τον λογον
  – he writes the word
γραφει τους λογους
  – he writes the words

3.4 Translate

1. ὁ λογος ἀληθης ἐστιν.	The word is true.
2. οἱ λογοι ἀληθεις εἰσιν.	The words are true.
3. οὑτος ὁ λογος ἀληθης ἐστιν.	This word is true.
4. οὑτοι οἱ λογοι ἀληθεις εἰσιν.	These words are true.
5. ἀληθης ἠν ὁ λογος.	The word was true.
6. ἀληθης ἠν ὁ λογος του Ἰησου.	The word of Jesus was true.
7. γραφει τον λογον.	He writes the word.
8. γραφει τους λογους.	He writes the words.
9. ὁ Μαρκος γραφει τους λογους. γραφει τους λογους του Ἰησου. οὑτοι οἱ λογοι του Ἰησου ἀληθεις εἰσιν.	Mark writes the words. He writes the words of Jesus. These words of Jesus are true.
10. ὁ Ἰησους ἠν προς τον θεον. οὑτος ἠν ἐν ἀρχῃ προς τον θεον.	Jesus was with God. He was in the beginning with God.
11. οὑτοι εἰσιν οἱ λογοι του Ἰησου και οἱ λογοι του Μαρκου.	These are the words of Jesus and the words of Mark.

3.5

You have begun to learn the following Greek words. Notice the English words that are like them. Many English words are derived from Greek words.

Greek word	Compare
ἡ ἀρχη – the beginning	archetype – original model
	archaeology – study of things from earlier times
ὁ θεος – God, the God	theism – belief in God
	theology – study of God
ὁ λογος – the word	logic, theology, archaeology
Ἰησους – Jesus	Jesus
Μαρκος – Mark	Mark
ἐν – in	enter, in
ἐστιν – he is, she is, it is	is
εἰσιν – they are	is
γραφει – he writes, she writes	graph, paragraph, graffiti
και – and	
προς – towards, with	
ἀληθης – true	

3.6 Test the progress you have made

Read the questions and write down which answers you think are correct. For example, in question 1 if you think that Ἰησους ἐστιν means "Jesus is", write down: 1 (c).

Progress test 1

Which translation is correct?

1. Ἰησους ἐστιν.
   (a) The word is.
   (b) Jesus was.
   (c) Jesus is.

2. ὁ λογος ἠν.
   (a) The word was.
   (b) The word is.
   (c) God was.

3. οὑτος ἐστιν ὁ λογος.
   (a) God is the word.
   (b) This is the word.
   (c) These are the words.

4. οὑτοι οἱ λογοι ἀληθεις εἰσιν.
   (a) These words are true.
   (b) This word is true.
   (c) He writes true words.

5. γραφει τους λογους του Ἰησου ὁ Μαρκος.
   (a) Jesus is writing these words.
   (b) He is writing the words of Jesus and of Mark.
   (c) Mark is writing the words of Jesus.

Now check your answers by looking at the key on page 280. Three right is good; four or five right is excellent. If you scored only one or two, do not worry. Continue the course as far as the end of lesson 6, then turn back and do this test again.

Introduction to lessons 4–6

When you have mastered lessons 4, 5, and 6 you will have made a great advance towards your goal of reading the New Testament in Greek. In each lesson you will learn a few important new forms. You will learn them one small step at a time, but for purposes of reference all the forms are listed here.

In lessons 4 and 5 you will learn the forms of λεγω – I am saying, I speak:

One person – singular
λεγω – I am saying
λεγεις – you are saying
λεγει – he is saying

More than one person – plural
λεγομεν – we are saying
λεγετε – you are saying
λεγουσιν – they are saying

In lesson 6 you will learn the forms of λογος – a word, and ὁ – the:

Singular
ὁ λογος – the word   < subject >
τον λογον – the word   < object >
του λογου – of the word
τῳ λογῳ – with the word

Plural
οἱ λογοι – the words
τους λογους – the words
των λογων – of the words
τοις λογοις – with the words

Copy these forms in large letters on a sheet of paper. Put it where you will see the forms every day.

Lessons 4–6 should be studied as a group. When you do lessons 4 and 5 you will probably have some questions in your mind which you will find answered in lesson 6.

LESSON 4

λεγω – I am saying, I say

4.1

λεγω – I am speaking, I speak
λεγεις – you are speaking, you speak
λεγει – he is speaking, he speaks

Note that the endings show who is speaking:

-ω – I   -εις – you, thou   -ει – he, she, it.

Each of these endings refers to only one person.

Note that as Greek uses the same ending for he, she, or it, λεγει could also mean "she is speaking", or "she speaks". If you are reading a whole passage of Greek, you will be able to tell which is meant. To save space in this book, -ει forms are usually translated as "he...", but bear in mind that they could equally well mean "she...", or "it...".

4.2

λεγω – I am saying, I say   The ending -ω
      I am speaking, I speak   indicates I
γραφω – I am writing, I write

So: λεγω τον λογον – I am saying the word
                  I am speaking the word

      γραφω τους λογους – I am writing the words.

Translate

1. λεγω τους λογους.	I am saying the words.
2. τον λογον γραφω.	I am writing the word.
3. γραφω τους λογους.	I am writing the words.
4. γραφω τους λογους του Μαρκου.	I am writing the words of Mark.
5. λεγω λογους ἀληθεις.	I am saying true words.
6. λεγω τον λογον.	I am saying the word.
7. λεγω τον λογον του θεου.	I am saying the word of God.

4.3 Translation

λεγω – I say, I speak, I tell, I am saying...

Note that when we wish to translate λεγω into English we have to choose from several English words. Consider λεγω αὐτῳ. αὐτῳ means "to him". So we may translate λεγω αὐτῳ as "I say to him", "I speak to him", "I tell him", or "I am telling him".

In 4.2 no. 7, λεγω τον λογον του θεου, "I am speaking God's word" might be a better translation than "I am saying the word of God". When you check your own translations by uncovering the right-hand columns in this book, do not ask yourself "Have I used exactly the same words in my translation?" but "Have I expressed the same meaning?"

4.4

λεγεις – you are saying, you say
γραφεις – you are writing, you write

The ending -εις indicates you (when addressing one person only)

So: λεγεις τον λογον αὐτῳ – you are saying the word to him
λεγεις λογον αὐτῳ – you are saying a word to him
'Ιησου, λεγεις λογους – Jesus, you are speaking words.

Translate

1. λεγεις τους λογους αὐτῳ.	You are saying the words to him.
2. λεγεις λογους αὐτῳ.	You are saying words to him.
3. γραφεις τον λογον.	You are writing the word.
4. γραφω λογον.	I am writing a word.
5. 'Ιησου, λεγεις τους λογους.	Jesus, you are speaking the words.
6. 'Ιησου, λεγεις τους λογους του θεου.	Jesus, you are speaking the words of God.
7. 'Ιησου, λεγεις αὐτῳ τους λογους του θεου.	Jesus, you are telling him the words of God.

4.5

λεγει – he is saying, he says
γραφει – he is writing, he writes
ἀναγινωσκει – he is reading, he reads

The ending -ει indicates he, she, or it

So: λεγει τους λογους του θεου – he speaks the words of God
ὁ προφητης λεγει τους λογους – the prophet speaks the words

11

ἀναγινωσκει λογους ὁ Μαρκος – Mark reads words
ἀναγινωσκει λογους ἡ Μαρια – Mary reads words.

Translate

1. λεγει τους λογους.	He speaks the words.
2. ὁ προφητης γραφει τους λογους.	The prophet writes the words.
3. ὁ Μαρκος ἀναγινωσκει τους λογους.	Mark reads the words.
4. ὁ Μαρκος ἀναγινωσκει τους λογους του προφητου.	Mark reads the words of the prophet.
5. λεγω λογους και ὁ Μαρκος γραφει τους λογους.	I speak words and Mark writes the words.
6. γραφεις λογους και ὁ προφητης ἀναγινωσκει τους λογους.	You are writing words and the prophet is reading the words.

4.6 Progress test 2

Which translation is correct?

1. λεγεις τους λογους.
   (a) I am speaking the words.
   (b) You are speaking the word.
   (c) You are speaking the words.

2. λεγει λογον.
   (a) He speaks a word.
   (b) You speak a word.
   (c) I speak a word.

3. λεγω λογους ἀληθεις.
   (a) He speaks true words.
   (b) You speak true words.
   (c) I speak true words.

4. ὁ προφητης γραφει τους λογους,
   (a) He writes the word of the prophet,
   (b) The prophet writes the words,
   (c) The prophet speaks the words,

5. και ἀναγινωσκεις αὐτους.
   (a) and you read them.
   (b) and he reads them.
   (c) and she reads them.

Check your answers on page 280.

LESSON 5

λεγομεν – we are saying, we say

5.1

In lesson 4 you learned three forms which indicate a single person:

λεγω – I am saying	-ω – I
λεγεις – you are saying	-εις – you
λεγει – he is saying, she is saying	-ει – he, she, it

Now you will learn three forms which indicate more than one person:

λεγομεν – we are saying	-ομεν – we
λεγετε – you are saying	-ετε – you
λεγουσιν – they are saying	-ουσιν, -ουσι – they

Note the difference between

λεγεις – you say, thou sayest
and λεγετε – you say.

5.2

λεγομεν – we are saying, we say	The ending -ομεν
γραφομεν – we are writing	indicates
ἀναγινωσκομεν – we are reading	**we**

So: λεγομεν τους λογους και γραφομεν αὐτους
We are saying the words and we are writing them

γραφομεν τον λογον και ἀναγινωσκομεν αὐτον
We are writing the word and we are reading it.

Translate

1. γραφομεν τον λογον και
ἀναγινωσκεις αὐτον.

We write the word and you read it.

2. γραφει τους λογους και
ἀναγινωσκομεν αὐτους.

He writes the words and we read them.

3. ὁ προφητης λεγει τους λογους του
θεου και γραφομεν αὐτους.

The prophet speaks the words of God and we write them.

4. λεγομεν τους λογους του Ἰησου και
γραφει αὐτους ὁ Μαρκος.

We speak the words of Jesus and Mark writes them.

5. ὁ Μαρκος γραφει τον λογον και ἀναγινωσκομεν αὐτον.

Mark writes the word and we read it.

5.3

λεγετε – you are saying, you say
γραφετε – you are writing
ἀκουετε – you are hearing

The ending **-ετε** indicates **you**, when addressing more than one person (plural or pl.)

So: λεγομεν τουτους τους λογους και ἀκουετε αὐτους
We speak these words and you hear them

γραφετε τουτον τον λογον και ἀναγινωσκω αὐτον
You write this word and I read it.

Translate

1. λεγετε τουτον τον λογον.

You speak this word.

2. ἀκουετε τουτον τον λογον.

You hear this word.

3. γραφετε τουτους τους λογους και ἀναγινωσκω αὐτους.

You write these words and I read them.

4. ὁ προφητης λεγει τουτους τους λογους και ἀκουετε αὐτους.

The prophet speaks these words and you hear them.

5. ἀναγινωσκετε τους λογους του προφητου και ἀκουομεν αὐτους.

You are reading the words of the prophet and we hear them.

5.4

λεγουσιν – they are saying, they say
ἀκουουσιν – they are hearing
ἀναγινωσκουσιν – they are reading

The ending **-ουσιν** or **-ουσι** indicates **they**

So: γραφουσιν τους λογους ἐν τῳ βιβλιῳ
They are writing the words in the book

οἱ προφηται ἀναγινωσκουσιν τους λογους του βιβλιου
The prophets are reading the words of the book.

Translate

1. οἱ προφηται γραφουσιν. τους λογους ἐν τῳ βιβλιῳ.

The prophets are writing the words in the book.

2. οἱ προφηται λεγουσιν τους λογους του θεου και ἀκουομεν τους λογους.

The prophets speak the words of God and we hear the words.

3. ἀναγινωσκετε τους λογους του
   βιβλιου και ἀκουουσιν αὐτους.

You read the words of the book
and they hear them.

4. ἀκουουσιν τους λογους και
   γραφουσιν αὐτους ἐν τῳ βιβλιῳ.

They hear the words and they
write them in the book.

5.5

Here are the forms of λεγω you have learned:

One person (singular)	More than one person (plural)
λεγω – I say	λεγομεν – we say
λεγεις – you say	λεγετε – you say
λεγει – he says	λεγουσιν – they say

The endings indicate the person:

-ω – I	-εις – you	-ει – he, she, it
-ομεν – we	-ετε – you	-ουσιν – they

The main part, or stem, indicates the meaning:

Verb	Stem
λεγω – I say	λεγ – say
γραφω – I write	γραφ – write
ἀκουω – I hear	ακου – hear
ἀναγινωσκω – I read	αναγινωσκ – read

5.6 Type of action – continuing or repeated

Compare these two sentences:

(a) I am writing the words – γραφω τους λογους

(b) I write the words – γραφω τους λογους

In (a), γραφω describes an action that is going on now; a continuous
action. We will represent this continuing present action by a line: —.
In (b), if the sentence is completed by the words "every day", so that it
reads "I write the words every day", then γραφω describes a repeated
action, or a series of repeated actions. We will represent this kind of
repeated action by a series of dots: ·····. So in Greek, a form like λεγω or
γραφω may represent either:

    continuing action —

or **repeated action** ·····

When we translate such forms into English we have to choose either an

5.6

English form that indicates continuing action: I am saying, I am writing —, or one that indicates repeated action: I say, I write ⋯⋯.

In short passages and single sentences like the ones in these early lessons it is not usually possible to choose one form rather than the other. So if you translate λεγομεν as "we are saying", and the check-column has "we say", do not be surprised. You are not wrong; either alternative is an acceptable translation.

5.7 Progress test 3

Which translation is correct?

1. ἀκουουσιν τους λογους.
   (a) We speak the words.
   (b) They hear the words.
   (c) We hear the word.

2. ἀναγινωσκομεν τον λογον.
   (a) They read the word.
   (b) We are reading the word.
   (c) You are reading the word.

3. γραφετε τα βιβλια.
   (a) You read the books.
   (b) He writes the books.
   (c) You write the books.

4. ἀναγινωσκει το βιβλιον.
   (a) We read the book.
   (b) You read the book.
   (c) She reads the book.

5. οἱ προφηται ἀκουουσι τους λογους του θεου.
   (a) The prophets hear the words of God.
   (b) The prophet hears the words of God.
   (c) The prophet hears the word of God.

Check your answers on page 280.

LESSON 6

λογος – a word   ὁ λογος – the word

6.1

In a simple sentence like

ὁ ἀποστολος	λεγει	τον λογον
The apostle	speaks	the word

there are three main parts: the subject, the verb, and the object.

16

The apostle – ὁ ἀποστολος – is the subject, the person who does something
speaks – λεγει – is the verb, indicating the action being done
the word – τον λογον – is the object, the thing done, or affected by the doing.

In English we usually show the subject by putting it before the verb, and the object by putting it after the verb.

In Greek it is usually the ending of the word which shows most clearly whether it is the subject or the object, not the order of words. Usually -ος indicates a **subject** and -ον indicates an **object**.

So: ὁ Μαρκος γραφει τον λογον
and γραφει τον λογον ὁ Μαρκος

both mean: Mark writes the word.

When we want to understand a Greek sentence we must always read it right through to the end, keeping alert to notice the various subject and object indicators.

6.2

λογος – a word   λογοι – words   -ος⎫ subject
ὁ λογος – the word   οἱ λογοι – the words   -οι⎭ endings

ὁ ⎫ the (indicating
οἱ ⎭ subject)

So: λογος ἀληθης – a true word

ὁ λογος ἀληθης ἐστιν – the word is true.

Translate

1. λογοι, λογος. | Words, a word.
2. ὁ λογος, οἱ λογοι. | The word, the words.
3. οἱ λογοι ἀληθεις εἰσιν. | The words are true.
4. ὁ λογος ἀληθης ἐστιν. | The word is true.

6.3

τον λογον – the word (object)   -ον ⎫ object
τους λογους – the words (object)   -ους ⎭ endings

τον ⎫ the (usually indicating
τους ⎭ the object)

6.3

So: γραφει *τους* λογους – he writes the words
γραφει *τους* λογους ὁ ἀποστολος – the apostle writes the words
ἀκουετε αὐτους – you hear them.

Translate

1. γραφει τους λογους.	He writes the words.
2. λεγομεν λογους.	We speak words.
3. γραφει λογον.	He writes a word.
4. γραφει τους λογους ὁ προφητης.	The prophet writes the words.
5. λεγετε τους λογους και ἀκουομεν αὐτους.	You speak the words and we hear them.
6. γραφεις τον λογον και ἀναγινωσκω αὐτον.	You write the word and I read it.

6.4

του λογου – of the word
των λογων – of the words

-ου ⎫ endings indicating
-ων ⎭ of

του ⎫ of the
των ⎭

So: ἡ ἀρχη *του* λογου
The beginning of the word

ἀναγινωσκει τους λογους *των* προφητ*ων*
He is reading the words of the prophets

ἀκουετε τον λογον *του* ἀποστολ*ου*
You hear the word of the apostle.

Translate

1. ἡ ἀρχη των λογων.	The beginning of the words.
2. ὁ λογος του προφητου.	The word of the prophet.
3. οἱ λογοι των προφητων.	The words of the prophets.
4. ὁ ἀποστολος γραφει τους λογους του Ἰησου.	The apostle writes the words of Jesus.
5. οἱ λογοι του ἀποστολου ἀληθεις εἰσιν.	The words of the apostle are true.
6. ἀκουομεν τους λογους των ἀποστολων και γραφομεν αὐτους ἐν τῳ βιβλιῳ.	We hear the words of the apostles and we write them in the book.

6.5

τῳ λογῳ – by the word, with the word	-ῳ ⎱ endings indicating -οις ⎰ by, with, for, etc.
τοις λογοις – by the words, with the words	τῳ ⎱ by the, τοις ⎰ with the, etc.

So: λεγουσιν λογοις – they speak by means of words
λεγουσιν τοις ἀποστολοις – they say to the apostles

γραφετε ἐπιστολας αὐτοις και λεγομεν αὐτοις
You write letters to them and we speak to them.

Translate

1. λεγω αὐτοις. — I am speaking to them.
2. γραφομεν τους λογους αὐτοις και ἀναγινωσκουσιν τους λογους. — We write the words to them (for them) and they read the words.
3. λεγεις λογοις. — You speak by means of words.
4. λεγετε τοις λογοις. — You speak by means of the words.
5. ὁ προφητης λεγει τῳ ἀποστολῳ τους λογους του θεου και ὁ ἀποστολος γραφει αὐτους ἐν τῳ βιβλιῳ. — The prophet speaks the words of God to the apostle and the apostle writes them in the book.

6.6 Progress test 4

Which is the better English translation?

1. λεγουσιν τους λογους οἱ ἀποστολοι.
   (a) They speak the words the apostles.
   (b) The apostles speak the words.

2. το βιβλιον ἀναγινωσκει ὁ προφητης.
   (a) The book he is reading the prophet.
   (b) The prophet is reading the book.

3. γραφει τουτους τους λογους ὁ Μαρκος.
   (a) Mark writes these words.
   (b) Mark writes these the words.

4. τους λογους αὐτου ἀναγινωσκομεν αὐτοις.
   (a) The words of him we are reading to them.
   (b) We are reading them his words.

Check your answers on page 280.

LESSON 7

αὐτος – he   οὑτος – this

7.1

αὐτος (he) has forms similar to λογος.

αὐτος – he, it   αὐτοι – they

So: αὐτος πιστευει ἀλλα αὐτοι οὐ πιστευουσιν
He believes but they do not believe.

Note that πιστευει by itself means "he believes". αὐτος is added for emphasis, usually when "he" is contrasted with another person or group.

Translate

1. αὐτοι λεγουσιν ἀλλα (but) αὐτος οὐ (not) λεγει. | They are speaking but he is not speaking.
2. αὐτοι γραφουσιν τους λογους ἀλλα αὐτος οὐ γραφει αὐτους. | They are writing the words but he is not writing them.
3. αὐτος ἀναγινωσκει τους λογους ἀλλα αὐτοι οὐκ (not) ἀναγινωσκουσιν αὐτους. | He reads the words but they do not read them.

7.2

αὐτον – him, it   αὐτους – them

Translate

1. ἀκουω τον λογον και γραφω αὐτον. | I hear the word and I write it.
2. ἀκουεις τους λογους και γραφεις αὐτους. | You hear the words and you write them.

7.3

αὐτου – of him, of it   αὐτων – of them

So: ἀναγινωσκετε το βιβλιον αὐτου
Lit. You are reading the book of him.

In English we do not say "the book of him", so we translate, "you are reading his book".

20

Translate

1. ἀναγινωσκομεν το βιβλιον αὐτου. | We are reading his book.
2. ἀναγινωσκομεν το βιβλιον αὐτων. | We are reading their book.
3. ἀκουω τους λογους αὐτου και γραφω αὐτους ἐν τῳ βιβλιῳ. | I hear his words and I write them in the book.

7.4

αὐτῳ – to him, for him   αὐτοις – to them, for them

Translate

1. λεγω αὐτῳ. | I am speaking to him.
2. λεγω αὐτοις. | I am speaking to them.
3. λεγετε αὐτοις τους λογους του θεου και αὐτοι γραφουσιν αὐτους ἐν τοις βιβλιοις αὐτων. | You speak to them the words of God and they write them in their books.

7.5

There are many other words with the same endings as αὐτος and λογος, for example: **ἀνθρωπος** – a man.

ἀνθρωπος – a man   < subject >   ἀνθρωποι – men
ἀνθρωπον – a man   < object >   ἀνθρωπους – men
ἀνθρωπου – of a man   ἀνθρωπων – of men
ἀνθρωπῳ – to a man, for a man   ἀνθρωποις – to men, for men

The forms of **ὁ** (the) which go with ἀνθρωπος are the same as those which go with λογος (see page 9). So, των ἀνθρωπων – of the men.

7.6 Words

Some words with endings like λογος:

	Compare
ὁ θεος – the god, God	theist – one who believes God exists
ὁ ἀνθρωπος – the man	anthropology – the study of man
ὁ ἀποστολος – the apostle, the envoy	apostle – a person sent by someone
ὁ θρονος – the throne, the seat	throne – a king's seat

21

ὁ οὐρανος – the sky, heaven
αὐτος – he, it

Compare
Uranus – one of the planets
autobiography – a person's life story written by himself

Note also:
λεγω τον αὐτον λογον – I say the same word
αὐτος ὁ θεος – God himself
ἀλλα – but (ἀλλ' before a vowel)
οὐ, οὐκ, οὐχ – not
Note that οὐ becomes οὐκ before a vowel and οὐχ before '(h).

So: λεγει αὐτῳ – he speaks to him
   οὐ λεγει αὐτῳ – he does not speak to him

   λεγει αὐτῃ ἀλλ' οὐ λεγει αὐτοις
   – he speaks to her but he does not speak to them

   ἀκουουσιν τους λογους – they hear the words
   οὐκ ἀκουουσιν τους λογους – they do not hear the words
   οὑτος – this man
   οὐχ οὑτος – not this man.

7.7 Translate

1. οἱ ἀποστολοι λεγουσιν τον λογον
του θεου και ἀκουομεν αὐτον.

The apostles speak the word of God and we hear it.

2. οἱ ἀνθρωποι λεγουσιν τους λογους
ἀλλα οὐκ ἀκουετε αὐτους.

The men speak the words but you do not hear them.

3. γραφουσιν τους λογους του Μαρκου
οἱ ἀποστολοι ἀλλ' αὐτος οὐκ
ἀναγινωσκει αὐτους.

The apostles write the words of Mark but he does not read them.

4. οὐκ ἀναγινωσκομεν τους λογους
των προφητων ἀλλα τους λογους
του ἀποστολου.

We are not reading the words of the prophets but the words of the apostle.

5. ὁ θρονος του θεου ἐν τῳ οὐρανῳ
ἐστιν, οὐκ ἐστιν ἐπι (on) της γης
(the earth).

The throne of God is in heaven, it is not on the earth.

6. ἐν ἀρχῃ ἐποιησεν (made) ὁ θεος
τον οὐρανον και την γην, και
ἐποιησεν τον ἀνθρωπον ἐπι της γης.

In the beginning God made the heaven and the earth, and he made the man on the earth.

7. και ἐποιησεν ἀνθρωπον.

And he made a man.

7.8

οὗτος – this, this man, this person, he

The forms of οὗτος have endings like λογος. Like the forms of ὁ (the) they begin with τ, except for the subject form.

So: (a) **οὗτος** ὁ ἀνθρωπος ἀναγινωσκει **τουτους** τους λογους τοις ἀνθρωποις **τουτοις**
This man is reading these words to these men

(b) **οὗτος** ἠν ἐν ἀρχῃ προς τον θεον
He was in the beginning with God.

Notice that "this man" may be expressed in Greek either as

οὗτος ὁ ἀνθρωπος (this the man)
or ὁ ἀνθρωπος οὗτος (the man this).

In sentence (a) both types of word order are found:

οὗτος ὁ ἀνθρωπος – this man
τοις ἀνθρωποις τουτοις – to these men.

Translate

1. οὗτοι εἰσιν οἱ λογοι.	These are the words.
2. οὗτος ἠν ὁ θρονος.	This was the throne.
3. οὗτοι ἠσαν οἱ θρονοι.	These were the thrones.
4. οὗτος ἐστιν ὁ ἀποστολος.	This is the apostle (*or* He is...)
5. γραφω τουτους τους λογους.	I am writing these words.
6. λεγω τοις ἀποστολοις τουτοις.	I am speaking to these apostles.
7. λεγω τουτους τους λογους του Ἰησου τοις ἀποστολοις αὐτου και αὐτοι γραφουσιν αὐτους ἐν τοις βιβλιοις αὐτων.	I am speaking these words of Jesus to his apostles and they are writing them in their books.
8. γραφεις τον λογον τουτον ἀλλα οὗτοι οἱ ἀνθρωποι οὐκ ἀναγινωσκουσιν αὐτον.	You are writing this word but these men are not reading it.

7.9 Translation

Notice again that the word order in Greek sentences is seldom the same as the word order in a good English translation.

Compare the following:

Greek	Literal English	English
ὁ λογος οὗτος	the word this	this word
οὗτος ὁ λογος	this the word	this word
αὐτος ὁ θεος	he the God	God himself
ὁ λογος αὐτου	the word of him	his word
οἱ λογοι αὐτων	the words of them	their words
ἀδελφοι μου οὗτοι εἰσιν	brothers of me these are	they are my brothers
ὁ τον λογον ἀκουων	the the word hearing	he who hears the message

Some writers have suggested that literal translations are good translations, but this is not so. A literal translation may be useful as a first step in helping us to understand the structure of a Greek sentence. We must then think how we can best express its meaning in our own language.

7.10 Progress test 5

Which translation is correct?

1. λεγομεν λογους.
   (a) We speak words.
   (b) They speak words.
   (c) We speak the words.

2. λεγετε τουτους τους λογους.
   (a) They speak these words.
   (b) You speak their words.
   (c) You speak these words.

3. λογον γραφω.
   (a) I hear a word.
   (b) I write a word.
   (c) You write a word.

4. γραφει τον λογον.
   (a) You write the word.
   (b) He writes the words.
   (c) He writes the word.

5. γραφουσιν τουτον τον λογον.
   (a) We write this word.
   (b) They write these words.
   (c) They write this word.

6. ἀναγινωσκεις τους λογους αὐτου.
   (a) You read these words.
   (b) You read his words.
   (c) You hear his word.

7. οὗτος ἦν ὁ λογος του προφητου και οὗτος ἐστιν ὁ γραφων αὐτον.
   (a) These are the words of the prophet and he is writing it.
   (b) This is the word of the prophet and this is the person writing it.
   (c) This was the word of the prophet and this is the person writing it.

8. αὐτος οὐκ ἐστιν ἐπι της γης ἀλλ᾽ ἐν τῳ οὐρανῳ.
   (a) These are not on the earth but in heaven.
   (b) He was not on the earth but in heaven.
   (c) He is not on the earth but in heaven.

Check your answers on page 280.

7.11

If you have not yet done so, write out neatly the Greek words in 3.3 and 7.6. Write each word or small group of words on a small card or piece of paper. On the other side of the card write the meaning. Carry these memory cards with you for some days and check from time to time that you know them all. Add these words:

λεγω – I am saying, I say	γραφω – I write
ἀκουω – I hear	ἀναγινωσκω – I read
ὁ προφητης – the prophet	το βιβλιον – the book
λεγων – saying	ὁ λεγων – the person saying

LESSON 8

λεγων – saying   ὁ λεγων – the person saying

8.1

λεγων – saying (one person: singular)
λεγοντες – saying (more than one person: plural)

So: (a) **λεγων τους λογους γραφει αὐτους**
         Saying the words he writes them
     or While saying the words he writes them

     (b) **ἀκουοντες του Ἰησου πιστευουσιν αὐτῳ**
         Hearing Jesus they believe in him
     or While they are listening to Jesus they trust in him.

8.1

These words λεγων, λεγοντες, ἀκουοντες refer to a continuing action: —.
In (a) he writes the words while the act of speaking is going on.
In (b) they believe in Jesus while the act of listening is going on.

Translate

1. ἀκουοντες τους λογους του Ἰησου πιστευομεν αὐτῳ.

   Hearing Jesus' words we believe in him.

2. ἀκουοντες αὐτου πιστευετε αὐτῳ.

   Hearing him you believe in him.

3. ἀκουοντες τους λογους πιστευουσιν αὐτοις.

   Hearing the words they believe them.

4. ἀκουων του Ἰησου πιστευεις αὐτῳ.

   Hearing Jesus you believe in him.

5. ἀκουων του Ἰησου πιστευω αὐτῳ.

   Hearing Jesus I believe in him.

6. ἀκουων τους λογους πιστευει αὐτοις.

   Hearing the words he believes them.

7. ἀκουει τους λογους ἀλλα οὐ πιστευει αὐτοις.

   He hears the words but he does not believe them.

8.2

ὁ λεγων – the person saying   οἱ λεγοντες – the people saying

Note that when ὁ (the) is followed by a form like λεγων, ὁ may be translated as "the person".

So: αὐτος ἐστιν ὁ λεγων τον λογον
      He is **the person saying** the word

      οὑτοι εἰσιν οἱ λεγοντες τους λογους
      These are **the people saying** the words.

Translate

1. αὐτος ἐστιν ὁ ἀκουων τον λογον.

   He is the person hearing the word.

2. οὑτος ἐστιν ὁ γραφων τουτον τον λογον.

   This is the person writing this word.

3. αὐτοι εἰσιν οἱ λεγοντες τουτους τους λογους.

   They are the people saying these words.

4. ἀκουων τους λογους γραφει αὐτους.

   Hearing the words he writes them.

5. οὑτοι εἰσιν οἱ ἀναγινωσκοντες το βιβλιον.

   These are the people reading the book.

26

8.3 Translating forms like ὁ λεγων into English

In order to aid our understanding of the Greek, it is helpful to begin by seeing that ὁ λεγων is "the person saying". But such an expression is not often used in English. We would usually translate ὁ λεγων as "he who says", or "the person who says".

So οἱ ἀναγινωσκοντες τα βιβλια (lit. the people reading the books) may be expressed in English as:

> The people who are reading the books
> *or* Those who read the books
> *or* The readers of the books.

ὁ ἀποστολος ὁ γραφων το βιβλιον (lit. the apostle the one writing the book) may be expressed in English as:

> The apostle who is writing the book
> *or* The apostle writing the book.

οἱ προφηται οἱ τα βιβλια ἐχοντες (lit. the prophets the ones having the books) may be expressed in English as:

> The prophets who have the books
> *or* The prophets with the books.

Translate

ὁ ἀποστολος ἀκουει τον λογον του Ἰησου, και ἀκουων τον λογον γραφει αὐτον ἐν τῳ βιβλιῳ. ὁ ἀποστολος ἐστιν ὁ γραφων το βιβλιον και οἱ λογοι αὐτου ἀληθεις εἰσιν. μακαριοι (blessed) εἰσιν οἱ ἀναγινωσκοντες το βιβλιον αὐτου.	The apostle hears the word of Jesus, and hearing the word he writes it in the book. The apostle is the person writing the book and his words are true. Blessed are those who read his book.

8.4 ὁτι – "..."

ὁτι is a linking word. It may mean "that" or "because" (8.7). But another common use of ὁτι is to show the beginning of quoted words. In New Testament Greek there are no inverted commas. ὁτι followed by a capital letter indicates words spoken or quoted.

So: οἱ λεγοντες ὁτι, Ἀποστολος ἐστιν, ἀληθεις εἰσιν
       Those who say, "He is an apostle," are true.

Note: ὁτι does not always occur before quoted words. In many cases a capital letter is the only indication of quoted or spoken words.

8.4

Translate

1. ὁ λεγων ὁτι Ὁ θεος ἐστιν ἐν τῳ οὐρανῳ, ἀληθης ἐστιν, ἀλλα ὁ λεγων ὁτι Ὁ θεος οὐκ ἐστιν ἐν τῳ οὐρανῳ, ψευστης (a liar) ἐστιν και οἱ λογοι αὐτου οὐκ ἀληθεις εἰσιν.	He who says, "God is in heaven," is true, but he who says, "God is not in heaven," is a liar and his words are not true.
2. ὁ λεγων ὁτι Ὁ θεος οὐκ ἀγαθος (good) ἐστιν, ψευστης ἐστιν και ὁ λογος του θεου οὐκ ἐστιν ἐν αὐτῳ.	He who says, "God is not good," is a liar and the word of God is not in him.
3. ἀγαθοι εἰσιν οἱ λογοι του ἀποστολου και μακαριος (blessed) ὁ ἀναγινωσκων αὐτους.	The words of the apostle are good and blessed is the person who reads them.
4. μακαριος ὁ λεγων τον λογον του θεου και μακαριοι εἰσιν οἱ ἀκουοντες.	Blessed is he who speaks the word of God and blessed are those who hear.
5. μακαριοι οἱ τον λογον του θεου ἀκουοντες και ποιουντες (doing).	Blessed are those who hear and do the word of God.

8.5 Words

Verbs with endings like λεγω (see 5.5):

Compare

γραφω – I write, I am writing — graph, anagram
ἀκουω – I hear, I listen — acoustic, acoustics
  ἀκουω τον λογον
  – I hear the word
  ἀκουω αὐτου – I hear him
ἀποστελλω – I send out, I send — apostle, apostolic
γινωσκω – I know — know, gnostic, agnostic
εὑρισκω – I find — heuristic
ἐχω – I have
λαμβανω – I take, I receive, I accept
ἀναγινωσκω – I read
πιστευω – I believe, I trust
  πιστευω τοις λογοις – I believe the words
  πιστευω τῳ Ἰησου – I believe in Jesus, I trust Jesus

Other words:
μακαριος – blessed, happy   ἡ Μαρια – Mary
ὁ Φιλιππος – Philip   ὁ Λουκας – Luke

28

8.6 Translate

1. ἡ Μαρια ἐχει το βιβλιον.	Mary has the book.
2. ἀκουουσιν τον λογον και λαμβανουσιν αὐτον.	They hear the word and receive it.
3. γινωσκετε τον Ἰησουν και πιστευετε αὐτῳ.	You know Jesus and you trust him.
4. ὁ Ἰησους εὑρισκει τον Φιλιππον και λεγει αὐτῳ ὁτι Μακαριος ὁ εὑρισκων τους λογους του θεου και πιστευων αὐτοις.	Jesus finds Philip and says to him, "Blessed is he who finds the words of God and believes them".
5. ὠτα (ears) ἐχων, ἀκουει.	Having ears, he hears.
6. ὠτα ἐχων, οὐκ ἀκουει.	Having ears, he does not hear. or Though he has ears he does not hear.
7. ὠτα ἐχοντες οὐκ ἀκουουσιν.	Though they have ears they do not hear.
8. γινωσκοντες τον Ἰησουν πιστευουσιν αὐτῳ, και λαμβανουσιν τους λογους αὐτου.	Knowing Jesus they trust him, and they accept his words.
9. ἀποστελλει τους ἀποστολους αὐτου προς την Μαριαν.	He sends his apostles to Mary.

8.7

Read through carefully, then do Progress test 6.

God sends his angel to Mary

ὁ θεος ἐν οὐρανῳ ἐστιν. και ἀποστελλει τον ἀγγελον αὐτου ἐκ (from) του οὐρανου προς την Μαριαν λεγειν (to speak) τους λογους αὐτου. και ἐρχεται (comes) ὁ ἀγγελος προς την Μαριαν και λεγει αὐτῃ (to her) τους λογους του θεου. και ἀκουει αὐτους ἡ Μαρια και γινωσκει ὁτι (that) ἀληθεις εἰσιν.

Τουτους τους λογους ἐγραψεν (wrote) ὁ Λουκας ἐν τῳ βιβλιῳ αὐτου, και ἀναγινωσκοντες το βιβλιον εὑρισκομεν τους λογους του ἀγγελου και τους λογους της Μαριας. και πιστευομεν αὐτοις ὁτι (because) ἀληθεις εἰσιν.

Μακαριος ὁ ἐχων τον λογον του θεου και πιστευων τῳ Ἰησου. και μακαριοι εἰσιν οἱ ἐχοντες το βιβλιον του ἀποστολου και ἀναγινωσκοντες αὐτο.

8.8 Progress test 6

Answer the following questions on 8.7.

1. Where does the passage say God is?
2. Who is sent to Mary?
3. Whose words does the angel speak to her?
4. What does Mary know about the words?
5. Who wrote these words in his book?
6. Who is reading the book?
7. Whose words do we find in the book?
8. Why do we believe the words?
9. What person is described as being blessed?
10. What people are described as being blessed?

Check your answers on page 280.

LESSON 9

καρδια – a heart   ἡ καρδια – the heart

9.1

As you study ἡ **καρδια**, the heart, you will see that the structure is similar to that of ὁ λογος, but there is a difference in the endings, and in the forms for "the".

ἡ καρδια – the heart	-α ⎱ subject
αἱ καρδιαι – the hearts	-αι ⎰ endings
	ἡ ⎱ the
	αἱ ⎰ (indicating subject)

So: ἡ **καρδια** αὐτου ἀγαθη ἐστιν – his heart is good

καθαραι εἰσιν αἱ **καρδιαι** αὐτων – their hearts are pure.

Translate

1. καρδια, καρδιαι.	A heart, hearts.
2. αἱ καρδιαι, ἡ καρδια.	The hearts, the heart.
3. ἀγαθαι εἰσιν αἱ καρδιαι αὐτων.	Their hearts are good.
4. ἡ καρδια αὐτου οὐκ ἐστιν καθαρα.	His heart is not pure.

9.2

την καρδιαν – the heart	-αν ⎫ object
τας καρδιας – the hearts	-ας ⎭ endings

την ⎫ the
τας ⎭ (indicating object)

So: γινωσκεις **την** καρδιαν αὐτου – you know his heart

καρδιαν ἐχει ἀγαθην – he has a good heart.

Translate

1. ὁ θεος γινωσκει τας καρδιας των ἀνθρωπων, και γινωσκει την καρδιαν τουτου του ἀποστολου.
God knows the hearts of the men, and he knows the heart of this apostle.

2. καρδιαν ἐχεις ἀγαθην και λαμβανεις τουτους τους λογους του θεου.
You have a good heart and you receive these words of God.

3. καρδιαν ἀγαθην ἐχων λαμβανεις τον λογον αὐτου.
Having a good heart you receive his word.

9.3

της καρδιας – of the heart	-ας ⎫ of
των καρδιων – of the hearts	-ων ⎭

της ⎫ of the
των ⎭

So: οἱ διαλογισμοι **των** καρδιων αὐτων
The thoughts of their hearts

αἰρω τους λογους ἀπο **της** καρδιας αὐτου
I take away the words from his heart.

Translate

1. γινωσκω τους διαλογισμους της καρδιας αὐτου.
I know the thoughts of his heart.

2. αἰρεις τον λογον του θεου ἀπο της καρδιας αὐτου.
You take away the word of God from his heart.

3. ὁ Ἰησους γινωσκει τους διαλογισμους των καρδιων αὐτων.
Jesus knows the thoughts of their hearts.

4. οὑτοι οἱ διαλογισμοι της καρδιας αὐτου οὐκ ἀγαθοι εἰσιν.
These thoughts of his heart are not good.

31

9.4

τη καρδια – with the heart, in the heart
ταις καρδιαις – with the hearts, in the hearts

-ᾳ ⎱ with, by,
-αις ⎰ in, to, for, etc.

τη ⎱ with the,
ταις ⎰ to the, etc.

The meaning indicated by these endings is usually shown by the rest of the sentence in which they occur (see also 42.1).

So: μακαριος ὁ καθαρος τη καρδια
   Blessed the pure in heart
or   Blessed is the pure in heart
or   How blessed the pure in heart!

   λεγουσιν ἐν ταις καρδιαις αὐτων...
   They say in their hearts...

Translate

1. μακαριοι οἱ καθαροι τη καρδιᾳ.	Blessed are the pure in heart.
2. λεγει ἐν τη καρδιᾳ αὐτου ὁτι Ὁ θεος οὐκ ἀγαθος ἐστιν.	He says in his heart, "God is not good".
3. μακαριος ὁ ἐχων τον λογον του Ἰησου ἐν τη καρδιᾳ αὐτου.	Blessed is he who has the word of Jesus in his heart.
4. μακαριοι οἱ ἐχοντες τουτους τους λογους των προφητων ἐν ταις καρδιαις αὐτων.	Blessed are those who have these words of the prophets in their hearts.

9.5 Translating καρδια into English

In 9.1–9.4 we have translated καρδια as "heart". In many New Testament passages "heart" is a suitable translation. In Matthew 5.8 we might translate μακαριοι οἱ καθαροι τη καρδιᾳ as, "Blessed are the pure in heart", or as, "How blest are those whose hearts are pure".

But in Revelation 18.7 ἐν τη καρδιᾳ αὐτης λεγει cannot be well translated as, "She says in her heart", because we do not normally use the word "heart" to refer to our processes of thinking. "She says in her mind" would perhaps be a better translation, but it is not the most natural way for an English person to express the meaning of ἐν τη καρδιᾳ αὐτης λεγει. We need to consider translations like "She says to herself", "She keeps telling herself", or "She thinks".

καρδια in New Testament Greek covers an area of meaning in which we find such English words as heart, mind, thoughts, intentions, attitude.

Those who are translating the New Testament into some other language must consider what words and idioms cover this area of meaning. For example, in some languages thoughts and emotions are described not by a word for the heart but by a word for the stomach.

9.6

Here are the forms of ἡ καρδια you have learned:

Singular

ἡ καρδια – the heart   < subject >

την καρδιαν – the heart   < object >

της καρδιας – of the heart

τη καρδιᾳ – with the heart

Plural

αἱ καρδιαι – the hearts

τας καρδιας – the hearts

των καρδιων – of the hearts

ταις καρδιαις – with the hearts

Note carefully the difference between:

    της καρδιας – of the heart

and   τας καρδιας – the hearts (object form).

9.7 Words

καρδια – heart, mind, attitude

Compare
cardiac

Words with the same endings as καρδια:

ἡ ἁμαρτια – the sin, sin

ἡ ἐκκλησια – the congregation, the church
   (note that ἐκκλησια refers to people,
   never to a building)

ἡ ἀληθεια – the truth (ἀληθης – true)

ἡ βασιλεια – the kingdom, the reign
   (βασιλευς – king)

ἡ ἡμερα – the day

hamartiology
ecclesiastical

basilica

ephemeral

Words with the same endings as ἡ:

ἡ γη – the earth, the land, the soil

ἡ ἐπιστολη – the letter, the epistle

αὑτη – she, it:
   ἡ βασιλεια αὑτης – her kingdom

αὑτη – this:

geology, geography
epistle, epistolary

    γραφει ταυτην την ἐπιστολην
  or γραφει την ἐπιστολην ταυτην } he writes this letter

ἐν ταυτη τη ἡμερᾳ – on this day

9.8 Translate

1. ὁ Παυλος γραφει τας ἐπιστολας και ἐν αὐταις εὑρισκομεν τον λογον της ἀληθειας.

Paul writes the letters and in them we find the word of truth.

2. λεγει ἐν τη καρδια αὐτης ὁτι Ἁμαρτιαν οὐκ ἐχω.

She says to herself, "I have no sin".

3. οἱ λεγοντες ὁτι Ἁμαρτιαν οὐκ ἐχομεν, οὐ την ἀληθειαν λεγουσιν.

Those who say, "We have no sin", do not speak the truth.

4. Παυλος γραφει ἐπιστολας ταις ἐκκλησιαις ταυταις και ἀναγινωσκομεν αὐτας.

Paul writes letters to these churches and we read them.

5. ὁ προφητης λεγει τους λογους του θεου τη Μαρια και αὐτη γραφει αὐτους ἐν τῳ βιβλιῳ αὐτης.

The prophet speaks the words of God to Mary and she writes them in her book.

6. και αὐτη ἐστιν ἡ ἐπιστολη ἡν (which) ὁ Παυλος γραφει και ἀναγινωσκεις αὐτην ἐν ταυτη τη ἡμερᾳ, και εὑρισκεις τον λογον της βασιλειας του θεου ἐν αὐτη.

And this is the letter which Paul is writing, and you are reading it on this day, and you find the word of the Kingdom of God in it.

7. ὁ ἀποστολος λεγει τον λογον τη ἐκκλησιᾳ και οἱ ἀνθρωποι ἀκουουσιν τον λογον της βασιλειας.

The apostle speaks the word to the congregation and the men hear the word of the Kingdom.

8. ἐν ταυταις ταις ἡμεραις ἀκουομεν τον λογον του Ἰωαννου (of John) και λαμβανομεν αὐτον ἐν ταις καρδιαις ἡμων (of us). και οὑτος ἐστιν ὁ λογος του Ἰωαννου,

Ὁ λεγων ὁτι Κοινωνιαν (fellowship) ἐχω μετα (with) του θεου, και ἐν τη σκοτιᾳ (darkness) περιπατων (walking) ψευστης ἐστιν και ἡ ἀληθεια οὐκ ἐστιν ἐν αὐτῳ.

ἀναγινωσκομεν τουτους τους λογους ἐν τη ἐπιστολη αὐτου, και ἀναγινωσκοντες αὐτην πιστευομεν τοις λογοις αὐτου.

In these days we hear the word of John and we receive it in our minds. This is John's message:

"He who says, 'I have fellowship with God' and walks in the darkness is a liar, and the truth is not in him."

We read these words in his letter, and reading it we believe his words.

9.9 Translation

In 9.8 no. 7, we translated ὁ ἀποστολος λεγει τον λογον τη ἐκκλησιᾳ as "The apostle speaks the word to the congregation". When we see that he speaks about the Kingdom, we might decide that an alternative translation of λεγει τον λογον would be better. We might translate it as "preaches the message to the congregation", or as "preaches to the congregation". See also 4.3.

9.10 Progress test 7

Which translation is correct?

1. ἐν ταυταις ταις ἡμεραις ἀκουομεν τον λογον του θεου.
   (a) In these days we hear the words of God.
   (b) On this day we hear the word of God.
   (c) In these days we hear the word of God.

2. μακαριοι οἱ ἐχοντες το βιβλιον του Ἰωαννου και ἀναγινωσκοντες αὐτο.
   (a) They have John's book and they read it.
   (b) Blessed are those who have John's book and read it.
   (c) Blessed is he who has John's book and reads it.

3. λεγει ἐν τῃ καρδιᾳ αὐτου ὁτι Οὐ πιστευω τῳ Ἰησου.
   (a) He says to himself, "I do not believe in Jesus".
   (b) He says in his heart, "I believe in Jesus".
   (c) She says to herself, "I do not believe in Jesus".

4. αὑται αἱ ἐπιστολαι ἀγαθαι εἰσιν.
   (a) This letter is good.
   (b) These letters are good.
   (c) These letters were good.

5. ἐν ταυταις ταις ἐπιστολαις του Παυλου εὑρισκομεν τον λογον της βασιλειας του θεου.
   (a) In this letter of Paul we find words of the Kingdom of God.
   (b) In these letters of Paul we find the word of God's Kingdom.
   (c) In Paul's letters we find the word of God's Kingdom.

Check your answers on page 280.

LESSON 10

ἡμεις – we   ὑμεις – you   ὁς – who

10.1

ἡμεις – we
ὑμεις – you (pl.)   -εις – subject ending

So: λεγομεν ἡμεις και ὑμεις ἀκουετε
We speak and you hear.

Translate

1. τους λογους γραφομεν ἡμεις και ὑμεις ἀναγινωσκετε αὐτους.

   We are writing the words and you are reading them.

2. λεγετε ὑμεις και ἡμεις ἀκουομεν.

   You are speaking and we are listening.

Note that γραφομεν by itself means "we write". ἡμεις can be added to it for emphasis. This is usually done when "we" are contrasted with another person or group:

  ἡμεις λεγομεν και ὁ Παυλος ἀκουει
  We are speaking and Paul is listening

  το βιβλιον ἀναγινωσκομεν ἡμεις ἀλλα ὑμεις οὐκ ἀκουετε
  We are reading the book but you are not listening.

10.2

ἡμας – us
ὑμας – you   -ας – object ending

So: ἀποστελλει ἡμας ὁ θεος ἀλλα ὑμεις οὐ λαμβανετε ἡμας
God sends us but you do not receive us.

Translate

1. ὁ θεος ἐστιν ὁ ἀποστελλων ἡμας.

   God is the one who is sending us.

2. τον Μαρκον γινωσκομεν ἀλλα ὑμας οὐ γινωσκομεν.

   We know Mark but we do not know you.

3. ὁ Μαρκος γραφει το βιβλιον και ὑμεις ἀναγινωσκετε αὐτο (it).

   Mark writes the book and you read it.

4. εὑρισκει ἡμας ὁ Παυλος ἀλλα ὑμας οὐκ εὑρισκει. || Paul finds us but he does not find you.

10.3

ἡμων – of us
ὑμων – of you (pl.)   **-ων – of**

So: ἀκουοντες τους λογους **ὑμων** πιστευομεν αὐτοις
Hearing your words we believe them.

Translate

1. ἀκουουσι τους λογους ἡμων.	They hear our words.
2. ἀκουει τους λογους ὑμων.	He hears your words.
3. ἡμεις ἀκουομεν τους λογους αὐτων.	We hear their words.
4. αὐτος γινωσκει τους διαλογισμους των καρδιων ὑμων.	He knows the thoughts of your hearts (minds).
5. αὑτη ἐστιν ἡ ἐπιστολη ἡμων.	This is our letter.
6. ὁ θεος ἐστιν μεθ᾽ ὑμων (with you).	God is with you.
7. ὁ προφητης μεθ᾽ ἡμων ἐστιν.	The prophet is with us.

10.4

ἡμιν – for us, to us
ὑμιν – for you, to you (pl.)   **-ιν – to, for**

So: λεγω **ὑμιν** – I speak to you, I say to you
ποιει **ἡμιν** βασιλειαν – he makes a kingdom for us

Note also:
ἀκουοντες τους λογους ἡμων, πιστευετε **ἡμιν**
Hearing our words, you believe **in us**
or Hearing our words, you trust **us**.

Translate

1. γραφει ἡ Μαρια τους λογους ἡμιν.	Mary writes the words for us (to us).
2. λεγει ὑμιν ὁ προφητης και ὑμεις λεγετε ἡμιν.	The prophet speaks to you and you speak to us.
3. ὁ τουτους τους λογους λεγων ἡμιν οὐ λεγει την ἀληθειαν.	The person who is saying these words to us is not speaking the truth.

10.4

4. ἡ ἀληθεια ἐν ὑμιν ἐστιν ἀλλα οὐκ ἐστιν ἐν ἡμιν.

The truth is in you but it is not in us.

5. οἱ λαμβανοντες τους λογους ὑμων ἐν ταις καρδιαις αὐτων εὑρισκουσιν την βασιλειαν του θεου.

Those who receive your words in their hearts find the Kingdom of God.

10.5

ὅς – who, which (he who)
ἥ – who, which (she who)
ὅ – which, that which, what

So: ὅς ἐχει ὠτα ἀκουει ἡμας – **he who** has ears hears us
ἥ ἐχει ὠτα ἀκουει ὑμας – **she who** has ears hears you

ὅ ἠν ἀπ' ἀρχης ἀπαγγελλομεν ὑμιν
   – **that which** was from the beginning we announce to you

and ὁ λογος ὅν λεγεις – the word **which** you say
ἡ ἐπιστολη ἥν ἀναγινωσκουσι – the letter **which** they read
το βιβλιον ὅ γραφει – the book **which** he writes.

Translate

1. οὑτος ἐστιν ὁ λογος ὅν λεγει.

This is the word which he speaks.

2. αὐτη ἐστιν ἡ ἐπιστολη ἥν γραφουσιν.

This is the letter which they are writing.

3. τουτο ἐστιν το βιβλιον ἐν ᾧ ὁ προφητης γραφει ἡμιν τους λογους του θεου και ὑμεις ἀναγινωσκετε αὐτο.

This is the book in which the prophet is writing for us the words of God and you are reading it.

4. ὅ ἠν ἀπ' ἀρχης ἀπαγγελλετε ἡμιν.

That which was from the beginning you announce to us.

10.6 Accents: ´ ` ˆ

The New Testament was originally written entirely in capital letters (see lesson 16). There were no marks to indicate a high tone (´) or a low tone (`) or a rising and falling tone (ˆ). The system of marks, called accents, is found in manuscripts from the ninth century AD onwards. You will find them used in printed texts of the New Testament. In this course we use accents only to distinguish a few words which might otherwise be confused. For example:

ἡ – the   ἥ – who, which, she who

38

ὁ – the	ὅ – that which
εἰ – if	εἶ – you are, thou art
τις – someone	τίς; – who?
τι – something	τί; – what? why?
μενω – I remain, I stay	μενῶ – I will remain

You can complete this course and read the New Testament without knowing anything more about accents. Those who need further information should consult the appendix on page 282.

10.7 Words

ἡμεις – we
ὑμεις – you
μετα – with
  μεθ' ὑμων – with you
ὁ ἀγγελος – the messenger, the angel
ἡ ἀγγελια – the message
ἀπο – from
  ἀπ' ἀρχης – from the beginning
ἀπαγγελλω – I announce, I bring back a report, I declare

ὁ Κυριος – the Lord, the owner
ὁ Χριστος – the Anointed One, the Messiah, the Christ
ἡ κοινωνια – the fellowship, the partnership, the sharing
ἡ σκοτια – the darkness
ὁς – who, which, he who
ἡ – who, which, she who
ὁ – which, that which, what
και – and, also, even

και is used to link words and sentences together. When και *begins* a sentence we may sometimes translate it into English as "so", "then", or "also". But very often we mark the end of one sentence and the beginning of another simply by using a full stop, followed by a capital letter. When και is the first word in a Greek sentence we usually do not need any other "translation" except the full stop. So we can translate και λεγει αὐτοις as "He says to them".

10.8 Translate

1. και λεγει αὐτοις, Ὁς ἐχει ὠτα ἀκουει τους λογους οὑς ἀπαγγελλουσιν ἡμιν οἱ ἀποστολοι.

He says to them, "He who has ears hears the words which the apostles announce to us".

2. και αὑτη ἐστιν ἡ ἀγγελια ἡν ἀπαγγελλομεν ὑμιν ἱνα (so that) και ὑμεις κοινωνιαν ἐχητε (you may have) μεθ' ἡμων και μετα του Κυριου Ἰησου Χριστου.

This is the message which we declare to you so that you also may have fellowship with us and with the Lord Jesus Christ.

3. ὃ ἦν ἀπ' ἀρχῆς ἀπαγγελλει ἡμιν ὁ || John declares to us that which was
   Ἰωαννης και ἀκουομεν τον λογον || from the beginning, and we hear
   αὐτου. || his word (*or* we hear what he says).

10.9

Read carefully:

The message which we declare

ὃ ἦν ἀπ' ἀρχῆς ὃ ἀκηκοαμεν (we have heard) ἀπαγγελλομεν ὑμιν ἱνα (so that)
και ὑμεις κοινωνιαν ἐχητε μεθ' ἡμων. και ἡ κοινωνια ἡμων μετα του κυριου ἡμων
Ἰησου Χριστου ἐστιν. και ταυτα (these things) γραφομεν ἡμεις ἱνα και ὑμεις
γινωσκητε τον θεον και τον κυριον ἡμων Ἰησουν Χριστον. και αὑτη ἐστιν ἡ
ἀγγελια ἡν ἀκηκοαμεν ἀπο του κυριου και ἀπαγγελλομεν ὑμιν ὁτι Ὁ θεος φως
ἐστιν και σκοτια οὐκ ἐστιν ἐν αὐτῳ.

10.10 Translating difficult words

When you come to a difficult word, or one you have forgotten, leave it
until you have finished reading the rest of the sentence. Then you may
see what it means. For example, in 10.9 you read the new word φως.
When you saw that the sentence said, "God is φως and darkness is not in
him", you could probably see that φως must mean "light".

When you are trying to find out the meaning of a Greek word, see
whether it reminds you of any English words. φως might remind you of
*phos*phorus (which glows) or of *pho*tograph (a picture "written" by *light*
on the film).

In 10.8 if you have forgotten αὑτη in αὑτη ἐστιν ἡ ἀγγελια ἡν ἀκηκοαμεν
ἀπο του κυριου, do not give up and do not waste time staring at the word
αὑτη. By the time you have said, "αὑτη is the message which we have
heard from the Lord" you will probably see or remember that αὑτη
means "this". In a few of the sentences and reading passages in this
course there are words you have not seen before. This is to give you
practice in working out the meaning of unknown words. Later on you
will learn to use a dictionary or lexicon, but the less you need to use it
the quicker you will be able to read.

The passage in 10.9 was based mainly on 1 John 1.1–5. You have
already made a great deal of progress towards reading parts of the New
Testament in Greek. In lesson 11 you will take another very important
step forward as you study the forms ἱνα λεγη (so that he may say), ἐαν
λεγη (if he says), ὁς ἀν λεγη (whoever says), and λεγωμεν (let us say).

10.11

Revise lessons 4, 5, and 6.

LESSON 11

ὃς ἂν λεγῃ – **whoever says**
ἐαν λεγῃ – **if he says**
ἱνα λεγῃ – **so that he may say**
λεγωμεν – **let us say**

11.1

Note the difference in English between (a) and (b) in the following:

1. (a) You are finding these lessons difficult
   (b) You may be finding these lessons difficult

2. (a) You are the man who finds these lessons easy
   (b) Whoever finds these lessons easy will be glad.

Both (a) sentences state a definite fact about a definite person.
Both (b) sentences state something about finding that is not definite.
In 1(b) "You may be finding..." does not state definitely that you are
finding them difficult – you may be finding them easy.
In 2(b) "Whoever finds..." does not refer to a definite person.

Now compare these:

3. (a) ὁ ἀνθρωπος **ὃς λεγει** τον λογον
      The man **who speaks** the word

   (b) **ὃς ἂν λεγῃ** τον λογον
      Whoever speaks the word

4. (a) ταυτα ἀπαγγελλομεν και κοινωνιαν **ἐχετε** μεθ᾽ ἡμων
      We declare these things and **you have** fellowship with us

   (b) ταυτα ἀπαγγελλομεν **ἱνα** κοινωνιαν **ἐχητε** μεθ᾽ ἡμων
      We declare these things **so that you may have** fellowship with us

5. (a) **ἀκουει** τουτους τους λογους
      He hears these words

   (b) **ἐαν ἀκουῃ** τουτους τους λογους...
      If he hears these words...
      or **If he should hear** these words...

11.1

6. (a) ταυτα λεγομεν
   We are saying these things

   (b) ἐαν ταυτα λεγωμεν...
   If we are saying these things...
   If we say these things...
   If we keep saying these things...

Notice that each (a) is definite, and each (b) is less definite.
Each verb in (b) has a vowel that is lengthened – compare:

4. (a) ἐχετε   (b) ἐχητε
5. (a) ἀκουει   (b) ἀκουῃ
6. (a) λεγομεν   (b) λεγωμεν

11.2 Words

ἐαν – if
    ἐαν ἐχῃ – if he has
ὁς ἀν – whoever
    ὁς ἀν λαμβανῃ – whoever receives
ἱνα – so that
    ἱνα πιστευωσιν – so that they may believe
ὁ ἀδελφος – the brother
ἡ ἀδελφη – the sister
ἡ ἀγαπη – the love
ἀγαπω (ἀγαπα-ω) – I love
Note the endings:
    ἀγαπ-**ω** – I   ἀγαπ-**ωμεν** – we
    ἀγαπ-**ᾳς** – you   ἀγαπ-**ατε** – you (pl.)
    ἀγαπ-**ᾳ** – he   ἀγαπ-**ωσιν** – they
μη – not. Compare:
    οὐκ ἐχομεν – we do not have: ἐαν μη ἐχωμεν – if we do not have
    ὁς ἀν ἐχῃ – whoever has: ὁς ἀν μη ἐχῃ – whoever does not have
    ὁ ἀγαπων – the person loving *or* he who loves
    ὁ μη ἀγαπων – the person not loving *or* he who does not love
ταυτα – these things

11.3 ὁς – who   ὁς ἀν – whoever

Translate

1. οὑτος ἐστιν ὁ ἀδελφος ὁς λαμβανει την ἀδελφην.	This is the brother who receives the sister.
2. ὁς ἀν λαμβανῃ τας ἀδελφας οὑτος λαμβανει ἡμας.	Whoever receives the sisters (he) receives us.

42

3. ὃς ἂν πιστευῃ τῳ ἀγγελῳ του
   κυριου, τῳ κυριῳ πιστευει· ἀλλα ὁ
   μη πιστευων τῳ ἀγγελῳ οὐ
   πιστευει τῳ κυριῳ.

Whoever believes the angel of the Lord believes the Lord: but the person who does not believe the angel does not believe the Lord.

11.4 ἐαν – if

Translate

1. ἐαν ἀγαπωμεν τους ἀδελφους
   λαμβανομεν την ἀγαπην του θεου ἐν
   ταις καρδιαις ἡμων.

If we love the brothers we receive the love of God in our hearts.

2. ἐαν ταυτην την ἀγγελιαν
   ἀπαγγελλωσιν ὑμιν, την ἀληθειαν
   λεγουσιν· ἀλλα ὁ μη λεγων την
   ἀληθειαν ψευστης ἐστιν.

If they declare this message to you, they are speaking the truth: but the person who does not speak the truth is a liar.

11.5 ἱνα – so that

Translate

1. ταυτα ἀπαγγελλετε ἡμιν ἱνα
   κοινωνιαν ἐχωμεν μεθ᾽ ὑμων και ἱνα
   ἀγαπωμεν τον θεον.

You declare these things to us so that we may have fellowship with you and so that we may love God.

2. ὃ ἠν ἀπ᾽ ἀρχης ἀπαγγελλομεν ὑμιν
   ἱνα και ὑμεις γινωσκητε τον θεον
   και τον Κυριον ἡμων Ἰησουν
   Χριστον.

That which was from the beginning we declare to you so that you also may know God and our Lord Jesus Christ.

3. ἀγαπω τους ἀδελφους ἀλλα οὐκ
   ἀγαπω τας ἀδελφας.

I love the brothers but I do not love the sisters.

11.6 Let us...

λεγωμεν – let us say
ἀγαπωμεν – let us love
μη λεγωμεν – let us not say
μη ἀγαπωμεν – let us not love

Compare

λεγομεν – we say
ἀγαπωμεν – we love
οὐ λεγομεν – we do not say
οὐκ ἀγαπωμεν – we do not love

Translate

1. λεγωμεν τους λογους.

|| Let us say the words.

2. ἀναγινωσκομεν την ἐπιστολην.	We are reading the letter.
3. ἀναγινωσκωμεν τας ἐπιστολας.	Let us read the letters.
4. πιστευωμεν τῳ θεῳ και ἀγαπωμεν αὐτον.	Let us trust in God and let us love him.
5. γινωσκομεν τους ἀδελφους ἀλλα οὐκ ἀγαπωμεν αὐτους.	We know the brothers but we do not love them.
6. γινωσκωμεν τας ἀδελφας και ἀγαπωμεν αὐτας.	Let us know the sisters and let us love them.
7. μη ἀγαπωμεν τον Μαρκον ἀλλα ἀγαπωμεν τον Κυριον.	Let us not love Mark but let us love the Lord.
8. ὁς ἀν λεγῃ ὁτι Ἁμαρτιαν οὐκ ἐχω, μη λαμβανωμεν τους λογους αὐτου. οὐκ ἀληθεις εἰσιν.	Whoever says, "I do not have sin", let us not receive his words. They are not true.

11.7 Continuing or repeated action

Note that all the forms of the verb you have learned so far usually represent either continuing action ── or repeated action ····· (see 5.6).

So: **γραφει**   he is writing ──
           or he writes ·····

    ἱνα γραφῃ   so that he may be writing ──
                or so that he may write ·····

    ὁ γραφων   the person writing ──
               or he who writes ·····

From lesson 20 onwards we shall also study forms which indicate completed action or single action.

11.8

Compare the following forms of λεγω:

Used in definite statements and definite questions		*Used in indefinite clauses and indefinite questions*
λεγω	I	λεγω
λεγεις	you	λεγῃς
λεγει	he, she, it	λεγῃ
λεγομεν	we	λεγωμεν
λεγετε	you (pl.)	λεγητε
λεγουσι(ν)	they	λεγωσι(ν)

11.9 Progress test 8

Which translation is correct?

1. ἐαν ταυτην την ἀγγελιαν ἀπαγγελλητε ἡμιν...
   - (a) So that we may announce this message to you...
   - (b) If we declare this message to you...
   - (c) If you declare this message to us...

2. μη ἀγαπωμεν τους ἀποστολους ἀλλα τον Κυριον.
   - (a) Let us love the apostles of the Lord.
   - (b) Let us not love the apostles but the Lord.
   - (c) If we love the apostles we also love the Lord.

3. ταυτη τη ἡμερα ὁ ἀδελφος και ἡ ἀδελφη λαμβανουσιν την βασιλειαν του θεου ἐν ταις καρδιαις αὐτων.
   - (a) On this day the sister and the brother receive the Kingdom of God in their hearts.
   - (b) On this day the brother and the sister receive God's Kingdom in their hearts.
   - (c) These are the brother and the sister who receive God's Kingdom in their hearts.

4. ὁς ἀν ἀναγινωσκη το βιβλιον του Ἰωαννου οὑτος ἐστιν ὁ ἀγαπων αὐτον.
   - (a) Whoever reads John's book, he is the one who loves him.
   - (b) Whoever reads John's book is the one whom he loves.
   - (c) The man who reads John's book, he is the one he loves.

5. ὁ ἡν ἀπ' ἀρχης ἀπαγγελλουσιν ὑμιν οἱ ἀποστολοι ἱνα κοινωνιαν ἐχητε μεθ' ἡμων.
   - (a) The apostles declare to us that which was from the beginning so that we may have fellowship with you.
   - (b) The apostles declare to you that which was from the beginning so that you may have fellowship with us.
   - (c) That which was from the beginning you declare to the apostles so that they may have fellowship with you.

Check your answers on page 280.

LESSON 12

ἐργον – a work   το ἐργον – the work
ὁ, ἡ, το – the

12.1

You have learned that some Greek words have endings like λογος, while others have endings like καρδια. In this lesson you will study το ἐργον as an example of a third type of Greek word. Some endings are the same as the endings of λογος, but not all.

το ἐργον – the work, the deed	-ον ⎱ subject
τα ἐργα – the works, the deeds	-α ⎰ endings
	το ⎱ the
	τα ⎰

So: το ἐργον ὃ ποιεις – the work which you do, the deed you are doing

τα ἐργα ἁ ποιεις – the deeds which you do,
                the works you are doing

τα ἐργα ἡμων – our deeds, our works, the things we do,
                the things we have done

τουτο το ἐργον – this act, this deed, this task.

Note that the endings -ον (singular) and -α (plural) are found in some English words derived from Greek, e.g. criterion, criteria; phenomenon, phenomena.

You will have noticed that there are several possible ways of translating ἐργον and ἐργα into English. In the right-hand check column we usually put only one translation. For example, for ταυτα ἐστιν τα ἐργα του θεου, we put "These are the works of God". If you translate it as "These are the deeds of God" or "These are the things God does", your translation is also correct.

When we are translating from the New Testament, the context may help us to decide how to translate. In Matthew 11.2, τα ἐργα του Χριστου means "The deeds Christ had done" or "The wonderful things Christ was doing"; but in John 6.28 τα ἐργα του θεου means "The things God wants us to do".

Translate

1. τουτο ἐστιν το ἐργον του θεου.	This is the work of God.
2. τουτο ἐστιν το ἐργον ὃ ποιει.	This is the work which he does.
3. ταυτα ἐστιν τα ἐργα του θεου.	These are the works of God.
4. ταυτα ἐστιν τα ἐργα ἁ ποιουσιν.	These are the deeds which they do.

Note that in nos. 3 and 4, ταυτα ἐστιν must be translated as "these are", and not as "these is". When plural words which take τα as "the" (e.g. ἐργα) are the subject of a sentence, they are usually followed by a singular form of the verb.

12.2

το ἐργον – the work, the deed
τα ἐργα – the works, the deeds

-ον⎫ object
-α ⎭ endings
(the same as the subject endings)

So: ὁ το ἐργον ποιων – the person doing the work
ὁ μη ποιων τα ἐργα – the person who does not do the deeds.

Translate

1. ποιει το ἐργον.	He does the work.
2. ὁ ποιων τα ἐργα.	The person doing the deeds.
3. ὁς ἀν ποιῃ ταυτα τα ἐργα...	Whoever does these acts...
4. ἐαν ποιῃ το ἐργον...	If he does the work...
5. γραφουσι τα βιβλια ἱνα ἀναγινωσκωμεν αὐτα.	They write the books so that we may read them.
6. οὑτοι εἰσιν οἱ μη ἀναγινωσκοντες τα βιβλια.	These are the people who are not reading the books.

12.3

του ἐργου – of the work
των ἐργων – of the works

-ου⎫ of
-ων⎭

So: ἡ ἀρχη του ἐργου – the beginning of the work.

12.3

Translate

1. ἡ ἀρχη των ἐργων του θεου.

   The beginning of the works of God.

2. αὐτη ἐστιν ἡ ἀρχη του ἐργου.

   This is the beginning of the work.

3. αὐτη ἠν ἡ ἀρχη του βιβλιου.

   This was the beginning of the book.

4. μη ἀναγινωσκωμεν τα βιβλια του ἀδελφου ἡμων ἀλλα τα βιβλια της ἀδελφης ὑμων.

   Let us not read our brother's books but your sister's books.

12.4

τῳ ἐργῳ – by the work
τοις ἐργοις – by the works

-ῳ } by, by means of,
-οις } with, in

So: μη ἀγαπωμεν λογῳ ἀλλα ἐργῳ
Let us not love in word but in deed

γινωσκω αὐτην τῳ ἐργῳ ὃ ποιει
I know her by the work which she does

πιστευω τοις ἐργοις αὐτου
I believe in his works
or I believe the miracles he does.

Translate

1. γινωσκομεν αὐτον τοις ἐργοις ἃ ποιει.

   We know him by the works which he is doing.

2. πιστευετε τοις ἐργοις αὐτου.

   You believe in his works.

3. πιστευουσι τοις ἐργοις ἡμων.

   They believe our works.

4. ἀναγινωσκεις τους λογους οὑς γραφω ἐν τῳ βιβλιῳ τουτῳ.

   You are reading the words which I am writing in this book.

12.5 Words

Compare

το ἐργον – the work, the deed, the action   energy
το τεκνον – the child
  το τεκνιον – the little child
το εὐαγγελιον – the good news, the good   evangel,
  message, the gospel (never used of a   evangelist
  book, always of a communicated message)

48

το βιβλιον – the book

το δαιμονιον – the demon

ὁ πονηρος – the evil one

πονηρος – evil, wicked

ποιεω (ποιω) – I do, I make

τουτο – this, this thing

ταυτα – these, these things

γαρ – for, because (γαρ is the second word in a Greek clause or sentence, never the first)

Compare

bibliography

demon

poetry

So: ὁ γαρ μη ἀγαπων τον ἀδελφον...

For he who does not love the brother...

ἠν γαρ αὐτων πονηρα τα ἐργα

(Lit. was for of them evil the deeds)

For their deeds were evil.

12.6 Translate

1. οἱ πιστευοντες τῳ Ἰησου τεκνα θεου εἰσιν ἀλλα οἱ μη πιστευοντες τεκνα του πονηρου εἰσιν και ποιουσιν τα ἐργα ἁ αὐτος ποιει.

Those who believe in Jesus are children of God but those who do not believe are children of the evil one and they do the deeds which he does.

2. τα δαιμονια πονηρα ἐστιν, πονηρα γαρ ἐστιν τα ἐργα αὐτων.

The demons are evil, for their deeds are evil.

3. οὐκ ἀγαπω τουτους τους ἀνθρωπους, ἐστιν γαρ αὐτων πονηρα τα ἐργα.

I do not love these men, for the things they do are evil (*or*, for their deeds are evil).

4. Τεκνια, μη ἀγαπωμεν λογῳ ἀλλα ἐν ἐργῳ και ἀληθειᾳ, και γαρ ὁ θεος ἀγαπη ἐστιν.

Little children, let us not love in word but in deed and truth, for God is love.

5. τουτο ἐστιν το βιβλιον ὁ γραφει ὁ Μαρκος.

This is the book which Mark is writing.

6. ταυτα γραφει ἐν τῳ βιβλιῳ τουτῳ ἱνα το εὐαγγελιον γινωσκητε και κοινωνιαν ἐχητε μετα του Κυριου ἡμων.

He writes these things in this book so that you may know the good news and have fellowship with our Lord.

12.6

7. καὶ λεγουσιν αὐτῳ οἱ Φαρισαιοι, Δαιμονιον ἐχεις και ἐν (through) τῳ ἀρχοντι (ruler) των δαιμονιων ἐκβαλλεις (you cast out) τα δαιμονια. και λεγει αὐτοις ὁ Ἰησους, Δαιμονιον οὐκ ἐχω, ἀλλα ποιω τα ἐργα του θεου και ἐκβαλλω τα δαιμονια ἐν τῃ δυναμει (power) αὐτου.

The Pharisees say to him, "You have a demon and through the ruler of the demons you cast out the demons". Jesus says to them, "I do not have a demon, but I do the works of God and I cast out the demons through his power".

12.7

You have now seen and translated all the forms for "the". Here they are in a table. Copy this table in large letters on a sheet of paper, and put it where you can see it every day.

Singular

ὁ	ἡ	το	subject (nominative)
τον	την	το	object (accusative)
του	της	του	of (genitive)
τῳ	τῃ	τῳ	by, with, to, for (dative)

Plural

οἱ	αἱ	τα	subject (nominative)
τους	τας	τα	object (accusative)
των	των	των	of (genitive)
τοις	ταις	τοις	by, with, to, for (dative)

The forms in column 1 go with all words which have ὁ = the: ὁ βασιλευς – the king; οἱ βασιλεις – the kings; ὁ πατηρ – the father; του πατρος – of the father. All nouns with ὁ are called masculine.

The forms in column 2 go with all words which have ἡ = the: ἡ καρδια – the heart; ἡ ἐρημος – the desert; ἡ πολις – the town; της γης – of the earth. All nouns with ἡ are called feminine.

The forms in column 3 go with all words which have το = the: το ὀνομα – the name; το γενος – the tribe; το φως – the light; ἐν τῳ φωτι – in the light. All nouns with το are called neuter.

Look at column 4. We can describe ὁ as nominative singular masculine, την as accusative singular feminine, τα as nominative or accusative plural neuter.

We shall discuss these grammatical terms in lesson 37 and study them in lessons 37, 39, and 42. It is not necessary to learn them at this stage in the course.

12.8

You have also read and translated forms of οὗτος – this, and ὅς – who.

	Masculine	Feminine	Neuter	
Singular				
	οὗτος	αὕτη	τοῦτο	nom.
	τοῦτον	ταὑτην	τοῦτο	acc.
	τούτου	ταύτης	τούτου	gen.
	τούτῳ	ταύτῃ	τούτῳ	dat.
Plural				
	οὗτοι	αὗται	ταῦτα	nom.
	τούτους	ταύτας	ταῦτα	acc.
	τούτων	τούτων	τούτων	gen.
	τούτοις	ταύταις	τούτοις	dat.

	Masculine	Feminine	Neuter	
Singular				
	ὅς	ἥ	ὅ	nom
	ὅν	ἥν	ὅ	acc.
	οὗ	ἧς	οὗ	gen.
	ᾧ	ᾗ	ᾧ	dat.
Plural				
	οἵ	αἵ	ἅ	nom.
	οὕς	ἅς	ἅ	acc.
	ὧν	ὧν	ὧν	gen.
	οἷς	αἷς	οἷς	dat.

You have already used and understood these forms. They are given here for reference purposes only.

LESSON 13

ποιεω (ποιω) – I do, I make

13.1

ποιω – I do, I make, I am doing...   Compare: λεγω
ποιουμεν – we do, we make...   λεγομεν

So: ταυτα ποιουμεν – we do these things

τουτο γραφομεν – we write this

τα ἐργα ἁ ποιω – the deeds which I do

οἱ λογοι οὑς λεγω – the words which I say.

A verbal form like λεγομεν has two parts:

(a) the stem, **λεγ**, which indicates the basic meaning
(b) the ending, **-ομεν**, which indicates the person.

In the form ποιουμεν we have:

(a) the stem, **ποιε**
(b) the ending, **-ομεν**

but the ε and ο of ποιεομεν have been combined so that ποιεομεν has become ποιουμεν.

Similar changes take place in other verbs with stems ending in a vowel (see ἀγαπαω in 11.2). Note that these verbs are written in dictionaries in their full form: καλεω, ἀγαπαω, πληροω. But in actual use, the vowel of the stem combines with the vowel of the ending to make the shorter or *contracted* ending, e.g. ποιω, ἀγαπω.

Translate

1. τουτο ποιω ἱνα πιστευῃς. | I am doing this so that you may believe.

2. ταυτα ποιουμεν ἡμεις ἱνα και ὑμεις πιστευητε. | We are doing these things so that you also may believe.

3. ταυτα λεγομεν ἱνα αὐτοι ποιωσιν τα ἐργα ἁ ποιουμεν. | We speak these things so that they may do the deeds which we do.

13.2

πoιεις – you do, you make...   Compare: λεγεις
πoιειτε – you (pl.) do, you make...   λεγετε

Translate

1. τουτο ποιειτε. | You are doing this.
2. τα έργα του πονηρου ποιειτε. | You do the works of the evil one.
3. έαν τα έργα αύτου ποιητε... | If you do his works...
4. το έργον αύτου ποιεις. | You are doing his work.
5. έαν το έργον του θεου ποιης... | If you do the work of God...

13.3

πoιει – he does, he makes...   Compare: λεγει
πoιουσιν – they do, they make...   λεγουσιν

Translate

1. τουτο ποιει ό Παυλος. | Paul is doing this.
2. τουτο ποιω. | I am doing this.
3. τουτο ποιουσιν. | They are doing this.
4. Ἰησου, ταυτα ποιεις. | Jesus, you are doing these things.
5. ταυτα ποιουσιν οί άποστολοι. | The apostles are doing these things.
6. ός άν ταυτα ποιη... | Whoever does these things...

13.4 Words

Compare

καλεω – I call, I invite | call, Para*cle*te
λαλεω – I talk, I speak | gloss*olalia*
περιπατεω – I walk about, I walk, I live | peripatetic
ζητεω – I seek, I look for
ή γλωσσα – the tongue, the language | *gloss*ary, *gloss*olalia
το φως – the light
   του φωτος – of the light | *photo*graph
το σκοτος or ή σκοτια – the darkness
έγω – I;   με – me;   μου – of me; | *ego*ism, me
   μοι – to me, for me
συ – you (thou);   σε – you;   σου – of you;
   σοι – to you, for you

13.5 Translate

1. οὑτος ἐστιν ὁ ἀδελφος μου.	He (this man) is my brother.
2. αὑτη ἐστιν ἡ ἀδελφη σου.	She is your sister.
3. ἐγω ταυτα γραφω ἀλλα συ οὐκ ἀναγινωσκεις αὐτα.	I am writing these things but you are not reading them.
4. ἡ γλωσσα μου λαλει σοι και τα ὡτα σου ἀκουει.	My tongue speaks to you and your ears hear.
5. λαλει ταυταις ταις γλωσσαις ἀλλα ἐγω οὐκ ἀκουω.	He speaks in these languages but I do not understand.
6. καλει σε ὁ Ἰησους ἱνα ἐν τῳ φωτι περιπατῃς.	Jesus calls you so that you may walk in the light.
7. οὐ ζητουμεν την σκοτιαν ἀλλα το φως.	We do not seek the darkness but the light.
8. μη ζητωμεν την σκοτιαν ἀλλα το φως και την ἀληθειαν.	Let us not seek the darkness but the light and the truth.
9. ὁ θεος φως ἐστιν και ἐν αὐτῳ σκοτια οὐκ ἐστιν. και καλει σε ὁ θεος ἱνα ἐν τῳ φωτι περιπατῃς, οἱ γαρ ἐν τῳ φωτι περιπατουντες τεκνα θεου εἰσιν, και αὐτον Κυριον καλουσιν. περιπατωμεν ἐν τῳ φωτι και μη περιπατωμεν ἐν τῳ σκοτει.	God is light and darkness is not in him. God calls you so that you may walk in the light, for those who walk in the light are children of God, and they call him Lord. Let us walk in the light and let us not walk in the darkness.
10. ζητειτε με ἱνα τους λογους μου ἀκουητε. ἀλλα, ἀδελφοι μου, ἐαν γλωσσαις λαλω ὑμιν οὐκ ἀκουετε. ὁ γαρ λαλων γλωσσαις οὐκ ἀνθρωποις λαλει ἀλλα θεῳ. οὐδεις (no one) γαρ ἀκουει τους λογους οὑς λεγει. μη λαλωμεν γλωσσαις ἐν τῃ ἐκκλησιᾳ.	You seek me so that you may hear my words. But, my brothers, if I speak to you in tongues, you do not understand. For he who speaks in tongues does not speak to men but to God, for no one understands the words he says. Let us not speak in tongues in the congregation.

13.6 Punctuation

In most editions of the New Testament (ἡ καινη διαθηκη) the following punctuation marks are used:

Compare English

1. Comma   ,   ,
2. Colon   ·   : or ;

3. Full stop　　　　.　　.

4. Question mark　　;　　?

5. Apostrophe　　'　　'
   to mark the dropping of a letter:
   μετα ἐμου becomes μετ' ἐμου – with me
   μετα ἡμων becomes μεθ' ἡμων – with us

13.7

Read carefully, making use when necessary of the notes at the end of each passage.

1. Love and light

ὁ ἀγαπων τον ἀδελφον αὐτου ἐν τῳ φωτι περιπατει, ἀλλα οἱ μη ἀγαπωντες τους ἀδελφους ἐν τῃ σκοτιᾳ εἰσιν και ἐν τῃ ϲκοτιᾳ περιπατουσι. τεκνια μου, ἀγαπωμεν ἀλληλους, ὁ γαρ θεος ἀγαπη ἐστιν· και μη ἀγαπωμεν λογῳ μηδε γλωσσῃ ἀλλα ἐν ἐργῳ και ἀληθειᾳ.

Notes:
ὁ ἀγαπων – lesson 8.1, 11.2	ἀλληλους – each other
μη – 11.2	ἀγαπωμεν λογῳ – 12.4
τεκνια – 12.5	μηδε – nor

2. Seeking God

και ἐγω ταυτα γραφω σοι ἱνα τον θεον ζητῃς ἐξ ὁλης της καρδιας σου· ὁ γαρ ζητων τον θεον ἐξ ὁλης της καρδιας αὐτου, εὑρησει αὐτον, καθως ἀναγινωσκεις ἐν τῳ βιβλιῳ του εὐαγγελιου, Ὁ ζητων εὑρισκει. ὁς γαρ ἀν αὐτον ζητῃ εὑρησει· και μακαριοι εἰσιν παντες οἱ ζητουντες και εὑρισκοντες αὐτον.

Notes:
ὁλος – whole	καθως – as
ἐξ – out of	παντες – all
εὑρησει – he will find	

13.8 Translation

Here are the last lines of 13.7.1:
και μη ἀγαπωμεν λογῳ μηδε γλωσσῃ ἀλλα ἐν ἐργῳ και ἀληθειᾳ.
This could be translated literally as, "And not let us love by word nor by tongue but by deed and by truth". Of course, this is not how we would naturally express these ideas in English. We must look for better ways to translate.

και μη ἀγαπωμεν is better translated as:
Let us not love...
or as Let us show love not by...

λογῳ and γλωσσῃ indicate love shown "by word" and "by tongue". Because New Testament writers, influenced by Hebrew idiom, often put side by side two ideas that we might rather combine, we might translate

μη...λογῳ μηδε γλωσσῃ
as not by the words we speak with our tongues.

ἐν ἐργῳ and ἀληθειᾳ indicate love expressed "by deed" and "by reality". So we might translate

ἐν ἐργῳ και ἀληθειᾳ
as by the things we actually do.

We could then translate

και μη ἀγαπωμεν λογῳ μηδε γλωσσῃ ἀλλα ἐν ἐργῳ και ἀληθειᾳ
as Let us show our love not by the words we speak with our tongues but by what we actually do.

In 13.7.2 we read: ὁ γαρ ζητων τον θεον ἐξ ὁλης της καρδιας αὐτου. This could be translated literally as, "The person for seeking the God out of whole of the heart of him". But it is clearly better to translate

ὁ γαρ ζητων τον θεον
as For the person who seeks God...
or as For he who seeks God...

ἐξ ὁλης της καρδιας αὐτου is better translated "with his whole heart" than "out of his whole heart". But even that is not very natural English. "Wholeheartedly" or "with all his heart", are better. So we might translate:

ὁ γαρ ζητων τον θεον ἐξ ὁλης της καρδιας αὐτου
as For the one who seeks God wholeheartedly...
or as For he who puts his whole heart into seeking God...

When we translate we must not ask ourselves, "How can I put these words into my language?" We must ask, "How can I express the meaning of these words in my language?"

LESSON 14

ἔλεγεν – he was saying, he used to say ----|

14.1

Compare:

(a) λεγει – he is speaking —, he speaks ·····
(b) ἔλεγεν – he was speaking —|, he used to speak ····|

(a) refers to a continuing or repeated action in the present
(b) refers to a continued or repeated action in the past.

ε before the stem of a verb is **a mark of past time.**

Translate

1. γραφει τας ἐπιστολας.	He is writing the letters.
2. ἔγραφεν ἐπιστολας.	He was writing letters.
3. λαμβανει το βιβλιον.	He takes the book.
4. ἐλαμβανεν τα βιβλια.	He was taking the books.
5. ἐπιστευεν τῳ ᾽Ιησου.	He was believing in Jesus.
6. πιστευει τῳ ᾽Ιησου.	He believes in Jesus.
7. ἀκουει λογους.	He hears words.
8. ἤκουεν τους λογους.	He was hearing the words.

14.2 Translating forms like ἔλεγεν

ἔλεγεν refers to continued or repeated action in the past.

So it may be translated into English as:

he was saying —|
or he used to say ····|

When we are translating a New Testament passage we have to choose a translation which will fit well in the passage. Consider these possible translations of και ἔλεγεν τοις μαθηταις:

So he said to the disciples

He was saying to the disciples

He began to say to the disciples

He went on to say to the disciples

He used to say to the disciples.

(In our right-hand check column we usually put the forms with "was" and "were", but always remember that forms with "used to" and other similar translations are also possible.)

14.3

ἔλεγεν – he was saying, he used to say, he said

ἔλεγον – they were saying, they used to say, they said

ἔβλεπεν – he was looking at

ἔβλεπον – they were looking at

Translate

1. λεγει τοις μαθηταις...	He is saying to the disciples...
2. ἔλεγεν τοις μαθηταις αὐτου...	He was saying to his disciples...
3. ἔλεγον αὐτῳ οἱ μαθηται...	The disciples said to him...
4. ἔβλεπεν τον Ἰησουν.	He was looking at Jesus.
5. ἔβλεπον τον ἀδελφον αὐτου.	They were looking at his brother.
6. βλεπουσι τας ἀδελφας αὐτου.	They are looking at his sisters.

14.4

ἔλεγες – you were saying   Compare: λεγεις

ἔλεγετε – you (pl.) were saying   λεγετε

Translate

1. ἔγραφες την ἐπιστολην ἡμιν.	You were writing the letter to us.
2. συ γραφεις ἐπιστολην μοι.	You are writing a letter to me.
3. ἔγραφες ταυτην την ἐπιστολην.	You were writing this letter.
4. ἔγραφετε ἐπιστολας.	You were writing letters.
5. ἀναγινωσκετε τας ἐπιστολας.	You are reading the letters.
6. ἀνεγινωσκετε τας ἐπιστολας.	You were reading the letters.
7. μη ἀναγινωσκωμεν την ἐπιστολην ἡν συ ἐγραφες.	Let us not read the letter which you were writing.

14.5

ἐλεγον – I was saying   Compare: λεγω
ἐλεγομεν – we were saying   λεγομεν

Note that only the context shows the difference between ἐλεγον – I was saying, and ἐλεγον – they were saying.

Translate

1. ἐγω Παυλος ἐλεγον ὑμιν ὁτι Ὁ θεος φως ἐστιν. | I, Paul, used to say to you, "God is light".
2. ταυτα ἐλεγομεν ὑμιν. | We were saying these things to you.
3. ἀγαπω σε και ταυτα ἐγραφον σοι ἱνα κοινωνιαν ἐχῃς μετα μου. | I love you and I was writing these things to you so that you may have fellowship with me.
4. ταυτα ἐγραφον ἡμιν οἱ ἀποστολοι. | The apostles were writing these things to us (for us).
5. ἐαν ταυτα γραφωσιν, την ἀληθειαν γραφουσιν. | If they are writing these things, they are writing the truth.
6. ἐγραφεν τα βιβλια ταυτα ἡ Μαρια. | Mary was writing these books.

14.6 Summary of forms

A

1. ἐλεγον – I was saying
2. ἐλεγες – you were saying
3. ἐλεγεν – he was saying

1. ἐλεγομεν – we were saying
2. ἐλεγετε – you were saying
3. ἐλεγον – they were saying

B

1. λεγω – I am saying
2. λεγεις – you are saying
3. λεγει – he is saying

1. λεγομεν – we are saying
2. λεγετε – you are saying
3. λεγουσιν – they are saying

Note

1. The type of action in all these forms in columns A and B is **continuing** or **repeated** action ‒‒‒.
2. ε before the stem is **a mark of past time**. So all the forms in column A indicate continued or repeated action in past time ‒‒‒ι.

14.6

3. The **endings** after the stem show the **person**:

	1st person	2nd person	3rd person
Singular	-ον – I	-ες – you	-εν – he, she, it
Plural	-ομεν – we	-ετε – you	-ον – they

4. The basic stem of the verb is not always its first part. For example, in English "standing" and "understanding" have the same basic stem: stand. Notice how the ε indicating past time comes immediately before the stem:

	Stem	
λεγω – I am saying	λεγ	ἐλεγον – I was saying
καλω – I am calling	καλε	ἐκαλουν – I was calling
ἀναγινωσκει – he is reading	γιν	ἀνεγινωσκεν – he was reading
περιπατει – he is walking	πατε	περιεπατει – he was walking
ἀποστελλουσι – they are sending	στελλ	ἀπεστελλον – they were sending

5. In grammar books the forms in column B (page 59) of λεγω (I am saying), are called present.

The forms in column A of ἐλεγον (I was saying), are called imperfect.

As we have seen, both the present and the imperfect tenses indicate continued or repeated action, and the *type* of action is often of more significance than the *time*. Note that, even in English, to describe "I go" as in the present tense can be misleading. Study this conversation:

"Do you go to school?"
"Yes, I go to school."

"I go to school" implies:

(i) I have been to school in the past
(ii) I go to school now, in the present
(iii) I expect to continue going to school.

"I go" may be described as being in the present tense, but it refers to past, present, and future time. So in John 15.18:

Εἰ ὁ κοσμος ὑμας μισει...
If the world hates you...

μισει (it hates) refers to any hatred "you" have encountered, do encounter, or will encounter from the world.

14.7 Words

ἀκολουθεω – I follow
    ἠκολουθει αὐτῃ – he was following her
βλεπω – I look at, I look, I see
διδασκω – I teach
    ὁ διδασκαλος – the teacher
    ἡ διδαχη – the teaching, the doctrine
ὁ μαθητης – the learner, the student, the disciple
ἀμην – truly, verily, amen

14.8 Translate

1. ἀκολουθω σοι.

I am following you.

2. ἠκολουθει τῳ Ἰησου ὁ Φιλιππος.

Philip was following Jesus.

3. οἱ μαθηται ἀκολουθουσιν τῳ Ἰησου και διδασκει αὐτους.

The disciples follow Jesus and he teaches them.

4. ἐβλεπεν ὁ διδασκαλος τους μαθητας.

The teacher was looking at the students.

5. οἱ μαθηται ἀκουουσιν την διδαχην του διδασκαλου ἱνα ποιωσιν τα ἐργα ἁ διδασκει αὐτους.

The disciples are listening to the doctrine of the teacher so that they may do the deeds which he teaches them.

14.9

Read carefully:

Disciples were following Jesus

1. Οἱ μαθηται του Ἰησου ἠκολουθουν αὐτῳ και ἐδιδασκεν αὐτους. και οἱ μαθηται του Ἰωαννου ἐλεγον αὐτῳ ὁτι Ἀκουομεν την διδαχην του Ἰησου και ἡ διδαχη ἠν διδασκει ἀληθης ἐστιν.

2. Και ἀφεντες (leaving) τον Ἰωαννην ἠκολουθουν τῳ Ἰησου. και ὁ Ἰησους βλεπων αὐτους ἀκολουθουντας αὐτῳ ἐλεγεν αὐτοις, Τί (what) ζητειτε; ἐλεγον αὐτῳ, Ἀκολουθουμεν σοι ἱνα την διδαχην ἡν συ διδασκεις ἀκουωμεν.

3. Και ἐλεγεν αὐτοις ἐν τῃ διδαχῃ αὐτου, Καλειτε με διδασκαλον και κυριον, και καλως (well) λεγετε, εἰμι (I am) γαρ. και ἐλεγεν αὐτοις, Ἀμην ἀμην λεγω ὑμιν, οὐκ ἐστιν μαθητης μειζων (greater) του διδασκαλου αὐτου.

61

14.10 Translation

In 14.9.2 we read: ἱνα την διδαχην ἡν συ διδασκεις ἀκουωμεν. We might translate this literally as "so that the teaching which you teach we may hear". But in English:

1. the word order must be changed – "so that we may hear the teaching which you teach", and
2. "the teaching which you teach", is not natural English. So the translator must find a better way. Consider:

   (a) so that we may hear the doctrine which you teach

   (b) so that we may listen to your teaching

   (c) so that we may hear what you teach.

A translator must not only ask, "How can I best express the meaning of these words in my language?" (13.8). He must also ask, "How can I best express the meaning of these words in my language so that they can be understood by those who will read them or hear them?" Look again at translations (a), (b), and (c) in the previous paragraph. If we expect our readers to have a good understanding of English, we might choose (a) or (b). If we expected their English to be limited, we would choose (c).

14.11

Revise lessons 7 and 8.

LESSON 15

ἐποιει – he was doing, he used to do ⁻⁻⁻|

15.1

ἐποιει – he was doing, he used to do   ποιει – he does
he was making,
he used to make

ἐποιουν – they were doing,   ποιουσι – they do
they were making

So: τουτο ἐποιουν – they were doing this
ταυτα ἐποιει ὁ Παυλος – Paul was doing these things.

Translate

1. ποιει τα ἐργα.	He does the works.
2. ἐποιει τα ἐργα ταυτα.	He was doing these works.
3. βλεπει το ἐργον ὃ ποιουσιν.	He sees the work which they do.
4. ἐβλεπεν το ἐργον ὃ ἐποιουν.	He saw the work they were doing.
5. ἐζητει τους περιπατουντας ἐν τῃ σκοτιᾳ.	He was looking for the people walking in the darkness.

15.2

ἐποιεις – you were doing, you were making	ποιεις – you do
ἐποιειτε – you (pl.) were doing, you (pl.) were making	ποιειτε – you do

So: ἐποιειτε τα ἐργα – you were doing the works

Translate

1. Ἰησου, ταυτα ἐποιεις.	Jesus, you were doing these things.
2. ποιεις τα ἐργα.	You are doing the deeds.
3. τουτο ἐποιει ὁ πονηρος.	The evil one was doing this.
4. ταυτα ἐποιειτε.	You were doing these things.
5. ἐζητειτε τον Ἰησουν.	You were seeking Jesus.
6. ἐκαλει τους ἀδελφους.	He was calling the brothers.
7. ἐκαλειτε τους ἀδελφους ὑμων.	You were calling your brothers.
8. ἐκαλεις τας ἀδελφας σου.	You were calling your sisters.
9. τουτο ποιειτε.	You are doing this.

15.3

ἐποιουν – I was doing, I was making	ποιω – I do
ἐποιουμεν – we were doing, we were making	ποιουμεν – we do

So: ψευστας αὐτους ἐποιουμεν – we made them liars
                            or we made them out to be liars.

15.3

Translate

1. ψευστην αὐτον ποιουμεν.	We make him a liar.
2. ψευστην ἐποιουμεν αὐτον.	We were making him a liar.
3. ταυτα ἐλαλουν ἐγω ἀλλα συ οὐκ ἠκουες.	I was saying these things but you were not listening.
4. οἱ μαθηται περιεπατουν ἐν τῳ φωτι.	The disciples were walking in the light.
5. γλωσσαις ἐλαλουμεν ἡμεις ἀλλα ὑμεις οὐκ ἠκουετε.	We were speaking in tongues but you were not understanding.

15.4 Questions

In a Greek text, a semi-colon (;) is used as a question mark. It is often sufficient to change a statement into a question:

τουτο λεγομεν – We say this   τουτο λεγομεν; – Do we say this?

τουτο λεγωμεν – Let us say this   τουτο λεγωμεν; – Should we say this?
or Are we to say this?

Translate

1. προφητης ἐστιν.	He is a prophet.
2. προφητης ἐστιν;	Is he a prophet?
3. προφητης ἠν;	Was he a prophet?
4. προφητης ἠν.	He was a prophet.
5. ταυτα ἐζητειτε.	You were seeking these things.
6. τουτο ἐζητειτε;	Were you seeking this?
7. ταυτα γραφομεν.	We are writing these things.
8. ταυτα γραφομεν;	Are we writing these things?
9. ταυτα γραφωμεν.	Let us write these things.
10. ταυτα γραφωμεν;	Should we write these things?

15.5

ἠγαπα – he was loving, he loved   ἀγαπᾳ – he loves
ἠγαπωμεν – we used to love, we loved   ἀγαπωμεν – we love

So: ὁ μαθητης ὁν ἠγαπα ὁ Ἰησους – the disciple whom Jesus loved.

Note that when the ε which shows past time is put before a stem that begins with a vowel, the vowel is usually lengthened by being combined with the ε.

So: ἀκουει – he hears   ἠκουεν – he was hearing
     εὑρισκουσι – they find   ηὑρισκον – they were finding
     ἐχει – he has   εἰχεν – he had, he used to have

Translate

1. ἀγαπᾳ ἡμας ὁ θεος.	God loves us.
2. ἠγαπα ὁ Ἰησους την Μαρθαν.	Jesus loved Martha.
3. οὑτος ἠν ὁ διδασκαλος ὁν ἠγαπατε.	This was the teacher whom you loved.
4. αὑτοι ηὑρισκον τα βιβλια ἁ εἰχεν ὁ Μαρκος.	They were finding the books which Mark had.

15.6 Words

βαπτιζω – I baptize
    ὁ βαπτιστης – the baptist, the baptizer
μαρτυρεω – I bear witness, I give evidence
    ὁ μαρτυς – the witness, the person who gives evidence
    ἡ μαρτυρια – the testimony, the witness, the evidence that is given
τηρεω – I keep watch over, I keep
ἡ ἐντολη – the commandment, the command
τίς; – who? which?
    τίνα; – whom?
    τίνος; – of whom?
    τίνι; – to whom, for whom?
    τίνες; – who? (pl.)
    τίσιν; – to whom? (pl.)
τί; – what? why?

15.7 Translate

1. Τίς ἐστιν και τί ποιει;

    Μαρτυς ἐστιν και μαρτυρει τῳ Ἰησου.

"Who is he and what does he do?"

"He is a witness and he bears witness to Jesus."

2. Τίς ἠν και τί ἐποιει;

    Ὁ βαπτιστης ἠν και ἐβαπτιζεν τους μαθητας αὐτου.

"Who was he and what was he doing?"

"He was the baptizer and he was baptizing his disciples."

3. *Τίνα ζητειτε;* "Whom do you seek?"

   Τον Χριστον ζητουμεν. "We seek the Messiah."

4. *Τίνες εἰσιν και τί ποιουσιν;* "Who are they and what do they do?"

   Μαθηται εἰσιν και τηρουσιν τας ἐντολας του Χριστου. "They are disciples and they keep the commandments of Christ."

5. *Τίνι λεγεις; και τίνα αὐτον καλεις; Λεγω τῳ Ἰωαννῳ και αὐτον τον βαπτιστην καλω.* "To whom are you speaking? And what do you call him?" "I am speaking to John and I call him the Baptist."

6. *Τί ἐδιδασκεν αὐτους; Ἐν τη διδαχη ἐλεγεν αὐτοις, Ἐγω οὐκ εἰμι (I am) ὁ Χριστος, ἀλλα μαρτυρω περι (about) αὐτου, και ἀληθης ἐστιν ἡ μαρτυρια μου ἡν μαρτυρω περι αὐτου ἱνα πιστευητε αὐτῳ.* "What was he teaching them?" "In his teaching he said to them, 'I am not the Messiah, but I bear witness about him, and my witness which I bear about him is true, so that you may believe in him.' "

15.8

Read carefully:

Keeping the commandments

Αἱ ἐντολαι του θεου οὐ πονηραι εἰσιν, και ἐτηρουν αὐτας οἱ ἀποστολοι και ἐδιδασκον τους ἀνθρωπους ἱνα τας ἐντολας αὐτου τηρωσιν. και ἐλεγεν ὁ Ἰωαννης ὁτι Ὁ ἐχων τας ἐντολας του θεου και τηρων αὐτας οὑτος ἐστιν ὁ ἀγαπων τον θεον· καθως εἰπεν ὁ Ἰησους, Ὁ ἐχων τας ἐντολας μου και τηρων αὐτας, ἐκεινος ἐστιν ὁ ἀγαπων με. ὁς γαρ ἀν ἐχη τας ἐντολας αὐτου και μη τηρη αὐτας, ἡ ἀγαπη του θεου οὐκ ἐστιν ἐν αὐτῳ. ἀλλα ἐαν τας ἐντολας αὐτου τηρωμεν, ἀληθως ἡ ἀγαπη του θεου ἐστιν ἐν ἡμιν.

Και τίς ἐστιν ἡ ἐντολη αὐτου; αὑτη ἐστιν ἡ ἐντολη αὐτου ἱνα ἀγαπωμεν ἀλληλους· καθως εἰπεν ὁ Ἰησους, Ἐντολην καινην διδωμι ὑμιν ἱνα ἀγαπατε ἀλληλους, καθως ἠγαπησα ὑμας ἱνα και ὑμεις ἀγαπατε ἀλληλους.

Notes:

καθως – as
εἰπεν – he said
ἐκεινος – that, that man, he
ἀληθως – truly
ἱνα – that

ἀλληλους – each other
καινη – new
διδωμι – I give
ἠγαπησα – I loved

LESSON 16

Α to Ω – Alpha to Omega

16.1 Capital letters

Here is John 1.1–2 in small letters and in capitals:

ἐν ἀρχῃ ἦν ὁ λογος και ὁ λογος ἦν προς τον θεον και θεος ἦν ὁ λογος οὗτος ἦν ἐν ἀρχῃ προς τον θεον.

ἘΝ ἈΡΧΗΙ ἪΝ Ὁ ΛΟΓΟΣ ΚΑΙ Ὁ ΛΟΓΟΣ ἫΝ ΠΡΟΣ ΤΟΝ ΘΕΟΝ ΚΑΙ ΘΕΟΣ ἫΝ Ὁ ΛΟΓΟΣ ὉΥΤΟΣ ἪΝ ἘΝ ἈΡΧΗΙ ΠΡΟΣ ΤΟΝ ΘΕΟΝ.

Here is the title of Mark's Gospel in *minuscule* (small) letters and in *uncials* (capitals):

ἀρχη του εὐαγγελιου Ἰησου Χριστου υἱου θεου.
ἈΡΧΗ ΤΟΥ ἘΥΑΓΓΕΛΙΟΥ ἸΗΣΟΥ ΧΡΙΣΤΟΥ ὙΙΟΥ ΘΕΟΥ.

Here are some common words in minuscule and in uncial letters:

ἡμερα ἩΜΕΡΑ } day		δοξα ΔΟΞΑ } glory	
ζωη ΖΩΗ } life		ἐρωταω ἘΡΩΤΑΩ } I ask	
ἐξοδος ἘΞΟΔΟΣ } exodus		ἐγγυς ἘΓΓΥΣ } near	

16.2 The alphabet and the names of the letters

α	Α	Alpha	ι	Ι	Iota	ρ	Ρ	Rho
β	Β	Beta	κ	Κ	Kappa	σ, ς	Σ	Sigma
γ	Γ	Gamma	λ	Λ	Lambda	τ	Τ	Tau
δ	Δ	Delta	μ	Μ	Mu	υ	Υ	Upsilon
ε	Ε	Epsilon	ν	Ν	Nu	φ	Φ	Phi
ζ	Ζ	Zeta	ξ	Ξ	Xi (ksi)	χ	Χ	Chi
η	Η	Eta	ο	Ο	Omicron	ψ	Ψ	Psi
θ	Θ	Theta	π	Π	Pi	ω	Ω	Omega

If you learn the order and names of the letters it will help you when you want to look up words in a dictionary or lexicon.

16.3 Uses of capital letters

When the first manuscripts of the New Testament books were written and copied, only capital letters (uncials) were used. Such manuscripts are therefore called uncial manuscripts.

In printed editions of the Greek New Testament, Ἡ ΚΑΙΝΗ ΔΙΑΘΗΚΗ, capital letters are used in three ways.

1. A capital letter is used for the first letter of spoken or quoted words and passages:

John 1.21   καὶ λεγει, Οὐκ εἰμι. Ὁ προφητης εἶ συ;
             He said, "I am not". "Are you the prophet?"

2. A capital letter is used for the beginning of a new paragraph, but not for every new sentence:

Mark 4.35   Καὶ λεγει αὐτοις ἐν ἐκεινῃ τῃ ἡμερᾳ...
             He said to them on that day...

3. A capital letter is used for names and titles:

John 1.44   ἦν δε ὁ Φιλιππος ἀπο Βηθσαιδα
             Philip was from Bethsaida

John 1.41   Εὑρηκαμεν τον Μεσσιαν, ὃ ἐστιν μεθερμηνευομενον Χριστος
             We have found the Messiah (which is translated "Christ").

16.4 Words

εἰμι – I am
    ἐσμεν – we are
    εἶ – you are (thou art)
    ἐστε – you (pl.) are
δε – but, and
    (like γαρ and οὐν, δε is the second word in a sentence or clause)
    ὁ δε – he,   οἱ δε – they
οὐδε – and not, nor
    οὐδε...οὐδε... – neither...nor...
ἐρωταω – I ask
    ἠρωτησεν – he asked
    ἠρωτησαν – they asked
εἰπεν – he said
    εἰπαν or εἰπον – they said
οὐν – so, therefore, then
    εἰπεν οὐν αὐτοις – so he said to them
    οἱ δε εἰπον αὐτῳ Τίς οὐν συ;
        – they said to him, "Then who are you?"

16.5 Translate

1. οἱ δε ἠρωτησαν αὐτον, Τίς εἶ; ὁ δε εἶπεν, Μαρτυς εἰμι και μαρτυρω τῳ Ἰησου.

They asked him, "Who are you?" He said, "I am a witness and I bear witness to Jesus".

2. οἱ δε εἶπαν, Μαρτυρες ἐσμεν, ὑμεις δε την μαρτυριαν ἡμων οὐ λαμβανετε οὐδε ἀκολουθειτε τῳ Ἰησου.

They said, "We are witnesses but you do not receive our witness nor do you follow Jesus".

3. συ μαθητης εἶ του Ἰησου και αὐτον Διδασκαλον καλεις· ἡμεις δε του Μωυσεως ἐσμεν μαθηται.

You are a disciple of Jesus and you call him "Teacher"; but we are disciples of Moses.

4. ὑμεις ἐστε το φως των ἀνθρωπων, ἡμεις δε ἐν τη σκοτια περιπατουμεν.

You are the light of men but we walk in the darkness.

5. οὐδε ἐκαλει αὐτους οὐδε ἐλαλει αὐτοις.

He was neither calling them nor speaking to them.

6. ὁ δε εἶπεν αὐτοις, Οὐκ εἰμι ὁ Ἡλειας. οἱ δε ἠρωτησαν αὐτον, Τίς οὖν συ;

He said to them, "I am not Elijah". They asked him, "Who are you then?"

7. οὐκ ἐστε ὑμεις οἱ καλουντες με ἀλλα ἐγω εἰμι ὁ καλων ὑμας.

You are not the ones calling me but I am the one who is calling you.

8. εἰπεν οὖν αὐτοις, Ἐαν τηρητε τας ἐντολας μου γινωσκετε τον θεον, ὁ γαρ μη τηρων αὐτας οὐδε γινωσκει τον θεον οὐδε ἀγαπᾳ αὐτον.

So he said to them, "If you keep my commandments you know God, for he who does not keep them neither knows God nor loves him".

16.6

Read carefully:

John's testimony and answers

Και αὐτη ἐστιν ἡ μαρτυρια του Ἰωαννου του Βαπτιστου ὁτε ἠρωτησαν αὐτον, Συ τίς εἶ; και εἰπεν αὐτοις, Ἐγω οὐκ εἰμι ὁ Χριστος. οἱ δε ἠρωτησαν αὐτον, Τίς οὖν συ; Ἡλειας εἶ; εἰπεν αὐτοις ὁ Ἰωαννης, Οὐκ εἰμι. Ὁ προφητης εἶ συ; ὁ δε εἰπεν αὐτοις, Οὐ. εἰπαν οὖν αὐτῳ, Τίς εἶ; τί λεγεις περι σεαυτου; και εἰπεν αὐτοις ὁ Ἰωαννης, Ἐγω φωνη βοωντος ἐν τη ἐρημῳ, καθως εἰπεν Ἠσαιας ὁ προφητης. και ἠρωτησαν αὐτον λεγοντες, Τί οὖν βαπτιζεις εἰ συ οὐκ εἶ ὁ Χριστος οὐδε Ἡλειας οὐδε ὁ προφητης;

Notes:
ὁτε – when   περι – about

σεαυτον – yourself
βοαω – I shout
βοωντος – of a person shouting

ἡ ἐρημος – the desert, the wilderness
τί οὖν – why then?
εἰ – if.

16.7 Translating 16.6

(a) οἱ δε ἠρωτησαν αὐτον, Τίς οὖν συ;
They asked him, "Who are you then?"

Τίς οὖν συ; is literally "Who then you?" In English we need:

1. to put in the word "are", and
2. to put "then" at the beginning or end of the question:
"Then who are you?" or "Who are you then?"

(b) Ἐγω φωνη βοωντος
Lit. I voice of one shouting

In English: "I am the voice of a person shouting" or "I am the voice of someone who is shouting".

(c) ἠρωτησαν αὐτον λεγοντες, Τί...;
Lit. They asked him, saying, "Why...?"

λεγοντες (saying) indicates that the words they said will follow. In written English we usually indicate this by inverted commas. So we can translate: "They asked him, 'Why...?' " or "They asked him this question, 'Why...?' "

16.8 Progress test 9

Which is the best English translation?

1. ἠρωτησεν αὐτον λεγων Τίς οὖν συ;
   (a) He asked him saying, "Who then are you?"
   (b) He asked him who he was.
   (c) He asked him, "Who are you then?"

2. και ἠρωτησαν αὐτον και εἰπαν αὐτῳ, Τί οὖν βαπτιζεις εἰ συ οὐκ εἶ ὁ Χριστος;
   (a) And they asked him and they said to him, "Why therefore do you baptize if you are not the Messiah?"
   (b) So they asked him this question, "Then why do you baptize people if you are not the Messiah?"
   (c) So they questioned him and they said to him, "If you are not the Messiah why do you baptize?"

3. *ἀδελφοι μου, οὐκ ἐντολην καινην γραφω ὑμιν.*
   (a) Brothers of me, not a commandment new I write to you.
   (b) My brothers, to you I am writing a commandment that is not new.
   (c) My brothers, it is not a new commandment that I am writing to
       you.

Check your answers on page 280.

16.9
Revise lessons 9 and 10.

LESSON 17

προς, εἰς, ἐν, ἐκ, ἀπο
ἐρχεται – he comes, he goes

17.1

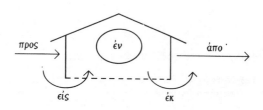

ἐρχεται – he goes, he comes   *ἐρχονται* – they go, they come

προς – to, towards

ἐρχεται προς τον οἰκον
He goes to the house *or*
He comes towards the house

17.1

εἰς – into

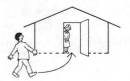

ἔρχεται εἰς τον οἶκον
He goes into the house *or*
He comes into the house

ἐν – in, inside

ἐν τῷ οἴκῳ εἰσιν
They are in the house

ἐκ – out of

ἔρχονται ἐκ του οἴκου
They come out of the house *or*
They go out of the house

ἀπο – away from, from

ἔρχονται ἀπο του οἴκου
They go away from the house *or*
They come away from the house

17.2 ἔρχεται

ἔρχεται – he goes; she goes; it goes; he comes...

The stem ερχ expresses a continuing movement. In the following diagram a woman is moving from A to B.

In English, if I am standing at A, I say: "She is going". If I am standing at B, I say: "She is coming". In English we have a choice of words for this one movement. In Greek the movement is expressed by one word: ἔρχεται.

72

Note also that in English, for the past simple of "I go" we use a different word: "I went". In Greek there are two different stems: ερχ and ελθ.

The stem **ερχ** indicates continuing or repeated action:

So: ἔρχομαι – I am going, I go.

The stem **ελθ** indicates completed or single action:

So: ἀπελθε – go away!   ἐλθων – having come, coming
ἦλθον – they went.

17.3 Words

ἔρχεται – he goes, he comes
          ἔρχονται – they go, they come
          (Note the endings: -εται – he, she, it; -ονται – they)
πρός – to, towards, up to, with
εἰς – into, in
          εἰς τον οἰκον – into the house
ἐν – in, inside, by means of
          ἐν τῳ οἰκῳ – in the house
ἐκ or ἐξ – out of, from
          ἐκ του οἰκου – out of the house, from the house
ἀπο – away from, from
          ἀπο του οἰκου – (away) from the house
εἰσερχεται – he goes into
          ἐξερχεται – he goes out
          ἀπερχεται – he goes away
ὁ οἰκος and ἡ οἰκια – the house, the home, the family
ἡ συναγωγη – the synagogue
το ἱερον – the Temple
ὁ ἱερευς – the priest
          οἱ ἀρχιερεις – the High Priests
ἦλθεν – he went, she went
          ἦλθον – they went

17.4 Translate

1. συ εἶ ὁ βαπτιστης ἀλλα ἐγω εἰμι ὁ ἱερευς. | You are the baptist but I am the priest.

2. ἐν τη συναγωγη οἱ μαθηται ἠρωτησαν αὐτον, Συ τίς εἶ; ὁ δε εἰπεν, Ὁ ἱερευς εἰμι. | In the synagogue the disciples asked him, "Who are you?" He said, "I am the priest".

3. ὁ ἱερευς ἔρχεται προς το ἱερον και εἰσερχεται εἰς το ἱερον. | The priest goes to the Temple and he goes into the Temple.

17.4

4. Ἔρχονται οἱ ἀπόστολοι εἰς τον οἶκον ζητουντες τον Ἰησουν, ἀλλα οὐχ εὐρισκουσιν αὐτον ἐν τῳ οἴκῳ. ἐξερχονται οὖν ἐκ του οἴκου και ἀπερχονται ἀπο του οἴκου προς την συναγωγην, και εὐρισκουσιν αὐτον ἐν τῃ συναγωγῃ. ὁ δε Ἰησους ἀποστελλει αὐτους προς τους Φαρισαιους.

The apostles go into the house looking for Jesus, but they do not find him in the house. So they come out of the house and go away from the house to the synagogue, and they find him in the synagogue. But Jesus sends them away to the Pharisees.

5. λαλει τον λογον του θεου.

He speaks the word of God.

6. οὐκ ἐλαλει τον λογον, οὐδε ἐν τῃ συναγωγῃ οὐδε ἐν τῳ ἱερῳ.

He was not speaking the word, neither in the synagogue nor in the Temple.

7. ἐρχεται ὁ ἀποστολος εἰς τας συναγωγας ἱνα τον λογον λαλῃ τοις ἀνθρωποις ἐν ταις συναγωγαις.

The apostle goes into the synagogues so that he may speak the word to the men in the synagogues.

8. ἐρχονται οἱ ἀποστολοι εἰς τας οἰκιας ὑμων ἱνα τους λογους του Ἰησου ἀπαγγελλωσιν ὑμιν.

The apostles come into your houses so that they may declare the words of Jesus to you.

9. ὁ ἐχων τας ἐντολας του θεου και τηρων αὐτας, οὑτος ἐστιν ὁ ἀγαπων τον θεον. ὁς δε ἀν μη τηρῃ αὐτας οὐκ ἀγαπᾳ αὐτον.

He who has the commands of God and keeps them, he is the person who loves God. But whoever does not keep them does not love him.

10. Ὁ δε Ἰησους ἠν ἐν τῳ ἱερῳ και ἐδιδασκεν τους μαθητας αὐτου. ἠλθον οὖν προς αὐτον οἱ Φαρισαιοι και ἠρωτησαν αὐτον, Τίς εἶ; ὁ Χριστος εἶ συ; ὁ δε εἰπεν αὐτοις, Ἐμαρτυρει περι ἐμου ὁ Ἰωαννης ἀλλα ὑμεις οὐκ ἐλαμβανετε την μαρτυριαν αὐτου.

Jesus was in the Temple and he was teaching his disciples. So the Pharisees came to him and asked him, "Who are you? Are you the Messiah?" He said to them, "John used to bear witness about me but you did not receive his testimony".

17.5

Read carefully in your Greek New Testament 1 John 1.5–7 (Ἰωαννου Α 1.5–7).

Notes:
ἀκηκοαμεν – we have heard
ἀπ᾽ = ἀπο

ἀναγγελλομεν – we are declaring, we announce

74

ὅτι – that
οὐδεμια – none, not one, not any
   (οὐδε – and not, μια – one)
ἐαν εἰπωμεν – if we should say
ψευδομεθα – we are lying
ὡς – as
μετ᾽ ἀλληλων – with each other
το αἱμα – the blood

ὁ υἱος – the son
καθαριζω – I cleanse
   (καθαρος – pure)
ἀπο πασης ἁμαρτιας
   – from every sin, from all sin
   (πας – every, all).
Compare ἀπο πασων των
   ἁμαρτιων – from all the sins.

LESSON 18

λεγειν – to say, to be saying ·····

18.1

   λεγει – he is saying, he says
   ὁς ἀν λεγη – whoever says
   λεγωμεν – let us say
   λεγων – saying
   ἐλεγεν – he was saying, he used to say

All these forms of λεγω indicate continuing —— or repeated ····· action.
Now note another verbal form that indicates continuing or repeated
action:

   λεγειν – to be saying, to say ⁼⁼⁼⁼
   ἀγαπαν – to love ⁼⁼⁼⁼

So:
Lk 7.24   ἠρξατο λεγειν προς τους ὀχλους περι Ἰωαννου
         He began **to** speak to the crowds about John

1 Jn 4.20   οὐ δυναται ἀγαπαν
         He is not able **to** love

1 Cor 14.5   θελω δε παντας ὑμας λαλειν γλωσσαις
         But I wish all of you **to** speak in tongues.

18.2

ἤρξατο – he began   -ατο – he, she, it
ἤρξαντο – they began   -αντο – they

So:

Mk 6.2   ἤρξατο διδασκειν ἐν τῃ συναγωγῃ
          He began to teach in the synagogue

Acts 2.4 ἤρξαντο λαλειν ἑτεραις γλωσσαις
          They began to speak in other languages.

Translate

1. ἤρξατο περιπατειν ἐν τῃ συναγωγῃ.	He began to walk about in the synagogue.
2. ἤρξαντο βαπτιζειν τους μαθητας αὐτων.	They began to baptize their disciples.
3. ἐρχονται προς τον οἰκον.	They go to the house.
4. ἤρξατο ἀποστελλειν τους ἀποστολους.	He began to send out the apostles.
5. ἐρχεται ἀπο του ἱερου.	He comes from the Temple.

18.3 Words

θελω – I wish, I want, I am willing
      ἠθελεν – he was willing
το θελημα – the will (what someone wants)
ἡ ἐξουσια – the authority (the power)
βαλλω – I throw, I put
      ἐκβαλλω – I throw out, I drive out, I send away
κηρυσσω – I preach, I proclaim
ἤρξατο – he began
      ἤρξαντο – they began

18.4 Translate

Ὁ δε Ἰησους ἐδωκεν (gave) ἐξουσιαν τοις ἀποστολοις αὐτου κηρυσσειν το εὐαγγελιον και ἐκβαλλειν τα δαιμονια. και ἤρξατο ἀποστελλειν αὐτους κηρυσσειν και ἐχειν ἐξουσιαν ἐκβαλλειν τα δαιμονια.

Jesus gave authority to his apostles to preach the good news and to cast out the demons. Then he began to send them out to preach and to have authority to cast out the demons.

Ἤρξαντο οὖν οἱ ἀπόστολοι κηρυσσειν το εὐαγγελιον της βασιλειας του θεου λεγοντες, Ἤγγικεν (it has come near) ἡ βασιλεια του θεου. ὅς ἀν θελῃ το θελημα αὐτου ποιειν, πιστευετω (let him trust) τῳ Ἰησου. και οἱ ἀπόστολοι ἐμαρτυρουν τῳ Ἰησου ἐν ταις συναγωγαις και ἐν τῳ ἱερῳ ἀλλα οἱ Φαρισαιοι οὐκ ἠθελον την μαρτυριαν αὐτων λαμβανειν· αὐτοι γαρ οὐκ ἠθελον το θελημα του θεου ποιειν.

So the apostles began to preach the good news of the Kingdom of God saying, "The Kingdom of God has come near. Whoever wants to do his will, let him trust in Jesus". The apostles were bearing witness to Jesus in the synagogues and in the Temple but the Pharisees were not willing to receive their testimony; for they themselves were not willing to do the will of God.

18.5

Read carefully Mark 11.27–30 (κατα Μαρκον 11.27–30).

Notes:

παλιν – again
Ἱεροσολυμα – Jerusalem
περιπατουντος αὐτου (lit. him walking) – as he was walking
ποιος; – what?

ἠ – or
ἐδωκεν – he gave
ἐπερωτησω – I will ask
ἑνα – one
ἀποκριθητε – Answer!

18.6 Progress test 10

Which is the correct translation?

1. τίς ἠρξατο διδασκειν ἐν τῳ ἱερῳ;
   (a) What did he come to teach in the Temple?
   (b) Who comes to teach in the Temple?
   (c) Who began to teach in the Temple?

2. ἐρχονται οἱ ἀποστολοι κηρυσσοντες το εὐαγγελιον.
   (a) The apostles began to preach the gospel.
   (b) The apostles come preaching the gospel.
   (c) The apostles come to preach the gospel.

3. βαλλωμεν τα βιβλια εἰς την θαλασσαν.
   (a) We throw the Bible into the sea.
   (b) Let us throw the books into the sea.
   (c) Let us throw the book into the sea.

4. τίς εἶ συ και τίνες εἰσιν οὑτοι;
   (a) Who are you and who is he?
   (b) Who am I and who are these men?
   (c) Who are you and who are these men?

5. οἱ ἱερεις οὐκ ἐκαλουν ἡμας εἰς την οἰκιαν ἀλλα εἰς το ἱερον.
   (a) The priests are not calling us into the house but into the Temple.
   (b) We were not calling the priests into the house but into the Temple.
   (c) The priests were not calling us into the house but into the Temple.

Check your answers on page 280.

18.7

Revise lessons 11 and 12.

LESSON 19

λεγων, λεγουσα, λεγον – saying

19.1

Lesson 12.7 gives the three kinds of forms of "the" in Greek, which indicate masculine, feminine, and neuter nouns. For example:

Masculine	Feminine	Neuter
ὁ ἀνηρ – the man	ἡ γυνη – the woman	το τεκνον – the child
ὁ λογος – the word	ἡ καρδια – the heart	το ἐργον – the work

In the same way, λεγων (saying) has three different kinds of endings, according to the gender (masculine, feminine, or neuter) of the word it goes with. Study the following examples:

> ἠλθεν ὁ ἀνηρ ταυτα λεγων
> The man came saying these things
>
> ἠλθεν ἡ γυνη ταυτα λεγουσα
> The woman came saying these things
>
> ἠλθεν το τεκνον ταυτα λεγον
> The child came saying these things.

Notice the difference in meaning between these pairs of sentences:

ἀκουει του ἀποστολου ταυτα λεγοντος
He hears the apostle saying these things
ἀκουει του ἀποστολου **του** ταυτα λεγοντος
He hears the apostle **who is** saying these things

βλεπει ἀποστολον τουτο ποιουντα
He sees an apostle doing this
βλεπει τον ἀποστολον **τον** τουτο ποιουντα
He sees the apostle **who is** doing this

ἐβλεπεν τας γυναικας τουτο ποιουσας
He used to see the women doing this
ἐβλεπεν τας γυναικας **τας** τουτο ποιουσας
He used to see the women **who were** doing this.

In this last sentence the Greek says: "He used to see the women the (ones) this doing". We have to express the meaning in an English way: "He used to see the women who were doing this".

Translate

1. βλεπει τους ἀποστολους ταυτα ποιουντας.	He sees the apostles doing these things.
2. οἱ τουτο ποιουντες ποιουσι το θελημα του θεου.	The people who are doing this are doing the will of God.
3. βλεπομεν τον ἀνθρωπον τον τουτο ποιουντα.	We see the man who is doing this.
4. ἐρχεται ἡ γυνη ταυτα ποιουσα.	The woman comes doing these things.
5. ὁ Μαρκος λεγει τῃ γυναικι τῃ ταυτα ποιουσῃ, Τίς εἶ;	Mark says to the woman who is doing these things, "Who are you?"

19.2 Translating into English

1. Compare sentences (a) and (b):

   (a) ὁ ἀνηρ ἐρχεται κηρυσσων το εὐαγγελιον
   (b) ἐρχεται ὁ ἀνηρ ὁ το εὐαγγελιον κηρυσσων.

Sentence (a) is literally, "The man comes preaching the good news". This is quite clear and understandable English.
Sentence (b) is literally, "Comes the man the the gospel preaching". This is not a natural way to express the meaning in English. We must find a better way – perhaps, "The man who preaches the gospel is coming".

2. Note ἐχων – having.

In English the idea expressed by ἐχων can often be well expressed by using the word "with".

So: βλεπω ἀγγελον **ἐχοντα** ἐξουσιαν
I see an angel **with** authority
or I see an angel **who has** authority

Mk 6.34 ἠσαν ὡς προβατα **μη ἐχοντα** ποιμενα
They were like sheep **without** a shepherd
or They were like sheep **that do not have** a shepherd.

19.3 Words

ὁ ἀνηρ – the man, the husband
    ἀγαπᾳς τον ἀνδρα σου – you love your husband
ἡ γυνη – the woman, the wife
    ἀγαπᾳς την γυναικα σου – you love your wife
ὁ υἱος – the son
ὁ πατηρ – the father
    ὁ υἱος του πατρος – the son of the father
ἡ μητηρ – the mother
    λεγει τῃ μητρι αὐτου – he says to his mother
ἡ φωνη – the voice, the sound
    ἀκουω την φωνην or ἀκουω της φωνης – I hear the voice
διδωμι – I give
προσκυνεω – I worship
    προσκυνω αὐτῳ or προσκυνω αὐτον
    – I worship him, I pay homage to him

19.4 Translate

1. οὑτος ἐστιν ὁ ἀνηρ.	This is the man.
2. εἰσερχεται ὁ ἀνηρ εἰς την συναγωγην.	The man goes into the synagogue.
3. ἐρχεται ὁ ἀνηρ κηρυσσων το εὐαγγελιον.	The man comes preaching the gospel.
4. ἀκουομεν αὐτου λεγοντος τους λογους.	We hear him speaking the words.
5. ἡ μητηρ και ὁ πατηρ ἀγαπωσι τον υἱον αὐτων και ἀκουουσι της φωνης αὐτου.	The mother and the father love their son and they listen to his voice.
6. ἐρχεται ἡ γυνη εἰς την οἰκιαν.	The woman comes into the house.

7. ἔρχονται αἱ γυναικες προς την οἰκιαν και βλεπουσι τους ἀνδρας αὐτων.	The women come to the house and they see their husbands.
8. διδωμι τα βιβλια τῳ πατρι μου και τῃ μητρι μου. ἐγω εἰμι ὁ υἱος αὐτων.	I give the books to my father and to my mother. I am their son.
9. ἐρχεται ὁ πατηρ ἐχων το βιβλιον.	The father comes with the book.
10. ἐρχεται ὁ πατηρ ὁ ἐχων το βιβλιον.	The father who has the book comes.
11. διδωμι ταυτα τῳ πατρι τῳ ἐχοντι το βιβλιον.	I give these things to the father who has the book.
12. ἐκαλει τον ἀνδρα τον το βιβλιον ἐχοντα.	He was calling the man who had the book.
13. ἐρχεται ἡ γυνη ταυτα λεγουσα.	The woman comes saying these things.
14. ἠρξατο ἡ γυνη ταυτα διδασκειν.	The woman began to teach these things.
15. εἰπεν οὐν τῳ ἀνδρι τῳ ἐχοντι το δαιμονιον, Τίς εἶ;	So he said to the man who had the demon, "Who are you?"

19.5 Forms of ὤν – being (εἰμι – I am)

	Masculine		Feminine		Neuter
Singular					
(ὁ)	ὤν	(ἡ)	οὐσα	(το)	ὄν
(τον)	ὄντα	(την)	οὐσαν	(το)	ὄν
(του)	ὄντος	(της)	οὐσης	(του)	ὄντος
(τῳ)	ὄντι	(τῃ)	οὐσῃ	(τῳ)	ὄντι
Plural					
(οἱ)	ὄντες	(αἱ)	οὐσαι	(τα)	ὄντα
(τους)	ὄντας	(τας)	οὐσας	(τα)	ὄντα
(των)	ὄντων	(των)	οὐσων	(των)	ὄντων
(τοις)	οὐσι(ν)	(ταις)	οὐσαις	(τοις)	οὐσι(ν)

So: οἱ ὄντες μετ' αὐτου – the people (being) with him
αἱ λεγουσαι – the women saying, the women who say.

Note also ὁ ὤν – he who is, ἡ οὐσα – she who is, το ὄν – that which is.

19.5

The forms of **ὤν** are the same as the endings of λεγων, λεγουσα, λεγον.
In translating, notice the difference in English between:

(a) βλεπει τον υἱον **τον ὀντα** ἐν τη οἰκια
 (Lit. He sees the son **the one being** in the house)
 English: He sees the son who **is** in the house

(b) ἐβλεπεν τον υἱον **τον ὀντα** ἐν τη οἰκιᾳ
 (Lit. He used to see the son **the one being** in the house)
 English: He used to see the son who **was** in the house.

The forms of καλων – calling (καλεω) are similar to the forms of λεγων,
but the final ε of the stem causes some small changes. Note, for
example:

(ὁ) **καλων**	(ἡ) **καλουσα**	(το) **καλουν**
(του) **καλουντος**	(της) **καλουσης**	(του) **καλουντος**

19.6 Translate

1. οὑτος ἐστιν ὁ ἀνηρ ὁ ὤν ἐν τη οἰκιᾳ. | This (He) is the man who is in the house.

2. ἐβλεπομεν τον ἀνδρα ὀντα ἐν τη οἰκιᾳ. | We used to look at the man while he was in the house.

3. ἐβλεπομεν τον ἀνδρα τον ὀντα ἐν τη συναγωγη. | We used to look at the man who was in the synagogue.

4. ἀκουει του ἀνδρος του ὀντος ἐν τῳ ἱερῳ. | He hears the man who is in the Temple.

5. λεγει τη γυναικι τη οὐση ἐν τη σκοτιᾳ. | He speaks to the woman who is in the darkness.

6. ἐκαλει τους ἀνδρας τους το ἐργον του θεου ποιουντας. | He was calling the men who were doing the work of God.

19.7

Read carefully John 4.17–24 (Κατα Ἰωαννην 4.17–24).

Notes:

ἀπεκριθη – she answered
καλως – well
ἐσχες – you have had
νυν – now
εἰρηκας – you have said
Κυριε – Sir (Lord)
θεωρω – I see

ὀρος – mountain
προσεκυνησαν – they worshipped
τοπος – place
δει – it is binding, it is necessary
ὡρα – hour
οἰδα – I know
σωτηρια – salvation

προσκυνητης – worshipper   πνευμα – spirit

19.8 Progress test 11

Which is the best English translation?

1. ἀπεκριθη ἡ γυνη και εἰπεν, Οὐκ ἐχω ἀνδρα.
   (a) The woman answered and she said, "I do not have a man".
   (b) The woman answered and said, "I do not have a husband".
   (c) The woman replied, "I do not have a husband".

2. και νυν ὁν ἐχεις οὐκ ἐστιν σου ἀνηρ.
   (a) and now whom you have is not of you a husband.
   (b) and now the man you have is not your husband.
   (c) and now you have a man who is not your husband.

3. ἐν Ἱεροσολυμοις ἐστιν ὁ τοπος ὁπου προσκυνειν δει.
   (a) in Jerusalem is the place where to worship it is binding.
   (b) the place where God should be worshipped is in Jerusalem.
   (c) in Jerusalem is the place where it is necessary to worship.

4. και γαρ ὁ πατηρ τοιουτους ζητει τους προσκυνουντας αὐτον.
   (a) and for the Father seeks such people the people worshipping him.
   (b) for it is worshippers like these whom the Father seeks.
   (c) for the Father wants such people to worship him.

Check your answers on page 280.

Introduction to lessons 20–25

In 17.5, 18.5, and 19.7 you have read passages from the New Testament. You have already made a great deal of progress towards your aim of being able to read and translate New Testament passages. In lessons 20–25 you will take another enormous step forward. Do not be surprised if you find these lessons somewhat difficult. By the time you reach lesson 25 the basic idea of this group of lessons will probably be fixed in your mind: it is repeated in all six lessons.

Lessons 20–25 are about a type of action: single or completed action.

Until now you have chiefly studied verbal forms which indicate continuing or repeated action ▭▭▭ (see 5.6, 14.1–2, 14.6, 18.1).

You will now study forms which indicate single · or completed ￢ action.

For example:

ποιησας doing (once) ·
    or having done ⌐

βαλων throwing (once) ·
    or having thrown ⌐

φαγων eating (once) ·
    or having eaten ⌐

Marks of single · or completed ⌐ action

Compare:

1.		2.
(a) ποιησας	– doing · – having done ⌐	ποιων – doing ⁓
(b) βαλων	– throwing · – having thrown ⌐	βαλλων – throwing ⁓
(c) φαγων	– eating · – having eaten ⌐	ἐσθιων – eating ⁓

In column (1) note the three most common marks of a single · or completed ⌐ action:

(a) σ between the stem and the ending (lessons 20, 21) *or*

(b) a shortened stem (lessons 22, 23, 25) *or*

(c) a different stem (lessons 22, 24).

When you have completed lesson 25 you will have laid nearly all the foundations on which you will build your knowledge of New Testament Greek. Most students find lesson 20 difficult, but by the time they have done lesson 25, if they look back at lesson 20 they find that it has become easy.

LESSON 20

ποιησας – having done ⌐

ποιησας – having done, doing (once)

Compare (a) and (b):

1. (a) ἐρχεται ταυτα **ποιων**
   He comes **doing** these things
   (b) τουτο **ποιησας** ἀπερχεται
   Having done this he goes away

2. (a) ἠλθεν **κηρυσσων** το εὐαγγελιον ἐν ταις συναγωγαις
   He went **preaching** the gospel in the synagogues
   (b) **κηρυξας** το εὐαγγελιον ἀπηλθεν
   Having preached the gospel he went away.

Note
(i) that in 1(a) and 2(a) the action expressed by **ποιων** and **κηρυσσων** is continued or repeated.
In 1(a) he continues to do these things while he is coming; in 2(a) he repeatedly preached in a number of synagogues.

(ii) that in 1(b) and 2(b) the action expressed by **ποιησας** and **κηρυξας** is completed action.
In 1(b) after he has done this, he goes away; in 2(b) he preached the gospel and then went away after he had completed his preaching.

Note also that **σ** between the stem and ending is the commonest mark of completed or single action. When the stem of the verb ends in a consonant, the added σ changes the consonant. For example:

κηρυσσω – I preach	**κηρυξας** – having preached
σωζω – I save	**σωσας** – having saved
πεμπω – I send	**πεμψας** – having sent

20.2

English words ending in -ing (for example, doing) are called *participles*. All Greek words like **ποιων** (doing) and **ποιησας** (having done) are participles.

20.2

Translate

In the following sentences, translate the participles as literally as possible:

1. (a) ἐρχονται ταυτα ποιουντες.	They come doing these things.
(b) ταυτα ποιησαντες ἀπερχονται.	Having done these things, they go away.
2. (a) ἠλθεν μαρτυρων τῳ Ἰησου.	He came bearing witness to Jesus.
(b) μαρτυρησας ἀπηλθεν.	Having borne witness, he went away.
3. (a) ἠλθον κηρυσσοντες ἐν ταις συναγωγαις.	They went preaching in the synagogues.
(b) κηρυξαντες ἐξηλθον ἐκ της συναγωγης.	Having preached, they went out of the synagogue.
(c) ἀποστελλει αὐτους κηρυσσειν.	He sends them off to preach.
4. (a) εὑρισκουσιν αὐτον ἐν τῳ ἱερῳ ἀκουοντα των διδασκαλων.	They find him in the Temple listening to the teachers.
(b) ἀκουσας των διδασκαλων ἐξηλθεν ἐκ του ἱερου.	Having listened to the teachers he went out of the Temple.
5. (a) ἐρχεται διδασκων αὐτους.	He comes teaching them.
(b) διδαξας αὐτους ἀπηλθεν.	Having taught them, he went away.
(c) ἠρξατο διδασκειν αὐτους.	He began to teach them.
6. (a) ζωην (life) διδωμι τοις προσκυνουσιν με.	I give life to the people worshipping me.
(b) ζωην διδωμι τοις προσκυνησασιν με.	I give life to the people having worshipped me.

20.3 Translating participles into English: ποιων and ποιησας

When you translated the sentences in 20.2 you were probably aware that some of the translations in the check-column did not express the meaning in a very natural English way.

Words like ποιων (doing), γραφων (writing), and κηρυσσων (preaching), can often be well translated using an English participle (-ing):

ἠλθεν Ἰωαννης **κηρυσσων** ἐν τῃ ἐρημῳ
John came **preaching** in the wilderness.

But sometimes we need to use different ways to express the meaning of a Greek participle in English. Consider:

(a) βλεπω ἀγγελον **ἐχοντα** εὐαγγελιον
I see an angel **who has** a message of good news

86

(b) ὢν ἐν τῃ οἰκιᾳ διδασκει τους μαθητας
While he is in the house he teaches the disciples

(c) ὦτα ἐχων οὐκ ἀκουει
Though he has ears he does not hear.

Words like ποιησας (having done), γραψας (having written), and κηρυξας (having preached), usually express completed ⁓ action. In English we seldom use sentences like "Having written the letter, he posted it". We are more likely to express the same basic idea by:

(a) When he had written the letter he posted it
or (b) He wrote the letter and posted it
or (c) He posted the letter he had written.

So we might translate:

ἀκουσας τους λογους ἐξηλθεν
as When he had heard the words he went out
or He heard the words and went out
or He went out when he had heard the words.

Look again at 20.2.
Find alternative translations for all the (b) sentences.

20.4

Notice that participles like ποιησας, γραψας, and κηρυξας may refer to events or actions which still lie in the future.

So: αὐριον **τουτο ποιησας** ἀπελευσεται
Tomorrow, **having done this,** he will go away
or Tomorrow, **when he has done this,** he will go away.

ποιησας is a completed action form. In this sentence it refers to an action that is still in the future, but at the time when the man goes away, the action will have been completed.

It is important to remember that completed or single action forms do not necessarily refer to past time, unless they also have an ε before the stem (lesson 21).

20.5

ὁ ποιησας – the doer ·
   he who has done ⁓
   he who had done ⁓
   he who did ⁓

20.5

In 8.2–3 you saw that ὁ can mean "the person".

So: ὁ ποιων – the person doing ⎯⎯⎯

In English we usually use other ways of expressing such continuing or repeated action: "he who is doing", "he who keeps doing", or "he who does".

ποιησας indicates a single or a completed action. So we can translate ὁ ποιησας τουτο or ὁ τουτο ποιησας as "the person who did this", "the person who has done this", " the person who had done this", "he who did this", or "he who will have done this".

Study these examples carefully:

⎯⎯⎯ μακαριοι εἰσιν **οἱ ποιουντες** το θελημα του θεου
Blessed are **those who do** the will of God

⎯ μακαριοι εἰσιν **οἱ ποιησαντες** το θελημα αὐτου
Blessed are **those who have done** his will

⎯ μακαριοι ἦσαν **οἱ ποιησαντες** το θελημα αὐτου
Blessed were **those who had done** his will

⎯⎯⎯ μακαριοι ἦσαν **οἱ ποιουντες** το θελημα αὐτου
Blessed were **those who were doing** his will

⎯⎯⎯ μακαριοι ἐσονται **οἱ ταυτα ποιουντες**
Blessed will be **those who do these things**
or Blessed will be **those who will be doing these things**

⎯ μακαριοι ἐσονται **οἱ τουτο ποιησαντες**
Blessed will be **those who have done this**
or Blessed will be **those who will have done this.**

20.6 Translate

1. Τίς ἐστιν ὁ ποιων το θελημα του θεου; Ὁ τας ἐντολας αὐτου τηρων ἐξ ὁλης της καρδιας αὐτου.	"Who is the person who does the will of God?" "He who keeps his commandments wholeheartedly."
2. Τίνες εἰσιν οἱ ταυτα ποιησαντες; Ἀποστολοι εἰσιν.	"Who are the people who have done these things?" "They are apostles."
3. ὁ θεος ἐποιει τον οὐρανον και την γην.	God was making the heaven and the earth.
4. ὁ θεος ἦν ὁ ποιων τον οὐρανον.	God was the one who was making the heaven.

5. Συ εἶ ὁ ποιησας την γην.	"You are the one who made the earth."
6. ἐν τῃ συναγωγῃ προσκυνουσιν τῳ ποιησαντι τους οὐρανους.	In the synagogue they worship him who made the heavens.
7. ἐν τοις ἱεροις προσκυνουσιν τοις μη ποιησασι την γην.	In the temples they worship those who did not make the earth.

20.7 Words

πεμπω – I send
    πεμπων – sending
    πεμψας – having sent
    ἐπεμψα – I sent
ἐκεινος – that (contrast οὑτος – this)
    ἐκεινη ἡ ἡμερα – that day
ἡ ὡρα – the hour
ἡ ζωη – the life
καθως – as
μειζων – greater, more important
    μειζων τουτου – greater than this
    μειζων ἐκεινου – greater than that

20.8 Translate

1. ἐν ταυτῃ τῃ ὡρᾳ ὁ Πατηρ ἀκουει την φωνην των προσκυνουντων αὐτῳ.	In this hour the Father hears the voice of those who are worshipping him.
2. ἐν ἐκεινῃ τῃ ἡμερᾳ προσκυνησαντες τῳ Πατρι ἐξηλθον ἐκ του ἱερου ἐκεινου.	On that day having worshipped the Father they went out of that temple.
3. ὁ προσκυνων τον θεον οὐκ ἐστιν μειζων του θεου οὐδε ἀποστολος μειζων του πεμψαντος αὐτον.	He who worships God is not greater than God nor is an apostle greater than he who has sent him.
4. ἐν ἐκεινῃ τῃ ὡρᾳ ἡλθεν ὁ Ἰησους ἀπο της συναγωγης και εἰπεν αὐτοις, Καθως ἐπεμψεν με ὁ Πατηρ και ἐγω πεμπω ὑμας.	In that hour (At that time) Jesus came from the synagogue and said to them, "As the Father sent me I also am sending you".
5. ἡλθες, Ἰησου, ἱνα ζωην ἐχωμεν και ἐν σοι ζωην εὑρισκομεν· συ γαρ εἰ ἡ ἀληθεια και ἡ ζωη. και μειζων των προφητων εἰ, καθως εἰπεν ὁ Ἰωαννης.	You came, Jesus, so that we might have life, and in you we find life; for you are the truth and the life. You are greater than the prophets, as John said.

6. ἐπεμπεν αὐτους βαπτιζειν ἀνδρας καὶ γυναικας. | He used to send them to baptize men and women.

7. μειζονα ἐργα διδωμι αὐτοις ποιειν. | I give them greater works to do.

20.9

Read carefully:

Life for the dead

ὁ μὴ τιμων τον υἱον οὐ τιμᾳ τον πατερα τον πεμψαντα αὐτον. Ἀμην ἀμην λεγω ὑμιν ὁτι Ὁ τον λογον μου ἀκουων καὶ πιστευων τῳ πεμψαντι με ἐχει ζωην αἰωνιον καὶ εἰς κρισιν οὐκ ἐρχεται ἀλλα μεταβεβηκεν ἐκ του θανατου εἰς την ζωην. ἀμην ἀμην λεγω ὑμιν ὁτι Ἐρχεται ὡρα καὶ νυν ἐστιν ὁτε οἱ νεκροι ἀκουσουσιν της φωνης του υἱου του ἀνθρωπου καὶ οἱ ἀκουσαντες ζησουσιν.

Notes:

τιμαω – I honour
αἰωνιος – eternal
κρισις – judgement
μεταβεβηκεν – he has passed
 (μεταβαινω – I cross over, I pass)

ἀκουσουσιν – they will hear
ζησουσιν – they will live

20.10

Revise lessons 13 and 14.

LESSON 21

ἐποιησα – I did, I made ⌐|
ἐγραψα – I wrote, I did write ⌐|

21.1

Compare:

(a) τουτο **ποιησας** – **having done** this: completed or single action ⌐
(b) τουτο **ἐποιησα** – **I did** this: completed or single action in past time ⌐|

(a) **ἐγραφομεν** ἐπιστολας – we were writing letters ⋯|
(b) **ἐγραψαμεν** ἐπιστολας – we wrote letters ⌐|

21.2

έποιησα – I did, I made
έποιησαμεν – we did, we made

έγραψα – I wrote, I did write
έγραψαμεν – we wrote

Translate

1. έποιησαμεν τα έργα έκεινα.
2. μειζονα έργα έποιησα.
3. έπεμψαμεν άγγελους προς αύτον.
4. έπεμπομεν αύτους προς αύτην.
5. έγραψα σοι την έπιστολην ταυτην.
6. έγραψαμεν έπιστολας ύμιν;
7. ταυτα ποιησαντες προσεκυνησαμεν τον θεον.
8. έγω έλαλουν γλωσσαις άλλα συ ούκ έλαλησας.

We did those deeds.
I did greater deeds.
We sent messengers to him.
We were sending them to her.
I wrote you this letter.
Did we write letters to you?
When we had done these things we worshipped God.
I used to speak in tongues, but you did not speak.

21.3

έποιησας – you did
έποιησατε – you (pl.) did

έκηρυξας – you preached
έκηρυξατε – you (pl.) preached

Translate

1. έκηρυξατε το εύαγγελιον τουτοις τοις άνδρασιν.
2. συ δε ούκ έκηρυξας αύτο έκειναις ταις γυναιξιν.
3. ταυτα έποιουμεν ήμεις άλλα ύμεις ούκ έποιησατε αύτα.
4. ποιειτε ταυτα τα έργα ά έγω διδωμι (I give) ύμιν ποιειν.
5. άκουσας την φωνην του υίου μου ήλθον προς αύτον και έδιδαξα αύτον.
6. Έδιδαξας τους μαθητας σου; Ναι, έδιδαξα αύτους.

You preached the good news to these men.
But you did not preach it to those women.
We were doing these things but **you** did not do them.
You are doing these works which I give you to do.
Having heard the voice of my son I went to him and I taught him.
"Did you teach your disciples?" "Yes, I taught them."

21.4

ἐποιησεν – he did, he made   ἠκουσεν – he heard
ἐποιησαν – they did, they made   ἠκουσαν – they heard

Translate

1. ἐποιησεν ὁ θεος την γην.	God made the earth.
2. ἠκουσαν τον λογον του ἀποστολου.	They heard the apostle's word.
3. ἠκουσατε αὐτου λεγοντος.	You heard him speaking.
4. ἠκουσατε αὐτων λεγοντων;	Did you hear them speaking?
5. ἠρξατο λαλειν αὐτοις και ἐδιδαξεν αὐτους την ἐντολην του Πατρος.	He began to speak to them and he taught them the commandment of the Father.
6. ἠκολουθησαν αὐτῳ οἱ ἀδελφοι;	Did the brothers follow him?
7. ἠκολουθουν αὐτῳ οἱ μαθηται;	Were the disciples following him?

21.5

Note carefully:

1. ἐποιει – he was doing   ἠκουεν – he used to hear

   ε before the stem of a verb is a mark of action in past time.

2. ποιησας – having done   γραψας – having written
   ἀκουσας – having heard

   σ between the stem and the ending is a mark of single or completed action.

3. ἐποιησα – I did, I had done   ἠκουσα – I heard
   ἐγραψα – I wrote   ἐκηρυξα – I preached

   σ between the stem and ending and ε before the stem, are marks of single or completed action in past time ⸚.

In English, completed action in past time is usually expressed by forms like "I preached", "I did", "I went" (past simple), but sometimes by forms like "I had preached" (pluperfect). Notice the translations of ἐγραψα in sentences (a) and (b):

(a) ἀναγινωσκετε την ἐπιστολην ἡν ἐγραψα
    You are reading the letter which **I wrote**

(b) ἀνεγινωσκετε την ἐπιστολην ἡν ἐγραψα
    You were reading the letter which **I had written**

21.6

Read carefully:

The father preached to his sons and sent a message to his wife
Ἦλθεν οὖν ὁ πατηρ προς τους υἱους αὐτου και ἐκηρυξεν αὐτοις. οἱ δε ἠκουσαν
της φωνης αὐτου ἀλλα οὐκ ἠθελησαν το θελημα του θεου ποιειν. ἀπηλθον οὖν εἰς
οἰκον αὐτων.

Ἐν ἐκεινη τη ἡμερᾳ ἐπεμψεν ὁ ἀνηρ προς την γυναικα αὐτου λεγων, Ἐκηρυξα
τον λογον τοις τεκνοις ἡμων ἀλλα οὐκ ἠθελησαν ἀκουειν οὐδε ἐπιστευσαν τῳ
Κυριῳ. και ἠρωτησεν αὐτη λεγων, Ἐκβαλωμεν αὐτους ἐκ της οἰκιας; ἡ δε
ἀπεκριθη λεγουσα, Ἀγαπη ὁ θεος και ἐδωκεν ἡμιν ἐντολην ἱνα ἀγαπωμεν
ἀλληλους. αὐτη ἡ ἐντολη μειζων ἐστιν παντων των ἐντολων. νυν οὖν τηρωμεν
την ἐντολην και μη ἐκβαλωμεν αὐτους.

21.7

Here are the forms of ἐποιησα which you have learned:

ἐποιησα – I did, I made, I had done, I had made

	Singular (one person)	Plural (more than one)
1st person	ἐποιησα – I did	ἐποιησαμεν – we did
2nd person	ἐποιησας – you did	ἐποιησατε – you did
3rd person	ἐποιησεν – he did	ἐποιησαν – they did

21.8

ποιησας – having done   ὁ ποιησας – he who has done

	Masculine		Feminine		Neuter	
Singular	(ὁ)	ποιησας	(ἡ)	ποιησασα	(το)	ποιησαν
	(τον)	ποιησαντα	(την)	ποιησασαν	(το)	ποιησαν
	(του)	ποιησαντος	(της)	ποιησασης	(του)	ποιησαντος
	(τῳ)	ποιησαντι	(τη)	ποιησαση	(τῳ)	ποιησαντι
Plural	(οἱ)	ποιησαντες	(αἱ)	ποιησασαι	(τα)	ποιησαντα
	(τους)	ποιησαντας	(τας)	ποιησασας	(τα)	ποιησαντα
	(των)	ποιησαντων	(των)	ποιησασων	(των)	ποιησαντων
	(τοις)	ποιησασιν	(ταις)	ποιησασαις	(τοις)	ποιησασιν

With the same endings as ποιησας: πας – every, all.

21.8

Note: πας ἀνθρωπος – every man
παντες οἱ ἀνθρωποι – all the men
παντες – all, all men
τα παντα – all things, everything
παν ὃ ἐποιησας – everything which you have done.

LESSON 22

βαλων – having thrown   ἐλθων – having gone ⸰

22.1

Study the following pairs:

1. (a) βαλλων – throwing
   (b) βαλων – having thrown

2. (a) λαμβανων – taking
   (b) λαβων – having taken

3. (a) εὑρισκων – finding
   (b) εὑρων – having found

4. (a) αἱρων – picking up
   (b) ἁρας – having picked up

5. (a) γινωσκων – knowing
   (b) γνους – having known

6. (a) ἀναβαινων – going up
   (b) ἀναβας – having gone up

7. (a) διδων – giving
   (b) δους – having given

In 1–7 each (a) word refers to a continuing or repeated action ‑‑‑‑.
Each (b) word refers to a completed or single action ⸰.
In each pair the stem indicating completed or single action ⸰ is shorter than the stem indicating continuing or repeated action ‑‑‑‑.

Note also:

8. (a) λεγων – saying
   (b) εἰπων – having said

9. (a) ἐρχομενος – going, coming
   (b) ἐλθων – having gone,
              having come

10. (a) ἐσθιων – eating
    (b) φαγων – having eaten

11. (a) τρεχων – running
    (b) δραμων – having run

12. (a) φερων – bringing
    (b) ἐνεγκας – having brought

In 8–12, completed or single action ⸰ is indicated by a different stem.

94

22.2 Translate

1. ἐξελθων ἀπηλθεν.	Having gone out he went away.
2. ἐξελθουσα ἀπηλθεν.	Having gone out she went away.
3. ἐξελθοντες ἠλθον προς την οἰκιαν.	Having gone out they went to the house.
4. ἠλθομεν κηρυσσοντες.	We came preaching.
5. κηρυξαντες ἀπηλθομεν.	Having preached we went away.
6. ἐβλεψαν αὐτον ἐρχομενον.	They looked at him as he was coming.
7. ἐξερχομενοι εἰπον αὐτῳ...	As they were going out they said to him...
8. εὑρων αὐτον εἰπεν αὐτῳ...	Having found him he said to him...
9. μη εὑροντες αὐτον ἀπηλθον.	Not having found him they went away.
10. μακαριοι οἱ εὑρισκοντες τον Χριστον.	Blessed are those who find the Messiah.
11. μακαριοι ἠσαν οἱ εὑροντες αὐτον.	Blessed were those who had found him.
12. αἱροντες τας ἐπιστολας ἐξερχονται.	Picking up the letters they go out.
13. ἀρας την ἐπιστολην ἐξηλθεν.	Having picked up the letter he went out.
14. ταυτα λαβοντες ἀπηλθομεν.	Having taken these things we went away.
15. ταυτα λαμβανοντες ἀπερχομεθα.	Taking these things we go away.
16. οἱ ἱερεις οἱ ἀναβαινοντες εἰς Ἱεροσολυμα...	The priests who are going up to Jerusalem...
17. οἱ ἱερεις οἱ ἀναβαντες εἰς Ἱερουσαλημ...	The priests who had gone up to Jesusalem...
18. ἐρχεται ταυτα διδων.	He comes giving these things.
19. ταυτα δους ἀπερχεται.	Having given these things he goes away.
20. ταυτα δοντες ἀπερχονται.	Having given these things they go away.

22.3 Translating participles

1. Participles such as ποιων, βαλλων, or ἐρχομενος refer to continuing or repeated action ⁻⁻⁻.

In a sentence beginning

    ἐξερχομενος εἰπεν τῇ μητρι αὐτου...

the action expressed by the participle was *continuing* at the time the action expressed by the verb εἰπεν took place.

In English we do not say

    Going out he said to his mother...

but As he was going out, he said to his mother...

or While he was going out, he said to his mother...

2. Participles such as ποιησας, βαλων, or ἐλθων refer to completed or single action ⁻.

In a sentence beginning

    ἐξελθων εἰπεν αὐτῇ...

the action expressed by the participle ἐξελθων, was *completed* before the action expressed by the verb εἰπεν took place.

In English we do not usually say

    Having gone out he said to her...

but When he had gone out he said to her...

or He went out and said to her...

In another type of completed action, the action expressed by the participle finds its completion in the action expressed by the main verb. See, for example, Mark 5.7:

    κραξας φωνῃ μεγαλῃ λεγει...

κραξας is from κραζω (I shout). Its form indicates a completed action. But we would be wrong to translate this either as, "Having shouted with a loud voice he says...", or as "He shouted with a loud voice and said...". Both of these "translations" wrongly suggest that he shouted first and then spoke afterwards. But in this case the action indicated by κραξας finds its expression and completion in the action expressed by λεγει, so we must translate:

    Shouting with a loud voice he said

or He shouted out.

Compare the use of ἀποκριθεις – answering (once), having answered:

    ἀποκριθεις εἰπεν – he replied *or* in reply he said.

We would be wrong if we translated this as "Having replied, he said" or as, "He answered and said", because he did not first answer and then speak. The action expressed by the participle ἀποκριθεις finds its completion not *before* but *in* the action expressed by the verb εἰπεν.

22.4 Words

εἰδον – I saw
    ἰδων – having seen, seeing
    ἰδε – Look! (used to attract or direct attention)
ὡς – as, like
    ὡς ἠν – as he was
    ὡς ἀγγελοι – like angels, as angels are
καθως – as, according as (κατα – according to, and ὡς – as)
περι – round, about
    μαρτυρω περι αὐτου – I bear witness about him
    περιπατεω – I walk about, I walk around, I walk
ἀναβαινω – I go up, I come up
    ἀναβαινων – going up
    ἀναβας – having gone up
καταβαινω – I go down, I come down
    καταβαινων – coming down
    καταβας – having come down
πας – all, every
    παντες ζητουσιν σε – they are all looking for you
    πας ὁ ὀχλος – the whole crowd
    πας λογος – every word
    πασαι αἱ παραβολαι – all the parables
    τα παντα – everything, all things

22.5 Translate

1. ἰδων τα παντα ἐξηλθεν.	When he had seen everything he went out.
2. ἡ δε γυνη ἰδουσα τα παντα ἐξηλθεν.	When she had seen everything the woman went out.
3. ὁ θεος εἰδεν τα παντα και ἀγαθα ἠν.	God saw all things and they were good.
4. περιπατησαντες ἐν τῳ ἱερῳ ἐξηλθον ἐκ του ἱερου παντες.	When they had walked round in the Temple they all went out of the Temple.

5. οἱ ἀποστολοι καταβαντες ἀπο Ἱεροσολυμων εἰσηλθον εἰς Καφαρναουμ.	When the apostles had gone down from Jerusalem they went into Capernaum.
6. καταβαινοντες ἀπο Ἱεροσολυμων λεγουσιν αὐτῳ, Τίς εἶ;	As they are coming down from Jerusalem they say to him, "Who are you?"
7. καταβαντες ἀπο Ἱεροσολυμων ἐλεγον αὐτῳ, Τί ποιεις; ὁ δε ἀποκριθεις εἰπεν, Ποιω το θελημα του Πατρος μου.	When they had come down from Jerusalem they said to him, "What do you do?" He replied, "I do the will of my Father".
8. εἰσιν ὡς ἀγγελοι και ἀναβαινουσιν εἰς τον οὐρανον.	They are like angels and they go up into heaven.

22.6

Read carefully, then answer the questions in Progress test 12.

John's witness and teaching

Και ἀναβας εἰς Ἱερουσαλημ εἰδεν παντας τους ἱερεις ἐρχομενους προς αὐτον, και ἐμαρτυρησεν αὐτοις περι του Χριστου. και ἐδιδασκεν ἐν τῳ ἱερῳ ὡς ἐξουσιαν ἐχων και οὐχ ὡς οἱ Φαρισαιοι. και εἰπεν πασι τοις μαθηταις αὐτου, Ἰδε, οὑτοι οὐ λαμβανουσι την μαρτυριαν ἡν μαρτυρουμεν περι του Χριστου, καθως εἰπον παντες οἱ προφηται.

Και προσκυνησαντες τῳ θεῳ ἐξηλθον ἐκ του ἱερου. και ἐξελθοντες κατεβησαν ἀπο Ἱερουσαλημ. και καταβαινων ὁ Ἰωαννης εἰδεν τον Ἰησουν ἀναβαινοντα. και ἰδων αὐτον εἰπεν τοις μαθηταις αὐτου, Ἰδε, ὁ Ἀμνος (Lamb) του θεου ὁ καταβας ἐκ του οὐρανου. οὑτος ἐρχεται, καθως εἰπον ὑμιν, ἱνα ποιῃ το θελημα του θεου του πεμψαντος αὐτον. οἱ δε ἀκουσαντες αὐτου λεγοντος και ἰδοντες τον Ἰησουν ἠκολουθησαν αὐτῳ.

22.7 Progress test 12

Questions on 22.6. The participles are all in the reading passage.

1. Which of the following participles indicate more than one person?
   (a) ἀναβας, (b) ἐρχομενους, (c) προσκυνησαντες, (d) καταβαινων, (e) ἀκουσαντες.

2. Which of the following participles indicate only one person?
   (a) ἐχων, (b) ἐξελθοντες, (c) ἀναβαινοντα, (d) ἰδων, (e) πεμψαντος, (f) ἰδοντες.

3. Which of these participles indicate completed action?
   (a) ἀναβας, (b) ἐρχομενους, (c) ἐξελθοντες, (d) καταβαινων, (e) καταβας, (f) πεμψαντος, (g) ἀκουσαντες, (h) λεγοντος.

4.Which of these participles indicate continuing action?
(a) ἐρχομενους, (b) ἐχων, (c) προσκυνησαντες, (d) ἀναβαινοντα.

Check your answers on page 280.

22.8

Before you do lesson 23, revise lessons 15–16, and read John 1.43–51 (κατα 'Ιωαννην 1.43–51).

Notes:
τη ἐπαυριον – on the next day
πολις – town
νομος – law
δολος – deceit
ἀληθως – truly
ποθεν – how
δυναται – it is able
προ – before
φωνησαι – to call
συκη – fig tree
ὀψη – you shall see
ἐπι – on
ἰδιος – own (one's own, his own, her own)
ἀνεῳγοτα – open, opened

LESSON 23

ἐβαλον – I threw   ἡρα – I picked up ⊣|

23.1

In 22.1 you saw that in pairs like:

(a) βαλλων	(a) εὑρισκων	(a) αἰρων
(b) βαλων	(b) εὑρων	(b) ἀρας

a shortened stem marks completed or single action.

23.1

Now compare:

>(a) ἔβαλλον – I was throwing, I used to throw ┈┈|
>(b) ἔβαλον – I threw, I did throw ┤|

So: (a) ἔβαλλον τα δικτυα εἰς την θαλασσαν
>I was throwing the nets into the sea

>(b) ἔβαλον το δικτυον εἰς την θαλασσαν
>I threw the net into the sea.

Here again the long stem, **βαλλ**, indicates continuing action.

The short stem, **βαλ**, indicates completed action.

In both ἔβαλλον and ἔβαλον, **ε** before the stem is a mark of past time.

So in ἔβαλεν (he threw), ἐβαλομεν (we threw), ἔβαλον (they threw), **ἐβαλ-** indicates a completed act of throwing, in past time.

By contrast, **βαλων** and **βαλλων** (throwing, casting), have no mark of time.

Note the possible ways of translating μακαριος ὁ βαλων το δικτυον:

>(a) Blessed (is) he who casts the net
>(b) Blessed (was) he who did cast the net
>(c) Blessed (will be) he who will cast the net.

In ὁ βαλων the short stem **βαλ** indicates a single · or completed ┤ action, but it does not indicate anything about the time of the action. According to the context in which ὁ βαλων comes, the time may be either (a) present, (b) past, or (c) future.

Now compare:

>ὁ **βαλων** το δικτυον (single or completed action)
>and ὁ **βαλλων** το δικτυον (repeated or continuing action).

When the context shows that it is necessary to emphasize the repetition or continuance of the action expressed by βαλλων, we may need to translate ὁ βαλλων as "he who keeps casting".

Compare:

>μακαριος ἠν ὁ **βαλων** το δικτυον
>Blessed was **he who cast** the net

>μακαριος ἠν ὁ **βαλλων** το δικτυον
>Blessed was **he who kept casting** the net.

23.2 Words

ἁμαρτανω – I sin (ἁμαρτια – sin)
    ἡμαρτανον – I was sinning
    ἡμαρτον – I sinned
αἱρω – I pick up, I take up
    ἡρα – I picked up, I took up
ὁ λιθος – the stone
ὁ σταυρος – the cross (σταυροω – I crucify)
ἡ πολις – the town, the city
    ἐκ της πολεως – out of the town
    ἐξω – outside
ἡ θαλασσα – the sea, the lake
το πνευμα – the wind, the spirit, the breath
ἀκαθαρτος – impure, unclean
ἐρωταω – I ask
    ἡρωτησα – I asked

23.3

ἐβαλον – I threw	ἐβαλλον – I was throwing
ἐβαλομεν – we threw	ἐβαλλομεν – we were throwing
Stem: βαλ ⁻	Stem: βαλλ ⁻⁻⁻

Translate

1. ἐγω ἐβαλον λιθον. — I threw a stone.

2. ἀρας τον λιθον ἐβαλον αὐτον ἐξω. — Having picked up the stone, I threw it outside.

3. ἐβαλλομεν λιθους. — We were throwing stones.

4. ἐξω βαλλομεν αὐτους. — We are throwing them out (outside).

5. ἐβαλομεν τουτους τους λιθους; — Did we throw these stones?

6. ἐβαλλομεν τους λιθους ἐκεινους. — We were throwing those stones.

7. ἐγω ἐβαλλον τα δικτυα εἰς την θαλασσαν ἀλλα συ οὐκ ἐβαλες αὐτα. — I used to cast the nets into the sea but you did not cast them.

23.4

ἐξέβαλες – you threw out	ἐξέβαλλες – you were throwing out
ἐξεβάλετε – you (pl.) threw out	ἐξεβάλλετε – you (pl.) were throwing out

Translate

1. ἐξεβάλλετε πνευματα ἀκαθαρτα.	You were casting out unclean spirits.
2. ἐξεβάλετε το πνευμα το ἀκαθαρτον;	Did you cast out the unclean spirit?
3. Ἰησου, ἐξέβαλες αὐτο ἐκ του ἀνδρος.	Jesus, you cast it out of the man.
4. ἐξεβάλομεν τον ἀνδρα ἐκ της πολεως.	We expelled the man from the town.
5. ἐξέβαλες αὐτην ἐξω της πολεως.	You drove her outside the town.

23.5

ἐβαλεν – he threw	ἐβαλλεν – he was throwing
ἐβαλον – they threw	ἐβαλλον – they were throwing

Notice the difference between:

ἀρας τους λιθους ἐβαλον αὐτους
Having picked up the stones I threw them

and ἀραντες τους λιθους ἐβαλον αὐτους
Having picked up the stones they threw them.

ἀρας is singular (one person): it shows that ἐβαλον is 1st person singular – I threw.
ἀραντες is plural: it shows that ἐβαλον is 3rd person plural – they threw.

Translate

1. ἡμαρτον εἰς τον θεον παντες.	They all sinned against God.
2. ἡμαρτανεν εἰς τον θεον.	He was sinning against God.
3. τίς ἡμαρτεν εἰς σε;	Who sinned against you?
4. εἰσελθοντες εἰς την συναγωγην ἐβαλον τα πνευματα ἀκαθαρτα ἐκ των ἀνδρων.	They went into the synagogue and cast the unclean spirits out of the men.

23.6

αἴρω – I pick up, I take up, I lift   **αἴρων** – picking up
ἦρα – I picked up, I took up   **ἄρας** – having picked up

Translate

1. αἴρει τον σταυρον. | He takes up the cross.
2. ἦρεν τον σταυρον αὐτου. | He took up his cross.
3. ἦραν τους σταυρους οἱ μαθηται. | The disciples lifted up the crosses.
4. ἄραντες τους λιθους ἐξηλθον. | Having picked up the stones they went out.
5. ἄρας τον λιθον ἐξηλθον. | Having picked up the stone I went out.
6. ὅς ἀν μη αἴρη τον σταυρον οὐκ ἐστιν μαθητης μου. | Whoever does not keep taking up the cross is not my disciple.

23.7 ε as a mark of past time

We have seen that past time is usually indicated by an ε before the stem, e.g. ἐβαλεν – he threw. Note carefully the following examples:

(a)   **ἦραν** – they picked up   **ἠγαπησαν** – they loved

Compare:

ἄρας – picking up (once), having picked up
ἦραν – they picked up.

The completed action stem of αἴρω is **αρ**. When ε is put before the stem it is not written εαρ, it becomes ηρ.

Compare:

αἴρει – he picks up | ἦρεν – he picked up
ἐρωτᾳ – he asks | ἠρωτησεν – he asked
ἀγαπᾳ – he loves | ἠγαπησεν – he loved
οἰκοδομεω – I build | ᾠκοδομησα – I built

See also 15.5.

(b)   **ἐξεβαλεν** – he threw out   **ἀπηλθεν** – he went away

You have seen that a word like ἐκβαλλω has three parts:

1. **ἐκ** – out, out of (a preposition)
2. **βαλλ** – the stem, which indicates throwing ⎓
3. **-ω** – the ending.

In ἐξεβαλλομεν (we were throwing out), the ε which indicates past time comes before the stem, not before the preposition. Note the following examples:

Basic meaning	I am —	I was —|	I did ⁻|
throw out	ἐκβαλλω	ἐξεβαλλον	ἐξεβαλον
announce	ἀπαγγελλω	ἀπηγγελλον	ἀπηγγειλα
go up	ἀναβαινω	ἀνεβαινον	ἀνεβην
go down	καταβαινω	κατεβαινον	κατεβην
answer	ἀποκρινομαι	ἀπεκρινομην	ἀπεκριθην
walk about	περιπατεω	περιεπατουν	περιεπατησα
go out	ἐξερχομαι	ἐξηρχομην	ἐξηλθον

23.8 Translating βαλλω and ἐκβαλλω into English

Words from the Greek stem βαλ cover a fairly wide area of meaning. So in translating βαλλω and ἐκβαλλω into English we shall often have to choose between several English words, according to the context in the Greek passage.

> βαλλω – I throw, I drop, I put, I bring
> ἐκβαλλω – I cast out, I expel, I drive out, I pull out, I take out,
> I produce.

In John 20.25:
> Ἐαν μη...**βαλω** τον δακτυλον μου εἰς τον τυπον των ἡλων...
> If I do not **put** my finger into the mark of the nails...

In Matthew 12.35:
> ὁ πονηρος ἀνθρωπος ἐκ του πονηρου θησαυρου **ἐκβαλλει** πονηρα
> The evil man **produces** evil things from his store of evil
> or The bad man **brings** bad things **out** of his treasure of bad things.

23.9

Read John 9.35–38.

Notes:
ἱνα πιστευσω – so that I may
believe

ἑωρακας – you have seen
ἐφη – he said

LESSON 24

ἐσθιω – I am eating ⁓ ἐφαγον – I ate ⊣
λεγειν – to be saying ⁓ εἰπειν – to say ·

24.1

ἐσθιω τον ἀρτον – I eat the loaf
ἐφαγον τους ἀρτους – I ate the loaves

Re-read 22.1. Note carefully examples 8–12. In each pair of participles it is a change of stem which shows the change from continuing or repeated action ⁓ to single or completed action ⊣. In this lesson we study a number of very common verbs in which one stem indicates continuing or repeated action (present stem), but a different stem indicates single or completed action, or action where there is no reference to continuation or repetition (aorist stem). Note carefully the words, stems, and types of action in 24.2.

24.2 Words

Action ⁓	Present stem	Aorist stem	Action ⊣
ἐρχομαι – I go	ερχ	ελθ	ἠλθον – I went
τρεχω – I run	τρεχ	δραμ	ἐδραμον – I ran
λεγω – I say	λεγ	ειπ	εἰπον – I said
φερω – I carry	φερ	ενεγκ	ἠνεγκα – I carried
ὁραω – I see	ὁρα	ιδ	εἰδον – I saw
ἐσθιω – I eat	εσθι	φαγ	ἐφαγον – I ate

24.3 Translate

1. λαμβανων τους ἀρτους ἐσθιει αὐτους.

   Taking the loaves he eats them, or He keeps taking the loaves and eating them.

2. λαβων τον ἀρτον ἐφαγεν αὐτον.

   Having taken the loaf he ate it, or He took the loaf and ate it.

3. ἐδραμον οἱ μαθηται προς τον Κυριον και προσεκυνησαν αὐτῳ.

   The disciples ran to the Lord and worshipped him.

4. ἐξηλθεν φερων τους ἀρτους και φαγων αὐτους εἰσηλθεν.

|| He went out carrying the loaves and when he had eaten them he came in.

24.4

Read carefully:

Mary and some loaves

Τρεχει οὐν Μαρια ἡ Μαγδαληνη προς Σιμωνα Πετρον και λεγει αὐτῳ, Ὁ Λουκας ἠρεν τους ἀρτους ἐκ του οἰκου και ἐδραμεν προς την συναγωγην. ἀποκριθεις δε ὁ Πετρος εἰπεν αὐτῃ, Ἐγω οὐκ εἰδον αὐτον.

Τρεχει οὐν ἡ Μαρια προς την συναγωγην και εἰσελθουσα ὁρᾳ τους μαθητας ἐσθιοντας τους ἀρτους. οἱ δε μαθηται φαγοντες τους ἀρτους ἐδραμον ἐκ της συναγωγης.

24.5 λεγων – saying   εἰπων – having said

Forms like:

ποιων – doing   ποιησας – having done

are called *participles* (see 20.2).

Those which indicate continuing or repeated action ⸏⸏⸏ are called present participles.

Those which indicate completed or single action ⸏ are called aorist participles.

Continuing or repeated action	Completed or single action
ἐρχομενος – coming, going	ἐλθων – having come, coming
τρεχων – running	δραμων – having run, running
λεγων – saying	εἰπων – having said, saying
φερων – carrying, bringing	ἐνεγκας – having brought, bringing
ὁρων – seeing	ἰδων – having seen, seeing
ἐσθιων – eating	φαγων – having eaten, eating
ἀποκρινομενος – answering	ἀποκριθεις – having answered, answering

Translate

1. εἰδομεν αὐτους ἐρχομενους. || We saw them coming.

2. δραμων προς αὐτην εἰπεν αὐτῃ,
'Ορω τους ἀνδρας φεροντας γυναικα
προς σε. 'Ιδουσα αὐτους εἰπεν
αὐτοις, Διδωμι ὑμιν τους ἀρτους
τουτους. και φαγοντες τους ἀρτους
ἀπηλθον.

Running to her he said to her, "I
see the men bringing a woman to
you". When she saw them she said
to them, "I give you these loaves".
When they had eaten the loaves
they went away.

3. ἠνεγκαν τον ἀνθρωπον προς τον
'Ιησουν και ἐνεγκαντες ἀπηλθον.

They carried the man to Jesus and
when they had brought him they
went away.

24.6 λεγειν – to be saying   εἰπειν – to say

Forms like:

    λεγειν – to say   ποιειν – to be doing, to do ▭
and εἰπειν – to say   ποιησαι – to do ·

are called *infinitive*.

Those which indicate continued or repeated action are called present
infinitive (whether the time of the action is past, present, or future).

Those which indicate single action, or action without reference to its
continuance or repetition, are called aorist infinitive.

Continuing action ▭	*Single action* ·
ἐρχεσθαι – to be coming, to come	ἐλθειν – to come
τρεχειν – to be running, to run	δραμειν – to run
λεγειν – to be saying, to say	εἰπειν – to say
φερειν – to be carrying, to carry	ἐνεγκαι – to carry
ὁραν – to be seeing, to see	ἰδειν – to see
ἐσθιειν – to be eating, to eat	φαγειν – to eat

Translate

1. θελω παντας τους ἀρτους ἐσθιειν.
I am willing to eat all the loaves.

2. οὐ θελει τον ἀρτον φαγειν.
He does not want to eat the loaf.

3. ἠλθεν ταυτα λεγειν.
He came to say these things.

4. οὐκ ἠθελεν τουτο εἰπειν.
He was not willing to say this.

5. ἠρξαντο προσερχεσθαι προς τον
'Ιησουν.
They began to come towards
Jesus.

24.7

24.7 Progress test 13

Which translation is correct?

1. ἤρξαντο διδασκειν τους ἀκουοντας αὐτων.
   (a) They began to teach those who were listening to them.
   (b) They came to teach their disciples.
   (c) He came to teach those who listened to him.

2. ἤνεγκα αὐτην προς τους μαθητας ἀλλα αὐτοι οὐκ ἠδυναντο θεραπευειν αὐτην.
   (a) They brought her to the disciples and they were able to heal her.
   (b) He brought her to the disciple but he could not heal her.
   (c) I brought her to the disciples but they were not able to heal her.

3. ἀναβαντες εἰς Ἱεροσολυμα εἰσηλθομεν εἰς το ἱερον.
   (a) They went up to Jerusalem and went into the Temple.
   (b) Going up to Jerusalem they went into the Temple.
   (c) When we had gone up to Jerusalem we went into the Temple.

4. καταβαινοντων αὐτων ἀπο Ἱεροσολυμων ἠλθεν γυνη προς αὐτον.
   (a) While they were going down from Jerusalem a woman came to him.
   (b) When they had gone down from Jerusalem a woman came to him.

5. καταβαντων αὐτων εἰπεν αὐτοις, Που ἐρχεσθε;
   (a) While they were going down he said to them, "Where are you going?"
   (b) When they had gone down he said to them, "Where are you going?"

Which do you think is the better English translation?

6. εὑρων αὐτον εἰπεν, Συ πιστευεις εἰς τον υἱον του ἀνθρωπου;
   (a) Having found him he said, "Are you believing into the Son of Man?"
   (b) When he found him he said, "Do you believe in the Son of Man?"

7. ἀπεκριθη ἐκεινος και εἰπεν, Και τίς ἐστιν, Κυριε, ἱνα πιστευσω εἰς αὐτον;
   (a) The man replied, "Sir, who is he, that I may believe in him?"
   (b) That man answered him and said, "And who is he, Sir, so that I may believe in him?"

8. Which of the following participles indicate continuing or repeated action?
   (a) ἐρχομενος, (b) ἐλθων, (c) λεγων, (d) ἰδων, (e) ὁρων.

9. Which of the following infinitives indicate single action?
   (a) ποιησαι, (b) ποιειν, (c) δραμειν, (d) ἐνεγκαι, (e) φαγειν.

Check your answers on page 280.

24.8

Revise lessons 17 and 18.

LESSON 25

καταβαινοντος αὐτου – while he was coming down ‾‾‾
καταβαντος αὐτου – when he had come down ⊣

25.1

Compare:

(a) Mt 17.9   καταβαινοντων αὐτων ἐκ του ὀρους...
              As they were coming down from the mountain...

(b) Mt 8.1   Καταβαντος δε αὐτου ἀπο του ὀρους...
           When he had come down from the mountain...

In (a) note the type of action indicated by καταβαινων (coming down) ‾‾‾.

Literally, καταβαινοντων αὐτων means "them coming down", but that is not good English. According to the context, we shall need a translation like:

     While they were coming down...
or As they came down...
or As they are coming down...

So: **καταβαινοντος αὐτου,** τουτο ποιουμεν
      While he **is** coming down, we are doing this

      καταβαινοντος αὐτου, τουτο ἐποιησαμεν
      While he **was** coming down, we did this.

The order of words in this kind of clause may be either (1) καταβαινοντος αὐτου, or (2) αὐτου καταβαινοντος.
Mark usually uses order (1). John usually uses order (2).

In (b) note the type of action indicated by καταβας (having come down) ⌐.

Literally, καταβαντος αὐτου means "Him having come down", but that is not good English. According to the context, we shall need a translation like:

> When he had come down...
> *or* When he has come down...

So: 1. **καταβαντων αὐτων** ἐποιησαμεν τουτο
When they **had** come down we did this

2. **καταβαντων αὐτων** ποιησομεν τουτο
When they **have** come down we will do this.

In (1) the action expressed by ἐποιησαμεν is in past time, and the action expressed by καταβαντων was completed before "we did this". So we translate: "When they had come down...". In (2) the action expressed by ποιησομεν lies in the future. The action expressed by καταβαντων also lies in the future, but it will be completed before "we do this". So we translate: "When they have come down...".

25.2 ὤν – being   ὀντος αὐτου – him being

The way we translate a phrase like ὀντος αὐτου will depend on the context.
Compare:

(a) Mk 14.3   **ὀντος αὐτου** ἐν Βηθανιᾳ...ἠλθεν γυνη
While he **was** in Bethany, a woman came

(b) Mk 14.66   **ὀντος του Πετρου** κατω ἐν τη αὐλη
While Peter **is** below in the courtyard
ἐρχεται μια των παιδισκων του ἀρχιερεως
there comes one of the servant girls of the High Priest.

(Note ἐρχεται – she comes. In English we would normally use past tenses in telling a story: "While Peter was down in the courtyard one of the High Priest's serving-maids *came* by". This use of a present form in a narrative about the past is called the historic present. It occurs frequently in Mark's Gospel.)

Translate

1. αὐτου καταβαινοντος οἱ μαθηται εἰπον αὐτῳ...	As he was going down the disciples said to him...

2. καταβαντος αὐτου ἀπο Ἰερουσαλημ ἀνεβησαν οἱ Φαρισαιοι προς Ἰερουσαλημ.	When he had gone down from Jerusalem the Pharisees went up to Jerusalem.
3. εἰσελθοντων αὐτων εἰς την πολιν, ἠλθον προς αὐτον αἱ γυναικες.	When they had gone into the city the women came to him.
4. ὀντος αὐτου ἐν Βηθανιᾳ ἐν τῃ οἰκιᾳ Σιμωνος ἠλθεν προς αὐτον γυνη ἐχουσα βιβλιον.	While he was in Bethany in Simon's house, a woman with a book came to him.

25.3

Note that the forms like καταβαινοντος, καταβαντων, αὐτου, and αὐτων which you have studied in 25.1–2 are all in the genitive case (see 12.7, 37.1). This construction, in which a noun or pronoun in the genitive case is linked to a participle in the genitive case, e.g. καταβαινοντος αὐτου, is called the genitive absolute.

25.4 Words

δια – because of, through
    δια τί; – why? (because of what?)
μετα – with, after
    μετα μου or μετ' ἐμου – with me
ἐμβαινω – I go into, I get in
το πλοιον – the boat
ἐτι – still
    ἐτι ἐσθιοντων αὐτων – while they were (are) still eating;
οὐκετι, μηκετι – no longer, not still, never again
διδωμι – I give
    ἐδωκεν – he gave
μειζων παντων – greatest of all, most important (lit. greater of all)

25.5 Translate

1. οὐκετι εἰμι ἐν τῃ οἰκιᾳ μετα σου.	I am no longer in the house with you.
2. οὐκετι ταυτα λεγομεν.	We no longer say these things.
3. μηκετι ταυτα λεγωμεν.	Let us no longer say these things.
4. δια τί ταυτα λεγωμεν;	Why should we be saying these things?

111

25.6

Read carefully:

1. While his brothers ate, Peter went to the boat
ἔδωκεν ὁ Μαθθαιος ἄρτους αὐτοις και ἔτι αὐτων ἐσθιοντων ἐξηλθεν ὁ Πετρος. και ἐξελθων ἀπηλθεν προς το πλοιον. και ἐμβαντος αὐτου εἰς το πλοιον, οἱ ἀδελφοι αὐτου φαγοντες παντας τους ἄρτους ἐξηλθον προς την θαλασσαν της Γαλιλαιας.

Και ἐμβαινοντων αὐτων εἰς το πλοιον εἰπεν αὐτοις ὁ Πετρος, Δια τί ἀκολουθειτε μοι; εἰπον οὐν αὐτῳ, Ἐτι σου ὄντος μεθ᾽ ἡμων ἐν τῃ οἰκιᾳ Μαθθαιου εἰπομεν σοι ὅτι Θελομεν ἐξελθειν μετα σου, ἀλλα συ οὐκ ἤκουσας τους λογους οὓς ἐλαλησαμεν.

2. Jesus is thrown out of the Temple
Και ὄντος αὐτου ἐν τῳ ἱερῳ μετα παντων των ἀποστολων αὐτου, ἠλθον προς αὐτον οἱ ἱερεις, και προσελθοντες ἠρωτησαν αὐτον Δια τί διδασκεις αὐτους ἐν τῳ ἱερῳ; και τίς ἔδωκεν σοι την ἐξουσιαν ταυτην; και ἐξεβαλον αὐτον ἔξω. Και ἀπελθοντων αὐτων εἰπεν τοις μετ᾽ αὐτου οὐσιν, Ἀμην λεγω ὑμιν, πας ὁ πιστευων εἰς ἐμε ἔχει ζωην αἰωνιον, ἀλλα παντες οἱ μη πιστευοντες οὐκ ἔχουσιν την ζωην οὐδε κοινωνιαν ἔχουσι μετα του Πατρος.

Και ἔτι αὐτου λαλουντος ἠλθεν προς αὐτον γυνη και ἠρωτησεν αὐτον λεγουσα, Τίς ἐντολη μειζων ἐστιν παντων των ἐντολων; και ἀποκριθεις εἰπεν αὐτῃ Ἀγαπησεις Κυριον τον θεον σου ἐξ ὅλης της καρδιας σου. αὐτη ἡ ἐντολη μειζων ἐστιν παντων των ἐντολων ἃς ἔδωκεν ὁ θεος τῳ Ἰσραηλ.

LESSON 26

ἀκουσω – I will hear βαλω – I will throw

26.1

Compare:

1. (a) ἀκουω – I am hearing
   (b) ἀκουσω – I will hear

2. (a) βαλλω – I am throwing
   (b) βαλω – I will throw

3. (a) λεγω – I am saying
   (b) ἐρω – I will say

4. (a) ἐρχομαι – I am coming
   (b) ἐλευσομαι – I will come

Each (b) word refers to action in future time.

Note the commonest marks of future time:

1. σ between the stem and the ending

or 2. a shortened stem

or 3. a different stem.

These are the same marks as the marks of single action (page 84).

Since action in the future has not yet taken place, it is not normally thought of as continuing action. But some verbs express a state or action which is by its nature continuous, for example:

ἐσομαι – I will be (εἰμι)
ἐξω – I will have (ἐχω).

ἐσομαι may be used with a participle which expresses continuing action: 1 Corinthians 14.9, ἐσεσθε...λαλουντες – you will be speaking.

26.2 Words

δοξαζω – I glorify, I praise
δοξασω – I will glorify
ἡ δοξα – the glory
σωζω – I save, I rescue, I heal
σωσω – I will save
σωσας – having saved
ὁ σωτηρ – the saviour
ἡ σωτηρια – the salvation
ζαω – I live
ζησω – I will live
ἡ ζωη – the life
το ζωον – the living creature
ζῳοποιεω – I make alive
ἐγειρω – I raise, I rise
ἐγερω – I will raise
ἐρχομαι – I come, I go
ἐλευσομαι – I will come, I will go

26.3 Translate

1. πιστευομεν τῳ θεῳ τῳ ζωντι και τῳ ζῳοποιουντι ἡμας.	We trust in the living God who makes us alive.
2. πιστευσομεν τῳ σωτηρι.	We will trust in the Saviour.
3. ἀκουσουσιν τον λογον της ζωης.	They will hear the word of life.
4. ἀκουσετε και ζησετε.	You will hear and you will live.

26.3

5. ἀκουσαντες ζησομεν.	When we have heard we will live.
6. ἐγειρει αὐτους ὁ Κυριος.	The Lord raises them.
7. ἐγερει αὐτον ὁ σωτηρ.	The Saviour will raise him.
8. σωσει αὐτην και αὐτη δοξασει τον σωσαντα αὐτην.	He will save her and she will praise the man who has saved her.
9. σωζει αὐτην και αὐτη δοξαζει τον σωζοντα αὐτην.	He is saving her and she is praising the man who is saving her.
10. ἐαν αὐτη σωζῃ αὐτον, αὐτος δοξασει την σωσασαν αὐτον.	If she saves him, he will praise the woman who has saved him.
11. ἐρχεται ἐν τῃ δοξῃ του Πατρος.	He comes in the glory of the Father.
12. ἐλευσεται ἐν τῃ δοξῃ του θεου και σωσει ἡμας ἀπο πασων των ἀμαρτιων ἡμων.	He will come in the glory of God and he will save us from all our sins.
13. οὐ ζητειτε την δοξαν του θεου οὐδε ποιειτε το θελημα αὐτου.	You do not seek the glory of God nor do you do his will.
14. οὐ ζητησομεν την δοξαν του Κυριου ἀλλα ποιησομεν τα ἐργα του πονηρου.	We will not seek the glory of the Lord but we will do the works of the evil one.
15. μηκετι ζητωμεν την δοξαν ἡμων ἀλλα ἀγαπωμεν τους ἀδελφους και ποιωμεν το θελημα του θεου ὁς ἐγερει ἡμας και ζωοποιησει ἡμας.	Let us no longer seek our glory but let us love the brothers and let us do the will of God who will raise us up and will make us alive.

26.4 Some grammatical terms

1. The main forms of the verb which show continuing or repeated action ⁓ are called *present*.
   So λεγει (he says), λεγων (saying), λεγειν (to say), are all present.

   Forms of the verb that are used in definite statements and definite questions are called *indicative*.
   So ἀκουει (he hears) and ἠκουσεν; (did he hear?) are both indicative.
   The forms of λεγω in 5.5 are the present indicative of λεγω.

2. Forms of the verb which show continuing or repeated action in past time ⁓| are called *imperfect*.
   So ἐβλεπεν (he was looking at) and ἐβαλλεν (he was throwing) are both imperfect.
   The forms of ἐλεγον in 14.6 are the imperfect indicative of λεγω. The forms of ἐποιουν in 15.1–3 are the imperfect indicative of ποιεω.

114

3. Forms of the verb which show completed or single action ⁻ are called *aorist*.

So ἦλθεν (he came), ἐλθών (having come), ἐλθεῖν (to come), ἐποιησεν (he did), ποιησας (having done), ποιησαι (to do), are all aorist.

The forms of ἐποιησα in 21.7 are the aorist indicative of ποιεω. 21.8 gives the forms of the aorist participle of ποιεω.

4. Forms of the verb that show future time ⊢ are called *future*.

So: ἀκουσω   ἀκουσομεν
     ἀκουσεις   ἀκουσετε
     ἀκουσει   ἀκουσουσιν

and βαλω   βαλουμεν
     βαλεις   βαλειτε
     βαλει   βαλουσιν

are the future indicative forms of ἀκουω and βαλλω.

26.5

Compare these indicative forms:

Meaning	Present	Imperfect	Aorist	Future
I write	γραφω	ἐγραφον	ἐγραψα	γραψω
I teach	διδασκω	ἐδιδασκον	ἐδιδαξα	διδαξω
I read	ἀναγινωσκω	ἀνεγινωσκον	ἀνεγνων	ἀναγνωσομαι
I have	ἐχω	εἰχον	ἐσχον	ἐξω
He goes up	ἀναβαινει	ἀνεβαινεν	ἀνεβη	ἀναβησεται
They take	λαμβανουσι	ἐλαμβανον	ἐλαβον	λημψονται
They go	ἐρχονται	ἠρχοντο	ἠλθον	ἐλευσονται
We send	ἀποστελλομεν	ἀπεστελλομεν	ἀπεστειλαμεν	ἀποστελουμεν

26.6 Translate

1. ἀπεστελλεν τους ἀποστολους και ἀποστελλει ἡμας. — He used to send the apostles and he is sending us.

2. ὁ Κυριος ἀπεστειλεν αὐτην και ἀποστελει ὑμας. — The Lord sent her and he will send you.

3. ἀναβαινετε ὑμεις και ἡμεις καταβησομεθα.	You are coming up and we will go down.
4. ἐδιδαξα σε και συ διδαξεις αὐτους και αὐτοι λημψονται την διδαχην σου.	I taught you and you will teach them, and they will receive your teaching.
5. γραφετε ἐπιστολας και ἡμεις ἀναγνωσομεθα αὐτας.	You will write letters and we will read them.
6. ἐλευσονται μετα των ἀγγελων ἐν τῃ δοξῃ του Πατρος.	They will come with the angels in the glory of the Father.
7. ἐχει ταυτα τα βιβλια ὁ Παυλος και ἐκεινα ἐξει.	Paul has these books and he will have those.

26.7

Read John 5.25–28 and John 6.31–33.

Notes on John 5.25–28:

νυν – now	οὑτως – thus
ὁτε – when	ἑαυτον – himself
νεκρος – dead	μη θαυμαζετε – don't be surprised
ὡσπερ – as	το μνημειον – the tomb

In verse 25 οἱ ἀκουσαντες ζησουσιν, ἀκουσαντες indicates completed action. Since the hearing is in the future we can translate, "Those who hear will live" *or* "Those who have heard will live".

Notes on John 6.31–33:

γεγραμμενος – written	διδους – giving
δεδωκεν – he has given, he gave	ὁ κοσμος – the world
διδωσιν – he gives	

LESSON 27

Questions: τίς; – who?   τί; – what? why?

27.1 Words

τίς; – who?
τί; – what? why?
        δια τί; – for what reason? why?

ποτε; – when?
    ποτε ἐλευσεται; – when will he come?
πως; – how? how is it that?
    πως λεγεις; – how is it that you say?
που; – where?
    που μενεις; – where are you staying?
ποθεν; – where from? how? (idiomatically: how on earth?)
    ποθεν ἐρχεται; – where does he come from?
    ποθεν με γινωσκεις; – how (on earth) do you know me?
ἀποκρινομαι – I answer
    ἀπεκριθη – he answered
    ἀποκριθεις – answering
οἰδα – I know
    (compare οἰδεν – he knows, and εἰδεν – he saw)
δυναμαι – I am able to, I can
    δυναται λαλειν – he is able to speak
μενω – I abide, I remain, I stay
    μενῶ – I will remain
κρινω – I judge
    κρινῶ – I will judge
    ὁ κριτης – the judge
οὐδε or μηδε – and not, nor
ὁτε – when

27.2 Translate

1. Τί ἐστιν; Οὐκ οἰδα τί ἐστιν.

"What is it?" "I don't know what it is."

2. Τί ποιησεις; Οὐ τί ἐγω θελω ἀλλα τί συ.

"What will you do?" "Not what I want but what you want."

3. Τίς ἐστιν και ποθεν ἐρχεται; Οὐκ οἰδαμεν τίς ἐστιν οὐδε ποθεν ἐρχεται.

"Who is he and where does he come from?" "We do not know who he is nor where he comes from."

4. εἰπον αὐτῳ, Τίνες εἰσιν και που μενουσιν; ἀποκριθεις εἰπεν μοι, Οὐκ οἰδα τίνες εἰσιν οὐδε που μενουσιν.

I said to him, "Who are they and where do they stay?" In reply he said to me, "I do not know who they are nor where they are staying".

5. πως δυναται Σατανας Σαταναν ἐκβαλλειν;

How is Satan able to be casting out Satan?

6. οὐ δυναμαι Σαταναν ἐκβαλειν.

I cannot cast out Satan.

7. οὐκ οἴδατε πως κρινει τουτους
τους ἀνθρωπους ὁ κριτης οὐδε
ποτε κρινεῖ ἐκεινους.

You do not know how the judge
judges these men nor when he will
judge those.

8. ὁτε ἐρχεται ἐρει αὐτοις Ὑμεις
ἐστε οἱ ἀδελφοι μου.

When he comes he will say to
them, "You are my brothers".

9. ἡρωτησεν αὐτον, Που ἐστιν ὁ
πατηρ σου; ὁ δε ἀπεκριθη, Συ οὐκ
οἰδας που ἐστιν οὐδε ποθεν
ἐρχεται, ἀλλα ἐγω οἰδα και
δοξασω αὐτον.

He asked him, "Where is your
father?" He answered, "You do
not know where he is nor where
he comes from, but I know and I
will glorify him".

10. ἡρωτησαν αὐτους λεγοντες, Ποθεν
δυνασθε ταυτα ποιειν;
ἀπεκριθησαν οὐν αὐτοις οἱ
μαθηται, Ὁ Κυριος ὁ πεμψας ἡμας
ἐκεινος ποιει ταυτα τα ἐργα και
μειζονα τουτων ποιησει ἱνα αὐτον
δοξαζητε.

They asked them, "How is it that
you are able to do these things?"
So the disciples answered them,
"The Lord who sent us does these
works and he will do greater ones
than these so that you may praise
him".

27.3 Questions beginning with οὐ and μη (not)

Compare:

    (a) "You can do this, can't you?"
    (b) "You can't do this, can you?"

The person who asks question (a) expects that the answer will be, "Yes,
I can". The person who asks question (b) expects that the answer will
be, "No, I can't". Of course, the answer actually given may be quite
different, but that does not matter. It is the *expected* answer which
determines the form of the question.
In questions in Greek:

    (a) οὐ, οὐκ, οὐχ, and οὐχι show that the questioner expects the
    answer, "Yes".

    (b) μη and μητι usually show that the questioner expects the
    answer, "No".

For example:

    (a) οὐ δυνανται ἐκβαλλειν τα δαιμονια;
    They are able to cast out the demons, aren't they?
    or They can cast out the demons, can't they?

    (b) μη δυνανται το δαιμονιον ἐκβαλειν;
    They are not able to cast out the demon, are they?
    or They can't cast out the demon, can they?

Study these examples (for some examples, alternative similar translations are given):

Lk 4.22   *Οὐχὶ υἱός ἐστιν Ἰωσὴφ οὗτος;*
Isn't this man Joseph's son?
Surely he's Joseph's son, isn't he?

Lk 23.39   *Οὐχὶ σὺ εἶ ὁ Χριστός;*
Are you not the Messiah?
You are the Messiah, aren't you?

Mk 14.19   *Μήτι ἐγώ;*
It isn't me, is it?
Surely it isn't me?

Jn 4.12   *μὴ σὺ μείζων εἶ τοῦ πατρὸς ἡμῶν Ἰακώβ;*
You are not greater than our forefather Jacob, are you?

1 Cor 12.29   *μὴ πάντες διδάσκαλοι;*
They are not all teachers, are they?

Note that in Mark 14.19, John 4.12 and 1 Corinthians 12.29, RSV fails to represent the meaning of *μή* properly.

Sometimes *μή* or *μήτι* is used when the questioner is doubtful (perhaps thinking the answer will be "no" but hoping it may be "yes"):

Mt 12.23   *Μήτι οὗτός ἐστιν ὁ υἱὸς Δαυίδ;*
Could he be the Son of David?

Jn 4.29   *μήτι οὗτός ἐστιν ὁ Χριστός;*
Could he be the Messiah?

27.4 Translate

1. *οὐ κρινεῖ ὁ θεὸς πάντας τοὺς ἀνθρώπους;* — God will judge all men (all the men) won't he?

2. *οὐχὶ οὗτός ἐστιν ὁ προφήτης;* — This man is the prophet, isn't he?

3. *μήτι οὗτός ἐστιν ὁ ἀπόστολος;* — Could he be the apostle? *or* He isn't the apostle, is he?

4. *οὐκ οἶδας ποῦ μένει;* — You know where he is staying, don't you?

5. *μὴ πάντες ἀπόστολοι; μὴ πάντες προφῆται; μὴ πάντες γλώσσαις λαλοῦσιν;* — They are not all apostles, are they? They are not all prophets, are they? They do not all speak in tongues, do they?

27.5

Read John 3.8–13.

Notes:
πνει – it blows
το πνευμα – the wind, the spirit
       (it is used in this passage with a double meaning)
ὑπαγω – I go away
οὑτως – thus, so
ὁ γεγεννημενος – the person who has been begotten (γενναω – I beget)
γενεσθαι – to happen (γινομαι – I become, I happen)
τα ἐπιγεια – things on earth
οὑδεις – nobody

LESSON 28

ἀνθρωπος ἀγαθος – a good man
οἱ ἁγιοι – the saints

28.1 Nouns and adjectives

Words like

(ὁ)	(ἡ)	(το)
λογος	καρδια	ἐργον
ἀνηρ	γυνη	τεκνον
βασιλευς	πολις	θελημα

are called *nouns*.

Gender of nouns:
Those with ὁ (the) are called *masculine* (m.) nouns.
Those with ἡ (the) are called *feminine* (f.) nouns.
Those with το (the) are called *neuter* (n.) nouns.

Words which can describe nouns, such as:

      ἀγαθος – good   μεγας – big   ἀκαθαρτος – impure
      κακος – bad   μειζων – bigger   καινος – new

πονηρος – evil   πολυς – much   παλαιος – old
ἀληθης – true   πλειων – more   πας – every

are called *adjectives*.

When an adjective describes a noun it has the same case (37.1), number (singular or plural), and gender as the noun. So:

ἀγαθος λογος   ἀγαθη καρδια   ἀγαθον ἐργον
ἀγαθοις λογοις   ἀγαθαις καρδιαις   ἀγαθοις ἐργοις
παντες βασιλεις   πασαι πολεις   παντα τεκνα

28.2 Words

ἀγιος – holy
   το Πνευμα το Ἁγιον *or* το Ἁγιον Πνευμα – the Holy Spirit
   οἱ ἁγιοι – the holy people, the saints
καινος – new
   ἡ καινη διαθηκη – the new covenant
   ἐντολην καινην διδωμι ὑμιν – I give you a new command
   ὁταν αὐτο πινω καινον – when I drink it new
καλος – good, fine
   ὁ ποιμην ὁ καλος – the good shepherd
   καλον το ἁλας – salt is good
κακος – bad, evil
   τί κακον ἐποιησεν; – what evil did he do?
   ἀποδιδων κακον ἀντι κακου – returning evil in place of evil
ἀλλος – other
   εἰδεν ἀλλους δυο ἀδελφους – he saw another pair of brothers
   ὁς ἀν γαμησῃ ἀλλην – whoever marries another woman
   ἀλλους ἐσωσεν – he saved other people
ὁλος – whole
   ὁλον το σωμα – the whole body
   ἡ οἰκια αὐτου ὁλη – his whole family
πρωτος – first
   ἠλθεν πρωτος – he came first
ἐσχατος – last
   ἐν τῃ ἐσχατῃ ἡμερᾳ – on the last day
ἰδιος – one's own
   ἠλθεν εἰς την ἰδιαν πολιν – he went to his own town
   ἠλθομεν εἰς την ἰδιαν πολιν – we went to our own town
   ἀνεβη εἰς το ὀρος κατ' ἰδιαν – he went up the mountain on his own

28.3

Note carefully the differences between:

(a) ἀγαθος ἀνθρωπος ⎫ a good man
   ἀνθρωπος ἀγαθος ⎭

(b) ὁ ἀνθρωπος ὁ ἀγαθος ⎫ the good man
   ὁ ἀγαθος ἀνθρωπος ⎭

(c) ἀγαθος ὁ ἀνθρωπος ⎫
   ὁ ἀνθρωπος ἀγαθος ἐστιν ⎬ the man is good
   ἀγαθος ἐστιν ὁ ἀνθρωπος ⎭

28.4 Translate

1. το πνευμα το ἀκαθαρτον.	The unclean spirit.
2. προφητης ἁγιος.	A holy prophet.
3. ἁγιος ὁ προφητης.	The prophet is holy.
4. διδαχη καινη.	A new teaching.
5. πασα διδαχη καινη.	Every new doctrine.
6. τίς ἡ καινη αὑτη διδαχη;	What is this new teaching?
7. εἰπεν τοις ἰδιοις μαθηταις.	He spoke to his own disciples.
8. παντες ζητουσιν την δοξαν την ἰδιαν.	They all seek their own glory, *or* All people seek their own glory.
9. καλον το ἐργον και οὐ κακον.	The deed is good and not bad.
10. οὐκ ἠσαν πρωτοι ἀλλα ἐσχατοι.	They were not first but last.
11. οὐχι ἠσαν ἐσχατοι;	They were last, weren't they?
12. μητι εἰσιν ἐσχατοι;	They aren't last, are they?
13. δυναται ἀλλους διδασκειν ἀλλα τα ἰδια τεκνα οὐκ ἐδιδαξεν.	He is able to teach others but he did not teach his own children.
14. ὁ κριτης κρινει τους κακους ἀλλα ἀγαθους οὐ κρινει.	The judge judges the evil people, but he does not judge good people.
15. ἐπιστευσεν αὐτος και ἡ οἰκια αὐτου ὁλη.	He himself believed and his whole family.

28.5

καλως – well (καλος – good, fine)
ἀληθως – truly (ἀληθης – true)
οὑτως – thus, like this, in this way, so (οὑτος – this)

Jn 13.13 καλως λεγετε, εἰμι γαρ – you say well, for I am
Jn 8.31 ἀληθως μαθηται μου ἐστε – you are truly my disciples
Jn 18.22 οὑτως ἀποκρινῃ τῳ ἀρχιερει; – do you answer the high priest thus?

Translate

1. διδασκαλιαν ἀληθη διδασκει.	He is teaching true doctrine.
2. ἀληθως ἐδιδασκεν αὐτους.	He was teaching them truly.
3. αὐτος καλως ἐδιδαξεν αὐτην.	He taught her well.
4. ὁ καλος καλως διδαξει ἡμας.	The good man will teach us well.
5. τί οὑτος οὑτως λαλει; βλασφημει.	Why does he speak in this way? He is blaspheming.

28.6

ὁ, ἡ, το (the) is called the *definite article*.

Note the way the definite article is used with adjectives:

1. ὁ, ἡ, οἱ, and αἱ usually refer to **people**.

> ὁ and οἱ are masculine – they refer to men,
> or to people in general.

> ἡ and αἱ are feminine – they refer to women.

So: οἱ πρωτοι – the first, those who are first
οἱ ἁγιοι – the holy ones, the saints (used chiefly of angels and of Christian people).

Compare:

> ὁ λεγων – he who says ἡ λεγουσα – she who says.

2. το and τα refer to **things**.

> το ἁγιον – that which is holy
> τα ἰδια – one's own things, one's own home
> τα ἐσχατα – the last things, the final state
> ποιω τα κακα – I do what is evil, I do evil things.

Compare:

τα ὀντα – the things which are (see lesson 19.5)
ἐδωκεν και τοις συν αὐτῳ οὐσιν
– he gave also to those who were with him
(τοις οὐσιν – to the people being).

28.7 Translate

1. μακαριοι οἱ ἐσχατοι· οἱ γαρ ἐσχατοι ἐσονται πρωτοι.	Blessed are those who are last, for the last shall be first.
2. ἠσαν οἱ πρωτοι ἐσχατοι και οἱ ἐσχατοι πρωτοι.	The first were last and the last first.
3. ἀληθως λεγεις ὀτι μακαριος ἐστιν ὁ ὠν μετα του Ἰησου.	You say truly that he who is with Jesus is blessed.
4. μακαριοι ἠσαν οἱ εἰσελθοντες εἰς το ἱερον το ἁγιον· αὐτοι γαρ εἰδον την δοξαν του θεου.	Blessed were those who had gone into the holy Temple, for they saw the glory of God.
5. οὐχι τα ἀγαθα ποιει ὁ καλος;	The good man does good, doesn't he?
6. ἀγαθοι και ἁγιοι οἱ ἐχοντες την ἐντολην την καινην και τηρουντες αὐτην.	Good and holy are those who have the new commandment and keep it.
7. ὁ θεος ἐποιησεν τα παντα ἐκ των μη ὀντων.	God made all things (everything) out of things that were not in existence.
8. Ἡρωδης ἐλεγεν ὀτι Ἰωαννης ἐστιν. ἀλλοι δε ἐλεγον ὀτι Ἠλειας ἐστιν. ἀλλοι δε ἐλεγον Οὐχ οὑτος ἐστιν ὁ Χριστος;	Herod said, "He is John". But others said, "He is Elijah", and others said, "This man is the Messiah, isn't he?"

28.8

Read Revelation 21.1–3 and John 7.51–52.

Notes on Revelation 21.1–3:
ἡτοιμασμενος – prepared
  (ἑτοιμαζω – I prepare,
  ἑτοιμος – ready)
ἡ νυμφη – the bride
κεκοσμημενος – adorned

ὁ νυμφιος – the bridegroom
ἡ σκηνη – the tent, the tabernacle,
  the dwelling
ἐσται – he will be
αὐτος ὁ θεος – God himself

Notes on John 7.51–52:
ἐραυνησον – search!

ἐγειρεται – he arises, he comes

28.9 Progress test 14

Which translation is correct?

1. εἶπεν φωνῃ μεγαλῃ, Καλον το ἁλας.
   (a) They said in a great voice that the salt was good.
   (b) He said in a loud voice, "This salt is bad".
   (c) He said in a loud voice, "Salt is good".

2. ἐτι αὐτων ταυτα λεγοντων ἀπηλθεν ἀπο του ἱερου.
   (a) When they had said these things he went out of the Temple.
   (b) While he was still saying these things he went away from the Temple.
   (c) While they were still saying these things he went away from the Temple.

3. καταβαντος αὐτου ἀπο του ὁρους, ἡρωτησαν αὐτον λεγοντες, Μη συ μειζων εἶ του Ἰακωβ;
   (a) When he had come down from the mountain they asked him this question, "You are not greater than Jacob, are you?"
   (b) While he was coming down from the mountain she asked him, "You are greater than Jacob, aren't you?"
   (c) When he had gone up the mountain they spoke to him. "Are you greater than Jacob?" they asked.

4. αὑται εἰσιν αἱ λεγουσαι ὁτι Οἱ πρωτοι ἐσονται ἐσχατοι και οἱ ἐσχατοι πρωτοι.
   (a) She was the person who said that the first would be last and the last first.
   (b) These are the women who keep saying, "The first will be last and the last will be first".
   (c) These are the women who said, "The last will be first and the first last".

5. Which of the following words are present indicative?
   (a) λεγοντες,   (b) λεγει,   (?) γραφομεν,   (d) γραψας,   (e) γραφεις,
   (f) καταβαινων, (g) καταβας, (h) καταβαινετε.

6. Which of the words in question 5 are participles?

Check your answers on page 280.

28.10

Revise lessons 21 and 22.

LESSON 29

γινομαι – I become, I happen   γιν ‾‾‾‾

γενομενος – having become   γεν ˥

29.1

γινομαι – I become, I come into being, I am made, I happen

γιν is the stem which shows continuing or repeated action ‾‾‾‾
γεν is the stem which shows completed or single action ˥

So: γινομενος – becoming   γενομενος – having become

  γινεται – it happens   ἐγενετο – it happened

  γινεσθαι – to be happening   γενεσθαι – to happen

Note the endings of the present indicative:

  γινομαι – I become   γινομεθα – we become

  γινῃ – you become   γινεσθε – you (pl.) become

  γινεται – he becomes   γινονται – they become

ἐσομαι (I will be), and **λημψομαι** (I will take, I will receive), have the same endings. They are future indicative.

The endings of **δυναμαι** (I can, I am able), are similar:

  δυναμαι – I can   δυναμεθα – we can

  δυνασαι – you can   δυνασθε – you (pl.) can

  δυναται – he can   δυνανται – they can

29.2 Words

ἐρχομαι – I go
  ἐλευσομαι – I will go
  ἠλθον – I went
δυναμαι – I am able to
  δυνησομαι – I will be able
  ἐδυναμην or ἠδυναμην – I could
ἀρχομαι – I begin
  ἠρξαμην – I began
ἀποκρινομαι – I answer, I respond (to a statement, question, or situation)
  ἀποκριθησομαι – I will answer
  ἀπεκριθην – I answered

πορευομαι – I travel, I go
  ἐπορευομην – I was going
  ἐπορευθην – I went
προσευχομαι – I pray
  προσηυχομην – I was praying
  προσηυξαμην – I prayed
ἁπτομαι – I touch
  ἡψαμην – I touched
  ἡψατο των ὀφθαλμων αὐτης – he touched her eyes
παλιν – again

29.3 Translate

1. δυναμεθα τουτο ποιειν.	We can do this.
2. οὐ δυναμεθα ταυτα ποιειν;	We can do these things, can't we?
3. ἐρχεσθε παλιν εἰς την πολιν.	You go into the town again.
4. ἐαν θελῃς, δυνασαι Σαταναν ἐκβαλλειν.	If you want to, you can cast out Satan.
5. πως δυναμαι Σαταναν ἐκβαλειν;	How am I able to cast out Satan?
6. ποθεν ἐρχονται και που πορευονται;	Where are they coming from and where are they going?
7. οὐκ οἰδαμεν ποθεν ἐρχῃ οὐδε που μενεις.	We do not know where you come from nor where you are staying.
8. ἡμεις οὐκ ἁπτομεθα αὐτου και αὐτος οὐκ ἡψατο αὐτης.	We are not touching him and he did not touch her.
9. και ἐγενετο ἐν ἐκειναις ταις ἡμεραις ἠλθεν Ἰωαννης βαπτιζων ἐν τῃ ἐρημῳ. και ἐβαπτισεν τον Ἰησουν και φωνη ἐγενετο ἐκ των οὐρανων λεγουσα, Συ εἶ ὁ υἱος μου.	It happened in those days that John came baptizing in the desert. He baptized Jesus and there was a voice from heaven saying, "You are my Son".

29.4 Infinitives

Continued or repeated action ⁓

ἐρχεσθαι – to be going, to go
γινεσθαι – to happen, to be
προσευχεσθαι – to be praying, to pray
ἀποκρινεσθαι – to be answering
(These are present infinitive)

Single action ·

ἐλθειν – to go
γενεσθαι – to happen, to be
προσευξασθαι – to pray
ἀποκριθηναι – to answer
(These are aorist infinitive)

29.5

29.5 Translate

1. οὐ δυνανται προσευξασθαι.	They are not able to pray.
2. ἠρξαντο προσευχεσθαι.	They began to pray.
3. πως δυναται τουτο γενεσθαι;	How can this happen?
4. εἰσηλθον εἰς το ἱερον το ἁγιον προσευξασθαι και ἠρξαμην προσευχεσθαι.	I went into the holy Temple to pray and I began to pray.
5. οὐκ ἐδυναντο ἀποκριθηναι.	They were not able to answer.
6. μη δυνασθε ἀποκριθηναι;	You can't answer, can you?
7. ἐρχεται παλιν προς αὐτον ἡ γυνη και ζητει αὐτου ἁψασθαι.	The woman comes to him again and seeks to touch him.
8. ἀρχομεθα παλιν ταυτα γραφειν.	We are beginning again to write these things.

29.6 Past tenses

Continued or repeated action in past time ‧‧‧|

ἠρχομην – I was coming
ἐπορευου – you were travelling
προσηυχετο – he was praying
ἡπτοντο – they were touching

(These are imperfect indicative)

Completed or single action in past time ˥|

ἠλθον – I came
ἐπορευθης – you travelled
προσηυξατο – he prayed
ἡψαντο – they touched

(These are aorist indicative)

29.7

Here are the imperfect and aorist indicative endings of προσευχομαι (I pray), and πορευομαι (I travel, I go):

	I	You	He	We	You (pl.)	They
Imperfect						
προσηυχ- ἐπορευ- }	-ομην	-ου	-ετο	-ομεθα	-εσθε	-οντο
Aorist						
προσηυξ-	-αμην	-ω	-ατο	-αμεθα	-ασθε	-αντο
ἐπορευθ-	-ην	-ης	-η	-ημεν	-ητε	-ησαν

128

Translate

1. ἐπορεύοντο πρὸς αὐτὸν ἀπὸ πασων τῶν πόλεων.	They were going to him from all the towns.
2. ἐξελθόντες ἐπορεύθησαν παλιν εἰς τας ἀλλας πολεις.	When they had gone out they went again to the other towns.
3. εἰσελθὼν εἰς τὸ ἱερον προσηυχετο.	He went into the Temple and prayed (began to pray).
4. εἰσελθὼν προσηυξατο.	He went in and prayed.
5. ἤρχοντο πρὸς αὐτὴν και ἥπτοντο αὐτης.	They were coming to her and touching her, or People kept coming to her and touching her.
6. ἦλθον πρὸς αὐτὸν και ἥψαντο αὐτου.	They came to him and touched him.
7. ταυτα ἐν Βηθανιᾳ ἐγενετο.	These things took place in Bethany.
8. ἐπορευθης εἰς την Γαλιλαιαν.	You travelled into Galilee.
9. ἐγω προσηυχομην ἀλλα συ οὐ προσηυξω.	I was praying but you did not pray.

29.8 Participles

Continuing or repeated action ⁓

ἐρχομενος – coming, going
γινομενος – happening
προσευχομενος – praying
πορευομενος – journeying
ἀρχομενος – beginning
(These are present participles)

Completed or single action ⊣

ἐλθων – having come, having gone
γενομενος – having happened
προσευξαμενος – having prayed
πορευθεις – having journeyed
ἀρξαμενος – having begun
(These are aorist participles)

Notice that we seldom translate a Greek participle simply by an English participle. For example:

ὁ ἀνθρωπος ὁ ἐρχομενος – the man **who is coming**

πορευομενων δε αὐτων, ἀπηγγειλαν τινες τοις ἀρχιερευσιν ἀπαντα τα γενομενα
While they were on their way, some people announced to the High Priests all **the things that had happened**

ἐκεινη πορευθεισα ἀπηγγειλεν **τοις** μετ᾽ αὐτου **γενομενοις**
She went and told the news **to those who had been** with him.

29.8

Note that we must translate aorist participles into English in different ways, depending on whether:

       (a) the action is completed before the action of the main verb
  or (b) the action is completed in the action of the main verb.

So: (a) *προσευξαμενος ἐξηλθεν*
        When he had prayed he went out

      (b) *προσευξαμενος εἰπεν, Συ Κυριε ἀγαθος εἶ*
        In his prayer he said, "Lord, you are good"
    or He prayed, "You, Lord, are good".

Translate

1. *προσευξαμενοι ἀπηλθομεν.*	When we had prayed we went away.
2. *προσευξαμενοι εἰπομεν, Ἡμεις ἁμαρτανομεν ἀλλα συ ἀγαπᾳς ἡμας και ἐσομεθα μετα σου ἐν τη δοξη της βασιλειας σου.*	In our prayer we said, "We are sinning but you love us and we shall be with you in the glory of your kingdom".
3. *πορευθεντες ἀπο της πολεως εἰπον αὐτῳ, Συ ἀγαθος εἶ τοις μετα σου γινομενοις. ὁ δε ἀποκριθεις εἰπεν, Τί με καλειτε ἀγαθον;*	When they had gone away from the town they said to him, "You are good to those who are with you". But he replied, "Why do you call me good?"
4. *πως δυναται ταυτα γενεσθαι;*	How can these things happen?
5. *ἠκουσεν Ἡρωδης τα γινομενα παντα.*	Herod heard all the things that were happening.
6. *ἠκουσεν Ἡρωδης τα γενομενα παντα.*	Herod heard all the things that had happened.

29.9

Read carefully:

Ἠλθεν παλιν εἰς το ἱερον και προσηυχετο. και ἐγενετο ἐτι αὐτου προσευχομενου ἠλθον προς αὐτον οἱ ἀρχιερεις και εἰπαν αὐτῳ, Δια τί ἡμεις οὐ δυναμεθα ταυτα τα ἐργα ποιησαι ἁ συ δυνασαι ποιειν; αὐτος δε οὐκ ἀπεκριθη αὐτοις. παλιν οὐν ἠρωτησαν αὐτον λεγοντες, Ποθεν ἠλθες και που ἐλευσῃ; ὁ δε ἀποκριθεις εἰπεν αὐτοις, Ὑμεις οὐκ οἰδατε, ἀλλα ὁ πιστευων ἐν ἐμοι ἐκεινος οἰδεν.

29.10

Read John 1.1–9.

Notes:
δι' αὐτου (δια αὐτου) – through him
χωρις – apart from, without
γεγονεν – (it) has happened, has come into being, has been made
φαινει – it shines
καταλαμβανω – I seize, I overcome, I grasp
φωτιζω – I give light to, I enlighten

LESSON 30

ποιησαι – to do · ἐκβαλειν – to throw out ·

30.1

Compare the words in column A with those in column B:

	A ⁝⁝⁝	B ·	
1.			
ποιεω – I do	ποιειν	ποιησαι	to do
σωζω – I save	σωζειν	σωσαι	to save
πιστευω – I believe	πιστευειν	πιστευσαι	to believe
ἀγαπαω – I love	ἀγαπαν	ἀγαπησαι	to love
ζαω – I live	ζην (ζην)		to live
πεμπω – I send	πεμπειν	πεμψαι	to send
διδασκω – I teach	διδασκειν	διδαξαι	to teach
προσευχομαι – I pray	προσευχεσθαι	προσευξασθαι	to pray
2.			
ἐκβαλλω – I throw out	ἐκβαλλειν	ἐκβαλειν	to throw out
πασχω – I suffer	πασχειν	παθειν	to suffer
λαμβανω – I take	λαμβανειν	λαβειν	to take
αἰρω – I pick up	αἰρειν	ἀραι	to pick up
καταβαινω – I go down	καταβαινειν	καταβηναι	to go down
διδωμι – I give	διδοναι	δουναι	to give

131

30.1

3.

	A ˷	B ·	
λεγω – I say	λεγειν	εἰπειν	to say
ἐσθιω – I eat	ἐσθιειν	φαγειν	to eat
ἐρχομαι – I go	ἐρχεσθαι	ἐλθειν	to go
φερω – I bring	φερειν	ἐνεγκαι	to bring
ὁραω – I see	ὁραν	ἰδειν	to see

4.

εἰμι – I am	εἰναι		to be

Note in column B three marks of single action, or of action without reference to its continuance:

    1. σ after the stem
or 2. a shorter stem
or 3. a different stem.

All the forms in columns A and B are called *infinitive*.
Those in column A are called *present infinitive* because they indicate continued or repeated action.
Those in column B are called *aorist infinitive* because they indicate single action, or an action considered in itself without reference to its continuance.

In English usage we do not usually draw so much attention to the type of action. So we normally translate both ποιειν ˷ and ποιησαι · as "to do". However, when the context seems to demand emphasis on the continuing nature of the action we may translate ποιειν as "to be doing" or "to keep doing".

30.2 Translate

1. θελω αὐτους πεμψαι προς σε.	I want to send them to you.
2. ἠρχοντο σωζειν ἡμας ἀπο των ἁμαρτιων ἡμων.	They used to come to save us from our sins.
3. οὐκ ἠλθομεν σωσαι τους ἁγιους ἀλλα τους πονηρους.	We did not come to save the holy people but the evil people.
4. οὐκ ἠλθεν καλεσαι ἀγαθους ἀλλα κακους.	He did not come to call good people but bad people.
5. ἠρξαντο φερειν τα τεκνα προς τον Ἰησουν.	They began to carry the children to Jesus.

132

6. ἤρξαντο φερειν αὐτους που ἤκουον ὁτι Ἰησους ἐστιν.	They began to carry them where they heard that Jesus was.
7. οὐκ ἐδυναντο αὐτον ἐνεγκαι προς τον σωτηρα.	They were not able to carry him to the Saviour.
8. ἤρξατο προσευξασθαι.	He began to pray.
9. ἀγαπωμεν τους ἀδελφους, το γαρ ἀγαπαν τους ἀδελφους καλον ἐστιν και οὐ κακον.	Let us love the brothers, for to love the brothers is good and not bad.

30.3 Words

κατα – according to
    κατα τον νομον – according to the Law
    κατ' ἰδιαν – privately, on one's own
    καθ' ἡμεραν – daily
καθως – according as, as, just as
οὑτως – thus, so
παρα – (1) beside, along by
    παρα την θαλασσαν – by the sea, along the shore
παρα – (2) contrary to
    παρα τον νομον – against the Law
ὁτι – that, because
πασχω – I suffer
    πασχειν – to be suffering
    παθειν – to suffer
δεω – I bind
    δει – it is binding, it is necessary
ἐξεστιν – it is lawful, it is permitted (ἐξουσια – authority)
    παντα ἐξεστιν – everything is lawful, all kinds of things are
                          permitted
πολυς – much (πολυς, πολλη, πολυ)
    πολλοι – many people
    πολυ – much
    πολλα – many things, much
    πολλα παθειν – to suffer many things, to suffer much
το λεγειν – speaking, speech (lit. "the to speak").
    καλον το λεγειν – speaking is good
    ἐν τῳ λεγειν αὐτον – while he is (was) speaking
    δια το ἐχειν αὐτους – because they have (had)
    δια το μη ἐχειν – because of not having
    ἐμοι το ζην Χριστος – for me to live is Christ
οἱ υἱοι Ἰσραηλ – the sons of Israel, the people of Israel

30.4 Translate

1. δει αὐτους πολλα παθειν.

It is necessary for them to suffer much.

2. δει ὑμας πολλα παθειν καθως ὁ Κυριος ὑμων ἐπαθεν.

You are bound to suffer greatly just as your Lord suffered.

3. οὐκ ἐξεστιν σοι τουτους τους ἀρτους φαγειν· παρα τον νομον ἐστιν ὁτι ἁγιοι εἰσιν.

It is not lawful for you to eat these loaves. It is against the Law because they are holy.

4. ἐξεστιν αὐτοις φαγειν τους ἀρτους ὁτι ἱερεις εἰσιν.

They are permitted to eat the loaves because they are priests.

5. οὐκ ἐξεστιν μοι τουτο ποιησαι ὁτι το τουτο ποιειν παρα νομον ἐστιν.

It is not permissible for me to do this because doing this is against the Law (unlawful).

6. δει ταυτα γενεσθαι καθως εἰπον οἱ προφηται.

These things are bound to happen as the prophets said.

7. παραπορευομενων αὐτων παρα την θαλασσαν ἠλθεν προς αὐτον λεπρος.

As they were going along beside the sea a leper came to him.

8. καθως Μωυσης ἐδιδαξεν πολλους των υἱων Ἰσραηλ οὐτως δει τον υἱον του ἀνθρωπου διδαξαι μαθητας πολλους.

As Moses taught many of the people of Israel it is necessary for the Son of Man to teach many disciples.

9. και ἐν τῳ διδασκειν αὐτον παρα την θαλασσαν πολλοι ἐπιστευσαν αὐτῳ.

As he was teaching beside the lake many people believed in him.

10. δια το μη προσευξασθαι οὐ λαμβανουσιν, ἀλλα οἱ προσευχομενοι κατα το θελημα του θεου οὐτοι λημψονται.

Because of not praying people do not receive, but those who pray according to the will of God, they will receive.

11. και ἐτι αὐτων ὀντων ἐν τῃ πολει, παλιν εἰπεν αὐτοις κατ᾽ ἰδιαν ὁτι Οἱ θελοντες πρωτοι εἰναι ἐσονται ἐσχατοι και πολλοι εἰσιν ἐσχατοι οἳ ἐσονται πρωτοι.

While they were still in the city, he said to them again privately, "Those who want to be first shall be last, and many are last who shall be first".

30.5

Read John 1.10–14.

Notes:

εἰς τα ἰδια – to his own place   οἱ ἰδιοι – his own people

134

παραλαμβανω – I receive
ὁσοι – as many as, all who
το αἱμα – the blood
ἡ σαρξ – the flesh
γενναω – I beget

σκηνοω – I encamp,
 I live in a tent, I dwell
μονογενης – only begotten, only Son
πληρης – full
χαρις – grace

30.6

Revise lessons 23 and 24.

LESSON 31

βαπτιζομαι – I am being baptized ⎯
ἐβαπτιζομην – I was being baptized ⎯⎯|

31.1

βαπτιζομαι – I am being baptized, I am baptized
παραδιδομαι – I am being betrayed, I am handed over

The endings of βαπτιζομαι are the same as those of γινομαι (29.1):

	Singular		Plural	
1st person	-ομαι	– I	-ομεθα	– we
2nd person	-ῃ	– you	-εσθε	– you
3rd person	-εται	– he, she, it	-ονται	– they

So: βαπτιζομεθα – we are being baptized
παραδιδονται – they are being betrayed, they are being handed
 over.

31.2

βαπτιζομαι ὑπο του ἀποστολου – I am being baptized
 by the apostle
κρινομεθα ὑφ᾽ ὑμων – we are being judged **by you**

When the action of the verb is done by a person, ὑπο = by.
Note: ὑπο becomes ὑπ᾽ before a vowel, ὑφ᾽ before ῾ (h).

135

31.2

Translate

1. βαπτιζονται ὑπο Ἰωαννου.	They are being baptized by John.
2. κρινεται ὑπο του Κυριου.	He is being judged by the Lord.
3. Ἰησου, παραδιδῃ ὑπο του Ἰουδα.	Jesus, you are being betrayed by Judas.
4. βαπτιζεται ὑπ' αὐτου ἡ γυνη.	The woman is being baptized by him.
5. ἀγαπωμεθα ὑπο του θεου.	We are loved by God.
6. βαπτιζεσθε παντες ὑπο Ἰωαννου του βαπτιστου.	You are all being baptized by John the Baptist.
7. οὐ βαπτιζομαι ὑφ' ὑμων.	I am not being baptized by you.
8. ἐρχονται προς Ἰωαννην ἱνα βαπτιζωνται ὑπ' αὐτου.	They come to John so that they may be baptized by him.

31.3

βαπτιζομαι **ὑδατι** or βαπτιζομαι **ἐν ὑδατι** – I am baptized **with water**

When the action of the verb is carried out by means of a thing, "by" or "with" is shown:

(a) by the form, or case, of the word – the dative case

So: βαπτιζεται **ὑδατι** – he is baptized **with water**
τῃ **ἀληθειᾳ** σωζεσθε – you are being saved **by the truth**

(b) by **ἐν** (followed by a word in the dative case)

So: βαπτιζομαι **ἐν ὑδατι** – I am being baptized **with water**
ἀποκτεινεται **ἐν μαχαιρῃ** – he is being killed **with a sword**.

There seems to be a similar use of ἐν in 2 Corinthians 5.19:

...ὁτι θεος ἡν **ἐν Χριστῳ** κοσμον καταλλασσων ἑαυτῳ
...that God was **by means of Christ** (*or* **through Christ**) reconciling the world to himself.

31.4 Words

τις – someone, anyone, a (compare τίς, 15.6)
τινες – some people, some
τι – something, anything
εἰς – one
Like ὁ, ἡ, το (12.7), εἰς has three forms: εἰς, μια, ἑν.

136

So: εἰς ἀνηρ ἀγαπᾳ μιαν γυναικα – one man loves one woman
        μια γυνη ἀγαπᾳ ἑνα ἀνδρα – one woman loves one man
οὐδεις and μηδεις – no one, nobody
οὐδεν and μηδεν – nothing
δυω – two, δεκα – ten, δωδεκα – twelve, τρεις – three, τριακοντα – thirty,
        τριακοσιοι – three hundred
το ὀνομα – the name
        του ὀνοματος – of the name
το ὑδωρ – the water
        του ὑδατος – of the water
το ὀρος – the mountain
ἀλαλος – dumb (λαλεω – I speak)
ἡ πιστις – the faith, the trust
        δια πιστεως – through faith
ἡ χαρις – the grace: grace, graciousness, favour
        When used with reference to God, χαρις indicates his attitude of
        loving favour and his consequent loving action.
παραδιδωμι – I hand on, I hand over
        παραδιδωμι την παραδοσιν – I hand on the tradition

31.5 Translate

1. ἐρχεται τις προς το ὑδωρ.	Someone is coming to the water.
2. βαπτιζει τινα ὑδατι.	He baptizes someone with water.
3. βαπτιζεται ἑν ὑδατι ὑπο τινος.	He is baptized with water by someone.
4. ἐρχεται γυνη τις προς το ὀρος.	A woman is coming towards the mountain.
5. ἑκ Ναζαρετ δυναται τι ἀγαθον ἑλθειν;	Is anything good able to come from Nazareth?
6. ἑκ της Γαλιλαιας δυναται τι ἀγαθον εἰναι;	Can anything good be from Galilee?
7. ἑαν τις φαγῃ ἑκ τουτου του ἀρτου ζησει εἰς τον αἰωνα.	If anyone eats from this loaf he will live for ever.
8. ἐρχεται εἱς των μαθητων και βαπτιζεται ὑδατι ὑπο Ἰωαννου ἑν τῳ ὀνοματι του θεου.	One of the disciples comes and is baptized with water by John in the name of God.
9. τῃ χαριτι σωζομεθα δια πιστεως, και οὐδεις σωζεται τοις ἐργοις αὑτου.	We are being saved by grace through faith and no one is being saved by the deeds he does.

137

31.5

10. καταβαινοντων των δωδεκα ἐκ του ὀρους, αὐτος ἀνεβη εἰς το ὀρος κατ᾽ ἰδιαν.

While the twelve were coming down from the mountain, he went up the mountain on his own.

11. ἀλαλος ἐστιν και οὐ δυναται μηδεν μηδενι λεγειν περι της πιστεως αὐτου.

He is dumb and is not able to say anything to anyone about his faith.

31.6 ἐβαπτιζομην – I was being baptized ⁻⁻⁻⁻|

Here are the endings of ἐβαπτιζομην. Note the **ε** in front of the stem which indicates past time.

	Singular	Plural
1st person	**-ομην** – I	**-ομεθα** – we
2nd person	**-ου** – you	**-εσθε** – you (pl.)
3rd person	**-ετο** – he, she, it	**-οντο** – they

Translate

1. ἐξεπορευοντο προς αὐτον οἱ Ἱεροσολυμειται παντες και πολλοι ἐβαπτιζοντο ὑπ᾽ αὐτου.

All the people of Jerusalem were going out to him and many were baptized by him.

2. ἐρχονται οἱ δωδεκα και λεγουσιν ὁτι Τρεις ἐχομεν ἀρτους και τριακοντα ἰχθυας.

The twelve come and say, "We have three loaves and thirty fishes".

3. οἱ δυο ἀποστολοι ἐπεμποντο ὑπο του Κυριου και ἐποιουν τα ἐργα αὐτου.

The two apostles were being sent by the Lord and they were doing his works.

4. οὐδεις σωζεται τοις ἰδιοις ἐργοις ἀλλα ἐσωζομεθα τη χαριτι του θεου.

No one is being saved by his own deeds but we were being saved by the grace of God.

31.7

βαπτιζεσθαι – to be baptized ⁻⁻⁻⁻
βαπτιζομενος – being baptized ⁻⁻⁻⁻

So: ἐν τῳ βαπτιζεσθαι αὐτον... – while he was being baptized...

βαπτιζομενων αὐτων, ἠλθεν γραμματευς τις
As they were being baptized a scribe came

Ἰησους ὁ λεγομενος Χριστος
Jesus, the man called the Messiah.

Translate

1. οὐκ ἤλθομεν βαπτιζεσθαι ἀλλα βαπτιζειν.	We did not come to be baptized but to baptize.
2. εἶδεν αὐτους βαπτιζομενους.	He saw them being baptized.
3. τρεις ἀποστολοι ἀποστελλονται ὑπο του Κυριου.	Three apostles are being sent by the Lord.
4. οἱ προφηται φερομενοι ὑπο Πνευματος Ἁγιου ἐλαλησαν.	The prophets spoke as they were carried along (*or* being carried along) by the Holy Spirit.
5. οἱ ἁγιοι δυνανται ὑπο του Πνευματος του Ἁγιου φερεσθαι.	The saints are able to be carried along by the Holy Spirit.
6. εἰσηλθεν εἰς ἀνθρωπος εἰς την οἰκιαν και ἐμεινεν ἐν τη οἰκιᾳ ἡμερας τριακοντα και μιαν.	One man went into the house and he stayed in the house for thirty-one days.

31.8

Read Mark 11.9–11.

Notes:

προαγω – I go in front   ὀψια or ὀψε – late
περιβλεπομαι – I look round at   ἠδη – already

31.9 Grammatical terms for verbal forms

This section and 33.11 are for reference. Do not expect to learn them all at once. You will not need to know grammatical terms in order to read and translate the New Testament. You may need to know them when you are studying commentaries which refer to the Greek text. Several forms are included here for the purpose of reference although you have not learned them yet. Do not spend time studying them now. You will come to them in later lessons.

A. Mood

1. Verbal forms which make a definite statement or question are called *indicative*.

So: λεγει – he says
      ἐβληθησαν – they were thrown
      ἠν – he was
      ἀγομεν; – are we going?

are all in the indicative mood.

2. Verbal forms which make an indefinite statement or question are called *subjunctive*.

So: (ἐαν) λεγῃ – (if) he says
(ἐαν) εἰπῃ – (if) he should say
ἀγωμεν – let us go
ἀγωμεν; – should we go?

are all in the subjunctive mood.
(Other uses of the subjunctive will be studied in later lessons.)

3. Verbal forms which express a direct command are called *imperative*.

So: ποιησον – do!
ἐξελθε – go out!
δος – give!
βαλλε – keep throwing!

are all in the imperative mood. (See lessons 40 and 41.)

4. Verbal forms which express "to..." are called *infinitive*.

So: ποιειν – to be doing
ποιησαι – to do
βαπτιζεσθαι – to be being baptized
βαπτισθηναι – to be baptized

are all in the infinitive mood.

5. A verbal form that can describe a noun is called a *participle*.

So: ποιων – doing
ποιησας – having done
ἐρχομενος – coming
βαπτισθεις – having been baptized

are all participles.

B. Tense

1. Forms which express continuing or repeated action are called *present* ‾‾‾.

So: ποιει – he does
ποιωμεν – let us do
ποιειν – to do
ποιων – doing

are all present.

2. Forms which express continuing or repeated action in past time are called *imperfect* ‾‾‾|.

So: ἐποιει – he was doing
     ἤρχετο – he was coming
     ἐβαπτιζετο – he was being baptized

are all imperfect.

3. Forms which express completed or single action are called *aorist* ˄.

So: ἐποιησεν – he did
     βαλωμεν; – should we throw?
     φαγων – eating
     βαπτισθηναι – to be baptized

are all aorist.

4. Forms which express action in future time are called *future* |˄.

So: ποιησομεν – we shall do
     ἐλευσονται – they will come
     ἐσεσθαι – to be

are all future.

5. Forms which express action in the past which has a continuing result are called *perfect* ˄|•.

So: πεποιηκα – I have done
     γεγραπται – it has been written
     γεγραφθαι – to have been written
     γεγραμμενος – having been written
     δεδωκεν – he has given

are all perfect. (See lesson 33.)

6. Forms which express action in the past which had a continuing result which is also in the past are called *pluperfect* ˄|•|.

So: πεπιστευκειν – I had trusted
     δεδωκει – he had given

are pluperfect. (See lesson 49.7.)

C. Voice

1. Forms which normally express action done by the subject (usually to someone or something else) are called *active*.

   So: βαλλω – I throw
   ἐβαλον – I threw
   βαλλων – throwing
   βαλλειν – to throw
   βαλλε – throw!

   are all active.

2. Forms which normally express action done to the subject by someone or something else are called *passive*.

   So: βαλλομαι – I am being thrown
   ἐβληθην – I was thrown
   βληθηναι – to be thrown
   βληθεις – having been thrown

   are all passive.

3. Forms which normally express action done by the subject and involving the subject rather than anyone else are called *middle*. (See lesson 45.1–4).

   So: ἐρχομαι – I come
   πορευεσθαι – to travel
   προσηυξαμην – I prayed
   προσευξασθαι – to pray
   προσευχομενος – praying
   προσευξαμενος – having prayed, praying

   are all middle.

Putting together A, B, and C we can partly describe verbal forms as follows:

λεγει – he says	present indicative active
εἰπωμεν – let us say	aorist subjunctive active
ἐρχεσθαι – to be coming	present infinitive middle
βληθηναι – to be thrown	aorist infinitive passive
γραψας – having written	aorist participle active
ἐρχομενος – coming	present participle middle
γεγραμμενος – written, having been written	perfect participle passive

31.10 Progress test 15

1. Which of the following infinitives indicate continuing — or repeated ····· action?

   (a) διδαξαι
   (b) διδασκειν
   (c) ἐλθειν
   (d) ἐρχεσθαι
   (e) ἀγαπαν
   (f) ζην
   (g) προσευξασθαι
   (h) βαλλειν
   (i) καταβαινειν
   (j) καταβηναι

2. Which of the following infinitives indicate single · action?

   (a) κηρυξαι
   (b) κηρυσσειν
   (c) ἐσθιειν
   (d) φαγειν
   (e) γραψαι
   (f) ἀραι
   (g) ἐλθειν
   (h) ἐρχεσθαι
   (i) βαλλεσθαι
   (j) βληθηναι

3. Which of the following participles indicate continuing or repeated action?

   (a) γινομενος
   (b) γενομενος
   (c) σωζοντες
   (d) σωσαντες
   (e) κρινων
   (f) τρεχων
   (g) δραμων
   (h) πασχων
   (i) παθων
   (j) πορευομενοι

4. Which of the following forms are passive?

   (a) βαλειν
   (b) βληθηναι
   (c) βαπτιζομαι
   (d) βαπτιζω
   (e) βαπτιζειν
   (f) βαπτιζεσθαι
   (g) ἐβαπτισθη
   (h) ἐβαπτισεν
   (i) βαπτιζομενος
   (j) βαπτιζων

Which is the best English translation?

5. Ἐγενετο ἀνθρωπος, ἀπεσταλμενος παρα θεου, ὀνομα αὐτῳ Ἰωαννης.
   (a) A man was sent from God whose name was John.
   (b) There was a man. He had been sent by God. His name was John.
   (c) A man came who had been sent by God. His name was John.

6. οὗτος ἠλθεν εἰς μαρτυριαν ἱνα μαρτυρηση περι του φωτος ἱνα παντες πιστευσωσιν δι' αὐτου.
   (a) This came into witnessing so that he might witness about the light so that all might believe through him.
   (b) He came as a testimony to bear witness to the light to bring all people to faith.
   (c) He came for the purpose of bearing witness, to bear witness to the light so that through him all people might believe.

Check your answers on page 280.

31.11

Read John 1.15–18.

Notes:
κραζω – I shout
ὀπισω – after
ἐμπροσθεν – before
πρωτος μου – (lit. first of me)
   before me, superior to me
πληρωμα – fullness

ἀντι – in place of
ὁ νομος – the Law
ἑωρακα – I have seen
πωποτε – ever
κολπος – bosom, lap
ἐξηγεομαι – I explain

LESSON 32

ἐβαπτισθην – I was baptized ⊣
βαπτισθεις – having been baptized ⊣

32.1

Compare:

1. (a) ἐβαπτισα – I baptized ⊣ (aorist indicative active)
    (b) ἐβαπτισθην – I was baptized ⊣ (aorist indicative passive)
2. (a) ἐποιησεν – he did, she did, it did ⊣
    (b) ἐποιηθη – it was done ⊣

Note that where the aorist active has σ between the stem and ending, the aorist passive usually has θ between the stem and ending.

Compare also:

ἐβαπτιζομεθα – we were being baptized ···⊣ (imperfect indicative
                                                     passive)
ἐβαπτισθημεν – we were baptized ⊣ (aorist indicative passive).

Translate

1. ἐβαπτισθητε ὑπ' αὐτου; | Were you baptized by him?
2. ἐσωθημεν ἀπο του πονηρου. | We were saved from the evil one.
3. οὐδεις ἐσωθη. | No one was saved.
4. ποτε ἐπεμποντο; | When were they being sent?

5. που ἐπεμφθησαν;
6. συ ἠγαπηθης. δια τί ἐγω οὐκ ἠγαπηθην;

Where were they sent?
You were loved. Why was I not loved?

32.2

Compare these infinitives (1) and participles (2):

1. (a) βαπτισθηναι — to be baptized · — (aorist passive)
   (b) βαπτισαι — to baptize · — (aorist active)
   (c) βαπτιζεσθαι — to be baptized ⁓ — (present passive)
   (d) βαπτιζειν — to baptize ⁓ — (present active)

2. (a) βαπτισθεις — having been baptized ⫟ — (aorist passive)
   (b) βαπτισας — having baptized ⫟ — (aorist active)
   (c) βαπτιζομενος — being baptized ⁓ — (present passive)
   (d) βαπτιζων — baptizing ⁓ — (present active)

Translate

1. οὐκ ἠλθεν βαπτισθηναι ἀλλα βαπτισαι.

He did not come to be baptized but to baptize.

2. βαπτισθεις ἐξηλθεν βαπτιζων παντας τους πιστευοντας.

When he had been baptized he went out baptizing all the believers.

3. ἐξηλθον οὐν προς αὐτον παντες βαπτισθηναι και ἐβαπτισθησαν ὑπ’ αὐτου και βαπτισθεντες ἀπηλθον προς την πολιν.

So they all went out to him to be baptized and they were baptized by him. When they had been baptized they went away to the town.

4. οὐκ ἐβαπτισθημεν ὑπο Παυλου; και οὐχι μειζονες ἐσμεν των βαπτισθεντων ὑπο Σιμωνος;

Were we not baptized by Paul? And are we not more important than those who have been baptized by Simon?

5. καλουσιν αὐτον και κρινουσιν αὐτον οἱ κριται ὁτι πολλα ἐποιει παρα τον νομον.

They call him and the judges judge him because he was doing many things against the Law.

6. κληθεντος αὐτου, ἐκρινεν αὐτον ὁ Πιλατος κατα τον νομον των Ῥωμαιων.

When he had been called, Pilate judged him according to the law of the Romans.

32.3 βαπτισθησομαι – I shall be baptized

Compare:

σωσω – I shall save (future indicative active)
σωθησομαι – I shall be saved (future indicative passive).

Note that **θησ** between the stem and the ending is a mark of the future passive.

Translate

1. ὁ πιστευσας και βαπτισθεις σωθησεται.	The person who has believed and been baptized will be saved.
2. οἱ μη πιστευσαντες κριθησονται.	Those who have not believed will be judged.
3. τουτο ποιηθησεται.	This will be done.
4. ταυτα ἐποιηθη.	These things were done.
5. καλουμεν το ὀνομα αὐτου Ἰησουν ἀλλα υἱος θεου κληθησεται.	We call his name Jesus but he shall be called the Son of God.

32.4 Words

Subject form (nominative)	Meaning	"Of" form (genitive)	Subject form (nominative)
Singular		*Singular*	*Plural*
ἡ κεφαλη	the head	της κεφαλης	αἱ κεφαλαι
ὁ ὀφθαλμος	the eye	του ὀφθαλμου	οἱ ὀφθαλμοι
το οὐς	the ear	του ὠτος	τα ὠτα
το στομα	the mouth	του στοματος	τα στοματα
ἡ χειρ	the hand, the arm	της χειρος	αἱ χειρες
ὁ πους	the foot, the leg	του ποδος	οἱ ποδες
το σωμα	the body	του σωματος	τα σωματα
το μελος	the limb	του μελους	τα μελη
το μερος	the part	του μερους	τα μερη
ἡ σαρξ	the flesh	της σαρκος	αἱ σαρκες

τυφλος – blind
κωφος – deaf, deaf and dumb
χωλος – lame

πιπτω – I fall
  ἐπεσεν – he fell
  προσεπεσεν αὐτῳ – he fell before him
  προσεπεσεν προς τους ποδας αὐτου – he fell at his feet
θεραπευω – I heal
ἐκτεινω – I stretch out
κρατεω – I take hold of, I grasp, I seize, I arrest
  ἐκρατησεν της χειρος αὐτης – he took hold of her hand
  οἱ στρατιωται ἐζητουν αὐτον κρατησαι – the soldiers were seeking to arrest him

32.5 Translate

1. ἡ χειρ και ὁ πους μελη εἰσιν του σωματος. — The arm and the leg are limbs of the body.

2. το στομα και τα ὠτα μερη εἰσιν της κεφαλης. — The mouth and the ears are parts of the head.

3. οὐ δυναται βλεπειν τι τοις ὀφθαλμοις αὐτου· τυφλος γαρ ἐστιν. — He cannot see anything with his eyes, for he is blind.

4. οὐ δυνανται περιπατειν· χωλοι γαρ εἰσιν. — They cannot walk, for they are lame.

5. οὐκ ἐδυναντο οὐδεν ἀκουσαι τοις ὠσιν αὐτων· κωφοι γαρ ἠσαν. ἀλλα νυν ἀκουουσιν, ὁ γαρ Ἰησους ἐθεραπευσεν αὐτους. — They were not able to hear anything with their ears, for they were deaf. But now they (can) hear, for Jesus healed them.

6. ἐκτεινας την χειρα αὐτου ἐκρατησεν του ποδος αὐτης. — Stretching out his hand he took hold of her foot.

7. ὠτα ἐχοντες, οὐκ ἀκουετε; και ὀφθαλμους ἐχοντες οὐ βλεπετε; — You have ears, can't you hear? You have eyes, can't you see? (Having eyes, do you not see?)

8. ποδας ἐχοντες οὐ περιπατουσι και στοματα ἐχοντες οὐκ ἐσθιουσιν, εἰδωλα γαρ εἰσιν. — Though they have legs (feet) they do not walk, though they have mouths they do not eat, for they are idols.

32.6

Read carefully:

A blind man was healed

ἠν δε ἀνθρωπος τις λεγομενος Βαρτιμαιος. τυφλος ἠν και οὐκ ἐδυνατο οὐδεν βλεψαι τοις ὀφθαλμοις αὐτου. οὑτος ἐλθων προσεπεσεν προς τους ποδας του Ἰησου. και αὐτος ἐκτεινας την χειρα ἡψατο των ὀφθαλμων αὐτου. και

147

32.6

ἐθεραπευθη ὁ τυφλος και ἀνεβλεψεν. και πολλοι χωλοι και κωφοι ἠλθον προς αὐτον και ἐθεραπευσεν αὐτους. τους κωφους ἐποιησεν ἀκουειν και τους χωλους περιπατειν.

32.7

Read 1 Corinthians 12.12–21 (Προς Κορινθιους Α 12.12–21).

Notes:

καθαπερ – just as	εἰ – if
εἰτε...εἰτε... – whether...or...	ὀσφρησις – smelling
δουλος – slave	ἑκαστος – each
ἐλευθερος – free	χρεια – need
ποτιζω – I cause to drink,	ἐθετο – he put, he has put
I give to drink	μεν...δε... – on the one hand...
παρα τουτο – for this reason	on the other hand...
ἀκοη – hearing	(see also 49.4 (c) and (g)).

32.8

Revise lessons 25 and 26.

LESSON 33

πεπιστευκα – I have trusted ⊣⊦
γεγραπται – it has been written, it is written ⊣⊦
οἰδα – I know ⊣⊦

33.1

Study the following sentences:

(a)   πεπιστευκα ὁτι συ εἶ ὁ Χριστος
      I have believed that you are the Messiah
   or I believe that you are the Messiah

(b)   ἠγγικεν ἡ βασιλεια του θεου
      The Kingdom of God has come near

(c)   ἡ πιστις σου σεσωκεν σε
      Your faith has saved you

148

(d)   χαριτι ἐστε σεσωσμενοι
      By grace you are saved
   or You have been saved by grace

(e)   ὡς γεγραπται ἐν τῳ Ἠσαιᾳ
      As it has been written in Isaiah
   or As it is written in Isaiah.

In these sentences the verbal forms πεπιστευκα, ἠγγικεν, σεσωκεν, σεσωσμενοι, and γεγραπται all refer to (1) an action or state in the past which has (2) a present or continuing result ⊣⊦

(a) πεπιστευκα indicates (1) I believed   (2) I still believe

(b) ἠγγικεν indicates   (1) it came near   (2) it is near

(c) σεσωκεν indicates   (1) you were saved   (2) you are safe
                     or (1) you were made well (2) you are well

(d) σεσωσμενοι indicates (1) having been saved   (2) being still safe

(e) γεγραπται indicates (1) it was written   (2) it can still be read.

Such verbal forms which indicate a past state or action with a present or continuing result are described as being in the *perfect* tense (31.9 B5). When we translate these perfect tense forms into English, if the emphasis is on the past action we can usually use forms with "has" or "have" in English:

   ὃ γεγραφα, γεγραφα – what I have written, I have written.

But if the context shows that the emphasis is on the present result, we may use a present tense in English:

   ὡς γεγραπται – as it is written, as it stands written, as Scripture says.

οἰδα (I know) is perfect in form, but present in meaning.
(The basic meaning of its stem ιδ is to see or perceive: the perfect form of οἰδα suggests that present knowing is a result of past perception.)

33.2

The perfect indicative active of πιστευω – I believe – is πεπιστευκα – I have believed (and I still believe).

Note the endings:

	Singular	Plural
1st person	-α – I	-αμεν – we
2nd person	-ας – you	-ατε – you
3rd person	-εν – he, she, it	-ασιν – they

33.2

γεγραφα (I have written), οἰδα (I know), ἠγγικα (I have come near) and other perfect active forms have the same endings.

Note that the perfect indicative active is usually marked by some of the following:

1. ε before the stem, as in other past tenses
2. κ between the stem and the ending
3. α in the ending (except 3rd person singular)
4. Repetition, or reduplication, of the initial consonant of the stem before the ε that marks past time.

33.3 Words

διδωμι – I give
    ἐδωκα – I gave
    δεδωκα – I have given
καλως – well
    καλως ἐχω – I am well
ἀληθως – truly
λαμβανω – I take, I receive
    εἰληφα – I have received
θνησκω – I die
    ⲧεθνηκα – I have died, I am dead
το μνημειον – the tomb
το ταλαντον – the talent: silver, worth over £100,000 (a denarius was a day's wage for Jewish labourers, and a talent was worth 10,000 denarii)
    ἐν ταλαντον – one talent
    πεντε ταλαντα – five talents

33.4 Translate

1. πεντε ταλαντα ἐδωκεν σοι ὁ βασιλευς, ἐγω δε ἐν ταλαντον εἰληφα.

The king gave you five talents but I have received one talent.

2. ζωην αἰωνιον δεδωκεν ἡμιν ὁ θεος.

God has given eternal life to us.

3. πεπιστευκαμεν ὁτι συ εἶ ἀληθως ὁ σωτηρ του κοσμου.

We have believed that you are truly the Saviour of the world.

4. ἐγω γινωσκω ὑμας και ὑμεις ἐγνωκατε και πεπιστευκατε την ἀγαπην ἡν ἐχει ὁ θεος ἐν ἡμιν.

I know you and you have known and believed the love which God has for us.

5. οἰδεν ἡ γυνη τον σωτηρα ἐν ᾧ πεπιστευκεν.

The woman knows the Saviour in whom she has believed.

6. ὃ γεγραφα, καλως γεγραφα.
What I have written, I have written well.

7. οἰδασιν ἀληθως τίς ἐστιν και που μενει.
They know truly who he is and where he is staying.

8. συ καλως παντα πεποιηκας και ἡμεις καλως ἐχομεν.
You have done all things well and we are well.

33.5

πεπιστευκως – having believed
    οἱ πεπιστευκοτες – those who have believed
τεθνηκως – having died
    ἡ τεθνηκυια – the woman who has died
εἰληφως – having taken, having received
εἰδως – knowing

Each of these verbal forms is a perfect participle active. They indicate past action with a continuing result. So οἱ ἐσχηκοτες (ἐχω – I have) means "the people who have had and still have". Compare:

Mt 25.20   ὁ τα πεντε ταλαντα **λαβων**
           The man who had received the five talents

Mt 25.24   ὁ το ἑν ταλαντον **εἰληφως**
           The man who had received one talent

λαβων is an **aorist** participle. It indicates a completed action: "he did receive them".

εἰληφως is a **perfect** participle. It indicates a past action with a continuing result: "he had received it and he still had it".

Note also: πεπιστευκεναι – to have believed, εἰδεναι – to know.
These are perfect infinitive active.

33.6 Translate

1. ἐξηλθεν ὁ τεθνηκως ἐκ του μνημειου, και ἐξελθοντος αὐτου οἱ μαθηται ἀπηλθον προς την πολιν εἰπειν το γεγονος τοις οὐσιν ἐν τη πολει.
The man who had died came out from the tomb. When he had come out, the disciples went away to the town to tell the people in the town what had happened.

2. μη εἰδοτες τας γραφας οὐ δυνανται ἀποκριθηναι οὐδεν.
Because they do not know the Scriptures (*or* Not knowing the Scriptures) they are not able to make any answer.

3. οὐκ εἰσελευσονται εἰς την
βασιλειαν του θεου δια το μη
αὑτους πεπιστευκεναι εἰς τον υἱον
αὑτου.

They will not enter into the
Kingdom of God because they
have not believed in his Son.

4. μακαριοι οἱ πεπιστευκοτες· αὑτοι
σωθησονται δια της χαριτος του
θεου.

Blessed are those who have
believed: they shall be saved
through the grace of God.

5. οἱ καλως ἐχοντες εἰδον τον
ἐσχηκοτα τον δαιμονιον και
ἐχαρησαν εἰδοτες ὁτι ἐθεραπευθη
ὑπο του Ἰησου.

Those who were well saw the man
who had had the demon and they
rejoiced, knowing that he had
been healed by Jesus.

33.7

γεγραπται – it is written   **τετελεσται** – it has been completed

γεγραμμενος – written   **πεπληρωμενος** – fulfilled

γεγραφθαι – to have been written

So: οἰδα ταυτα γεγραφθαι ὑπο των προφητων
I know these things to have been written by the prophets
or I know that these things were written by the prophets.

Translate

1. εὑρισκει ταυτα γεγραφθαι ὑπο των
ἀποστολων και οἰδεν ὁτι ἀληθη
ἐστιν.

He finds that these things were
written by the apostles and he
knows that they are true.

2. και ἐγενετο, καθως γεγραμμενον
ἐστιν.

And it happened, just as it is
written.

3. πεπληρωται, καθως γεγραπται ἐν
τῳ Ἡσαιᾳ τῳ προφητῃ.

It has been fulfilled, as it is written
in (the book of) Isaiah the
prophet.

4. χαριτι ἐστε σεσωσμενοι και οὐκ ἐξ
ἐργων ὑμων.

You are saved by grace and not as
a result of what you have done.

5. ἡ μητηρ εὑρεν το δαιμονιον
ἐξεληλυθος ἐκ του τεκνου αὐτης.

The mother found the demon
(already) gone out from her child.

33.8 Words

ὁ λαος – the people
ὁ ὀχλος – the crowd
ὁ καιρος – the time, the opportunity
ὁ βασιλευς – the king
ὁ νομος – the Law (often: the Law of Moses, the Torah)
ὁ γραμματευς – the scribe, the teacher of the Law
ὁ ἀρχιερευς – the chief priest
ἡ δυναμις – the power, the ability, the miracle (δυναμαι – I am able)
το ἐθνος – the race, the nation
    τα ἐθνη – the nations, the Gentiles
ἐγγιζω – I come near
    ἐγγυς – near
πληροω – I fulfil
    πληρης – full

33.9 Translate

1. οἰδαμεν ὁτι οἱ γραμματεις ἐδιδασκον τον λαον τον νομον καθως αὐτοι ἐδιδαχθησαν.

We know that the scribes used to teach the people the Law just as they themselves had been taught.

2. πεπληρωται ὁ καιρος και ἡγγικεν ἡ βασιλεια του βασιλεως των βασιλεων.

The time has been fulfilled and the Kingdom of the King of kings has come near.

3. ἠλθον οὐν οἱ ἀρχιερεις και οἱ γραμματεις προς τον Ἰησουν και ἡρωτησαν αὐτον, Τί γεγραπται ἐν τῳ νομῳ περι του Χριστου;

So the chief priests and the teachers of the Law came to Jesus and asked him, "What is written in the Law about the Messiah?"

4. τα ἐθνη οὐκ οἰδασιν τον νομον του Μωυσεως και οἱ Ἰουδαιοι οὐ τηρουσιν αὐτον.

The Gentiles do not know the Law of Moses and the Jews do not keep it.

5. ὁ Ἰησους περιπατει παρα την θαλασσαν και εἰδεν Σιμωνα και ἐκαλεσεν αὐτον· και προβας ὀλιγον εἰδεν ὀχλον πολυν και εἰπεν αὐτοις φωνῃ μεγαλῃ, Ἀκουετε, ἡγγικεν ἡ βασιλεια του θεου και ἡ δυναμις αὐτου.

Jesus was walking along beside the lake and saw Simon and called him.
    Going on a little way he saw a large crowd and said to them in a loud voice, "Listen, the reign of God has come near, and his power".

33.10 Translation: Πεπλήρωται ὁ καιρός (Mark 1.15)

In sentence 2 in 33.9 we translated Πεπλήρωται ὁ καιρός rather literally as, "the time has been fulfilled". RSV translates similarly, "the time is fulfilled". But what does this mean in English? We often think of prophecy being fulfilled, but not naturally of time being fulfilled (except perhaps in the sense of a period of service being brought to an end). "The time is fulfilled" is "translation English" rather than real English. So we have to ask ourselves, "In Mark 1.15 what does Πεπλήρωται ὁ καιρός really mean, and how can we best express the meaning in English?"

καιρός means time in the sense of "opportunity" or "special time".

NIV translates: "The time has come", which is clear and natural English but does not express the very important meaning of πληρόω (I fulfil). Most often in the New Testament πεπλήρωται and similar forms draw attention to the fulfilment of the great promises made by God to the Israelites in Old Testament times (Luke 24.44, Acts 13.32–33). We must include this important idea in our translation. We might translate πεπλήρωται ὁ καιρός as "the time of fulfilment has come".

33.11 Grammatical terms

To *parse* a verb is to describe its precise verbal form, by identifying its person, number, tense, mood, and voice.

1. Person
　　I and **we** are called first person.
　　Thou and **you** are called second person.
　　He, she, it, and **they** are called third person.

So:　λεγω, λεγομεν are first person
　　　λεγεις, λεγετε are second person
　　　λεγει, λεγουσιν are third person.

2. Number
　　I, you (thou), he, she, and it, all refer to one person or thing; they are called singular.
　　We, you, and they, all refer to more than one; they are called plural.

So:　λεγω, λεγεις, λεγει are all singular
　　　λεγομεν, λεγετε, λεγουσιν are all plural

　　　λεγει is third person singular
　　　λεγετε is second person plural.

3. Tense

Tense	Examples	Type of action
Present	ποιω, βαλλω, λεγω, ἐρχομαι	⁞⁞⁞⁞⁞
Imperfect	ἐποιουν, ἐβαλλον, ἐλεγον, ἠρχομην	⁞⁞⁞|
Future	ποιησω, βαλω, ἐρω, ἐλευσομαι	|⁞
Aorist	ἐποιησα, ἐβαλον, εἰπον, ἠλθον	⁞|
Perfect	πεποιηκα, βεβληκα, εἰρηκα, ἐληλυθα	⁞|•
Pluperfect	πεποιηκειν, βεβληκειν, εἰρηκειν, ἐληλυθειν	⁞|•|

4. Mood

Mood	Examples
Indicative	λεγει, λεγομεν, εἰπεν, ἐποιησεν, ἐποιηθη
Subjunctive	λεγη, λεγωμεν, εἰπη, ποιηση, ποιηθη
Imperative	ποιησον, ἐξελθε, διανοιχθητι
Infinitive	λεγειν, εἰπειν, ποιησαι, ἐρχεσθαι, βαπτισθηναι
Participles	λεγων, εἰπων, ποιησας, ἐρχομενος, βαπτισθεις

(For optative, see 49.1–3)

5. Voice

Voice	Examples
Active	ποιω, ποιη, ποιησαι, ποιησας
Middle	ἐρχομαι, ἐρχεσθαι, ἐρχομενος
Passive	ἐβαπτισθην, βαπτισθηναι, βαπτισθεις

Parsing verbal forms

Putting together 1–5 above:

λεγομεν (we say) is 1st person plural present indicative active of λεγω

βαλωμεν (let us throw) is 1st person plural aorist subjunctive active of βαλλω

ποιησον (do!) is 2nd person singular aorist imperative active of ποιεω

βαπτισθηναι (to be baptized) is aorist infinitive passive of βαπτιζω

ἐρχεσθαι (to come) is present infinitive middle of ἐρχομαι

λεγων (saying) is nominative singular masculine present participle active of λεγω.

33.11

When parsing a verbal form we need first to translate it literally and then to decide whether it is:

   (a) indicative, subjunctive, imperative, or optative
   (b) infinitive
or (c) a participle.

For (a) indicative, subjunctive, imperative, or optative, we must give:
   person, number, tense, mood, and voice.

For (b) infinitive, we must give:
   tense, mood, and voice.

For (c) a participle, we must give:
   case, number, gender (37.1), tense, mood, and voice.

33.12 Progress test 16

Which is the correct translation?

1. ἀπεστελλοντο οἱ μαθηται ὑπο του κυριου βαπτιζειν ὑμας.
   (a) The disciples send us from the Lord to be baptized.
   (b) The disciples were being sent by the Lord to baptize you.
   (c) The disciples are sent by the Lord to baptize you.

2. παντα τα μελη του σωματος πολλα ὀντα ἑν ἐστιν σωμα.
   (a) All the limbs of the body, being many, are in the body.
   (b) While the limbs of the body are many, it is one body.
   (c) All the limbs of the body, though they are many, are one body.

3. Συ εἶ Σιμων, συ κληθηση Κηφας ὃ ἑρμηνευεται Πετρος.
   (a) You are Simon, you will be called Cephas (which is translated "Peter").
   (b) You were Simon, you will be called Cephas, which means "Peter".
   (c) You are Simon, you will become Cephas (which is translated "Peter").

Which is the best English translation?

4. δια το αὐτον πολλακις πεδαις και ἁλυσεσιν δεδεσθαι και διεσπασθαι ὑπ' αὐτου τας ἁλυσεις και τας πεδας συντετριφθαι.
   (a) Because of him many times with fetters and with chains to have been bound, and to have been torn apart by him the chains and the fetters to have been smashed.
   (b) Because he had been many times bound with fetters and chains and the chains to have been broken by him and the fetters smashed.

156

(c) Because many times he had been bound with fetters and chains but had torn the chains apart and smashed the fetters.

Which is the correct description of the following verbal forms from questions 1–4?

5. ἀπεστελλοντο (1)
    (a) First person plural aorist indicative active of ἀποστελλω.
    (b) Third person plural imperfect indicative passive of ἀποστελλω.
    (c) Third person plural present indicative passive of ἀποστελλω.

6. ὀντα (2)
    (a) Third person plural present indicative of εἰμι.
    (b) Nominative singular masculine present participle of εἰμι.
    (c) Nominative plural neuter present participle of εἰμι.

7. κληθηση (3)
    (a) Third person singular aorist indicative passive of κλαιω.
    (b) Second person singular aorist indicative passive of καλεω.
    (c) Second person singular future indicative passive of καλεω.

8. δεδεσθαι (4)
    (a) Perfect infinitive passive of δεω (I bind).
    (b) Second person plural perfect indicative passive of δεω.
    (c) Third person singular perfect indicative active of δεω.

Check your answers on page 281.

LESSON 34

τιθημι – I am putting   διδωμι – I am giving
τιθεις – putting ⁼⁼⁼   διδους – giving ⁼⁼⁼
θεις – having put ⁼   δους – having given ⁼

34.1 Words

τιθημι – I put, I place, I put down, I appoint
  τιθεναι – to put ⁼⁼⁼
  θειναι – to put ·
  ἐπιτιθημι – I place on, I put on (ἐπι – on)
διδωμι – I give, I present
  διδου – give! keep giving! ⁼⁼⁼
  δος – give! ·
  παραδιδωμι – I hand over, I betray, I hand on (παρα – alongside)
  παραδοθηναι – to be handed over, to be arrested
  παραδοσιν παραδουναι – to hand on a tradition or teaching
ἱστημι – I cause to stand, I set up, I stand
  ἑστηκα – I stood
  ἀνιστημι – I stand up, I rise (ἀνα – up)
    ἀναστας – having got up, rising ·
  παριστημι – I stand beside
    ὁ παρεστηκως – the bystander
  ἀποκαθιστημι – I restore
    ἀπεκατεσταθη ἡ χειρ αὐτου – his arm was restored (Mk 3.5)
ἱημι
  ἀφιημι – I leave, I allow, I forgive, I let, I let go
  συνιημι – I understand
  συνηκα – I understood
φημι – I say
  ἐφη – he said
ἀπολλυμι – I destroy, I spoil, I ruin
  ἀπωλεσα – I destroyed
  ἀπολεσαι – to destroy ·
  ἀπωλομην – I perished

34.2 Translate

1. ἐπιτιθημι τας χειρας μου ἐπι της κεφαλης αὐτου.	I am laying my hands on his head.
2. διδομεν τα βιβλια τοις μαθηταις ἱνα διδωσιν αὐτα τῳ ἀρχιερει.	We give the books to the disciples so that they may give them to the High Priest.
3. οἱ ἀδελφοι διδοασιν τους ἀρτους ἡμιν ἱνα διδωμεν αὐτους τοις ἱερευσιν.	The brothers give the loaves to us so that we may give them to the priests.
4. Ἰουδας Ἰσκαριωθ ἐστιν ὁ παραδιδους τον Ἰησουν.	Judas Iscariot is the person who is betraying Jesus.
5. ἀφιετε αὐτοις πολλα ποιειν.	You allow them to do many things.
6. ὁ θεος ἀφιησιν ἡμιν παντας τας ἁμαρτιας ἡμων και ζωην διδωσιν ἡμιν ἐν Χριστῳ.	God forgives us all our sins and gives us life through Christ (in Christ).
7. Ἰησου, ἀπολλυς παντα τα ἐργα του πονηρου.	Jesus, you are destroying all the works of the evil one.
8. εἰπον τῳ Ἰησου, Οὐχι συ εἶ ὁ βαπτιστης; ὁ δε ἐφη αὐτοις, Οὐκ εἰμι.	They said to Jesus, "You are the baptizer, aren't you?" He said to them, "I am not".

34.3 διδο ⸗ δο ⸰

In **βαλλειν** (to throw, to be throwing), **βαλειν** (to throw), **αἰρων** (picking up), and **ἀρας** (having picked up), the longer stems **βαλλ** and **αιρ** indicate repeated or continuing action; the shorter stems **βαλ** and **αρ** indicate single or completed action.

Compare:

⸗

διδου – give! keep giving!
διδους, διδουσα, διδον
  – giving
διδοναι – to give, to keep giving

⸰

δος – give!
δους, δουσα, δον
  – having given, giving
δουναι – to give

So: τον ἀρτον **διδου** ἡμιν καθ᾽ ἡμεραν – give us the bread every day

   τον ἀρτον **δος** ἡμιν σημερον – give us the bread today

Note the following words and forms carefully:

Verb	Continued or repeated action stem ⁓	Completed or single action stem ⊣
τιθημι – I put	τιθε	θε
διδωμι – I give	διδο	δο
ἱστημι – I set up, I stand	ἱστα	στα
ἀφιημι – I forgive, I leave (ἀπο + ἱημι)	ἱε	ἑ
ἀπολλυμι – I destroy	ολλ	ολ
δεικνυμι – I show	δεικνυ	δεικ

So:
τιθεις – putting, placing	θεις – having put, putting
ἐπιτιθησιν – he is placing on	ἐπεθηκεν – he put on
διδοτε – give!	δοτε – give!
ἠφιεν – he was allowing	ἀφηκεν – he allowed
ἑστηκεν – he is standing	ἑστη – he stood
εἱστηκει – he was standing	ἀναστας – having stood up
ἀπολλυμεθα – we are perishing	ἀπολεσαι – to destroy
δεικνυμι – I show	δειξω – I will show
δεικνυειν – to show	δειξαι – to show

34.4 Translate

1. ἐπιθεις αὐτῃ τας χειρας αὐτου ἐθεραπευσεν αὐτην.

   He laid (lit. having laid) his hands on her and healed her.

2. ἐπεθηκεν τας χειρας αὐτης ἐπι του ποδος αὐτου και ἀπεκατεσταθη ὁ πους αὐτου.

   She laid her hands on his foot (leg) and his foot (leg) was restored.

3. εἰπεν αὐτῃ ὁ Ἰησους, Ἀφεωνται σοι αἱ ἁμαρτιαι σου.

   Jesus said to her, "Your sins are forgiven you".

4. ἀναστας ἠλθεν εἰς την πολιν και ἐδειξεν ἑαυτον τῳ ἱερει.

   He got up and went into the city and showed himself to the priest.

5. ἀναστασα ἠλθεν εἰς την πολιν δειξαι ἑαυτην τῳ ἱερει.

   She got up and went into the city to show herself to the priest.

6. ἀ ναστ αντες ἐξηλθομεν ἐκ της πολεως.

   We got up and went out of the city.

7. ἔδωκεν τον ἀρτον τη γυναικι.

He gave the loaf to the woman.

8. δεδωκεν ἡμιν τουτους τους ἀρτους.

He has given us these loaves.

9. οἱ παρεστηκοτες εἶπον ὁτι Μωυσης δεδωκεν ἡμιν τον νομον. ὁ δε ἐφη, Οὐ Μωυσης ἐδωκεν ὑμιν τον νομον ἀλλα ὁ Πατηρ μου διδωσιν ὑμιν τον νομον τον ἀληθινον.

The bystanders said, "Moses has given us the Law". He said, "It was not Moses who gave you the Law, but my Father is giving you the true Law".

10. εἰς των μαθητων αὐτου εἶπεν αὐτῳ, Ἡ μητηρ σου και οἱ ἀδελφοι ἑστηκασιν ἐξω.

One of his disciples said to him, "Your mother and brothers are standing outside".

11. λαβων ἀρτον και δους αὐτοις εἶπεν, Τουτο ἐστιν το σωμα μου.

Taking a loaf and giving it to them he said, "This is my body", *or* He took a loaf, gave it to them and said, "This is my body".

12. οἱ Φαρισαιοι οὐ διδοασιν ἡμιν την ζωην την αἰωνιον ἀλλα Ἰησους ζωην δεδωκεν ἡμιν.

The Pharisees are not giving us eternal life, but Jesus has given us life.

13. ἐκαλεσεν αὐτους ὁ Ἰησους και ἀφεντες τον πατερα αὐτων ἐν τῳ πλοιῳ ἠκολουθησαν αὐτῳ.

Jesus called them and leaving (having left) their father in the boat, they followed him.

14. ἐφη αὐτῳ ὁ βασιλευς, Οὐ δυναμαι ἀναστας ἀρτους δουναι σοι.

The king said to him, "I cannot get up and give you loaves".

15. ἀποκριθεις δε ὁ ἀρχιερευς ἐφη αὐτῳ, Δια τί αἰρεις ὁ οὐκ ἐθηκας;

The High Priest said to him in reply, "Why do you take up what you did not put down?"

16. ἠλθεν δουναι την ψυχην (life) αὐτου και εἶπεν ὁτι Ἐξουσιαν ἐχω θειναι την ψυχην μου και ἐξουσιαν ἐχω παλιν λαβειν αὐτην.

He came to give his life, and he said, "I have authority to lay down my life and I have authority to take it again".

17. οὐκ ἀκουετε οὐδε συνιετε.

You do not listen, nor do you understand.

18. οὐκ ἀκουετε οὐδε συνιετε;

Do you not listen, nor understand?

19. οὐ συνηκαν τί το θελημα του θεου ἀλλα ἐζητουν πως ἀπολεσωσιν τον Χριστον.

They did not understand what God wanted, but they were seeking how they might destroy the Anointed One.

34.5

Read Mark 2.22.

Notes:
οἶνος – wine
ἀσκος – wineskin
εἰ δε μη – but if not, otherwise

ῥηγνυμι – I break
ῥηξει – it will burst

34.6 Translation – areas of meaning

Hardly any word in English is exactly the same in meaning and usage as any Greek word. So when we are translating a Greek word into English we must always be ready to think carefully.

For example, φοβος covers a fairly wide area of meaning for which we use in English such words as "fear", "respect", and "reverence". Very often "fear" will do as a translation, but not always. In 1 John 4.18 we may translate φοβος οὐκ ἐστιν ἐν τη ἀγαπη as "There is no fear in love". But in translating Acts 9.31, πορευομενη τῳ φοβῳ του Κυριου, we must ask ourselves, "Were the members of the Christian community, the ἐκκλησια, walking or living in fear of the Lord or in reverence for him?" It is clear from the context that they revered him rather than feared him. So we might translate as "Walking in reverence for the Lord", or "Living in reverence for the Lord".

Look again at Mark 2.22, especially the words

και ὁ οἶνος ἀπολλυται και οἱ ἀσκοι.

NEB: and then the wine and the skins are both lost.

GNB: and both the wine and the skins will be ruined.

You will see that the NEB and GNB translators both had difficulty in translating ἀπολλυται. ἀπολλυμι covers a wide area of meaning for which we use several English words including: I destroy, I spoil, I ruin.

In Mark 2.22 ἀπολλυται combines the ideas of being lost and being ruined. When a wineskin bursts it is ruined but not lost; so the NEB translation is not very good. When wine flows out over the floor it is lost rather than being ruined; so the GNB translation is not very good. In an English translation we really need two different verbs to express (a) what happens to the wine, and (b) what happens to the skins. We might translate:

The wine is spilled and the skins are spoiled.

This translation has a similarity of sound in the words "spilled" and "spoiled" which fits the proverbial nature of the saying.

34.7
Revise lessons 27 and 28.

Introduction to lessons 35–52

You have already learned how to understand and translate most of the basic forms and constructions found in the Greek New Testament. In lessons 35–52 you will build on the foundations you have laid. There will not be so many forms that are entirely new to you.

From this point onwards there are fewer sentences and passages to translate from Greek into English and a greater concentration on the text of the New Testament itself. Many of the points we study will be illustrated by quotations from the New Testament. Some of them contain new words and you may find them difficult at first – they will be easier when you go over the lesson a second time.

When you go over a lesson again, you may want to cover the English translation of each quotation until you have made your own attempt to understand and translate it. When you uncover the translation remember to ask yourself, "Have I expressed the same meaning?" Do not ask, "Have I used the same words?" For example, in lesson 35.3 we have translated δει τον υἱον του ἀνθρωπου πολλα παθειν (Mark 8.31) as, "It is necessary for the Son of Man to suffer much". We have done this so that it is easier for a student to recall that δει means "it is binding" or "it is necessary", and that παθειν means "to suffer" (aorist infinitive). You may prefer to translate as: "The Son of Man is bound to suffer greatly" or "The Son of Man must undergo great sufferings".

Lessons 37, 39, and 42 contain a large amount of material to illustrate different ways in which prepositions are used. If you are studying them with a class it may be necessary to spend two class periods on each lesson, or to cover some of the material in out-of-class study. There are other lessons, especially 46 and 48–52, which are introductions to a wide field of study. It is advisable for students to read them through carefully before any discussion of them in class.

Lesson 44 is designed to give you some insight into the structures of Greek words. It should give you a groundwork of understanding as you go on to enlarge your vocabulary by reading the New Testament. It may be more useful for private study and reference than for class work. A knowledge of some common stems (44.7) will also be helpful if you wish to study classical Greek.

LESSON 35

καλος – good   καλως – well
εἱς, δυο, τρεις – one, two, three

35.1

In English, the words "bad" and "good" are adjectives. The words "badly" and "well" are adverbs. Compare carefully:

Adjectives	Adverbs
καλος – good	καλως – well
κακος – bad	κακως – in an evil way
	(κακως ἐχω – I am ill)
ὀρθος – upright, straight	ὀρθως – properly, correctly
ὁμοιος – like	ὁμοιως – similarly, in the same way
περισσος – excessive, surplus	περισσως – exceedingly, very much
	ἐκπερισσως – very excessively
περισσοτερος – greater, more excessive	περισσοτερως or περισσοτερον – more excessively, more
δικαιος – righteous, just	δικαιως – righteously, justly
ἀληθης – true	ἀληθως – truly
ταχυς – quick	ταχυ, ταχειον, or ταχεως – quickly
ταχιστος – very quick, quickest	ταχιστα – very quickly
	ὡς ταχιστα – as quickly as possible
εὐθυς – straight, level	εὐθυς or εὐθεως – immediately, at once, next, then
Note also: οὑτος – this	οὑτως – thus
	οὑτως...ὡστε... – so much...that...

35.2 Translate

1. οἱ δικαιοι δικαιως ἐποιησαν και ὁμοιως ὁ πονηρος κακως ἐλαλησεν.

The just men acted justly and similarly the evil man spoke in an evil way.

164

2. ἀληθως λεγεις ὁτι οἱ κακως ἐχοντες χρειαν (need) ἐχουσιν ἰατρου.	You say truly that those who are ill have need of a doctor.
3. και εὐθυς ἐθεραπευσεν τον κωφον ὁ ἰατρος και ὀρθως ἐλαλει.	Immediately (then) the doctor healed the dumb man and he began to speak properly.
4. εἰδεν ὁ Ἰησους την Μαριαν και εὐθυς ἐκαλεσεν αὐτην και αὐτη ἠκολουθει αὐτῳ.	Jesus saw Mary and immediately he called her and she followed (began to follow) him.
5. οὑτως γαρ ἠγαπησεν ὁ θεος τον κοσμον ὡστε τον υἱον αὐτου ἐδωκεν ἱνα πας ὁ πιστευων εἰς αὐτον μη ἀποληται ἀλλ' ἐχῃ ζωην αἰωνιον.	For God so loved the world that he gave his Son so that everyone who believes in him should not perish but have eternal life.

35.3

πολυ or **πολλα** – much, greatly: **πλειον** – more

ὀλιγον – a little (**ὀλιγος** – little, **ὀλιγοι** – few)

μονον – only

μαλλον – rather, much more

These are adjectival forms. We often need to use an adverb when translating them into English.

Note:

Lk 7.47   ἠγαπησεν πολυ
          She loved much *or* She loved greatly

Lk 7.42   τίς οὐν αὐτων πλειον ἀγαπησει αὐτον;
          So which of them will love him more?

Mk 5.36   Μη φοβου, μονον πιστευε
          Do not fear, only believe

Mk 5.38   θεωρει...κλαιοντας και ἀλαλαζοντας πολλα
          He sees people crying and wailing loudly

Mk 8.31   δει τον υἱον του ἀνθρωπου πολλα παθειν
          It is necessary for the Son of Man to suffer much

Rev 5.4   ἐκλαιον πολυ
          I wept much

Mk 5.26   μηδεν ὠφεληθεισα ἀλλα μαλλον εἰς το χειρον ἐλθουσα
          Not having been helped at all but rather having become worse

35.3

Acts 4.19   Εἰ δικαιον ἐστιν...ὑμων ἀκουειν μαλλον ἠ του θεου
            If it is right to listen to you rather than to God

Mk 10.48   ὁ δε πολλῳ μαλλον ἐκραζεν
            He shouted out much more
       or He shouted out all the more
       or He began to shout even louder

Lk 11.13   ποσῳ μαλλον ὁ πατηρ ὁ ἐξ οὐρανου δωσει πνευμα ἁγιον τοις αἰτουσιν αὐτον
            How much more will the heavenly Father give the Holy Spirit to those who ask him

Mk 1.19   προβας ὀλιγον
            Having gone on a little way

Mk 6.31   ἀναπαυσασθε ὀλιγον
            Rest for a little while

Lk 7.47   ᾡ δε ὀλιγον ἀφιεται, ὀλιγον ἀγαπᾳ
            But to whom little is forgiven, he loves little
       or But he loves little to whom little is forgiven.

Translate

1. εἰπεν ἡμιν, Ἐγω εἰμι το φως του κοσμου. ἀπηλθομεν οὐν ἀπ’ αὐτου ἠγαπησαμεν γαρ μαλλον το σκοτος ἠ το φως.

     He said to us, "I am the light of the world". So we left him, for we loved the darkness rather than the light.

2. ἀναστας εἰσηλθεν εἰς την συναγωγην και εὐθυς ἐδιδασκεν αὐτους πολλα, και ἐλεγεν, Μακαριον ἐστιν διδοναι μαλλον ἠ λαμβανειν.

     He got up and went into the synagogue. Then he taught them many things, and he said, "It is blessed to give (to keep giving) rather than to receive".

35.4

Note that the following phrases and words can often be best translated into English using adverbs rather than a preposition and a noun:

     μετα χαρας – with joy; **joyfully**, gladly

     μετα σπουδης – with enthusiasm, with energy; **enthusiastically**, energetically

     ἐπ’ ἀληθειας – in truth; **honestly**, truly, certainly

     καθ’ ἡμεραν – each day; **daily**

     παρρησιᾳ – with boldness; **boldly**, openly.

When we translate a Greek adverb we may sometimes use an adjective in English:

Jn 1.47 ᾽Ιδε ἀληθως ᾽Ισραηλιτης
Look, **truly** an Israelite.

We might translate:

There is a man who is a **genuine** Israelite

or, with GNB,

Here is a **real** Israelite.

35.5

Adverbs ending with **-θεν** usually show the place someone or something comes from:

ἠλθεν ἐκειθεν – he came **from there**

ἐλευσεται ἀνωθεν – he will come **from above**

ἐρχονται παντοθεν – they are coming **from all directions**

ἐληλυθα ἀλλαχοθεν – I have come **from another place**.

Note also:

ὀπισθεν – behind, after

ἐμπροσθεν – before, in front of

ἐσωθεν – inside, within, from within

ἀνωθεν – from above; from the beginning, over again.

Adverbs ending with **-χου** usually show where someone is going:

ἀγωμεν ἀλλαχου – let us go **elsewhere**

ἐξελθοντες ἐκηρυξαν πανταχου – they went out and preached
everywhere

καθως πανταχου διδασκω – as I teach **in every place**.

Adverbs ending with **-τε** usually show the time at which something happened:

τοτε – then, at that time

εἰτεν or εἰτα – then, next

ποτε – ever

παντοτε – always, on every occasion

οὐδεποτε, μηδεποτε – never.

35.5

Read carefully:

Ἐξηλθεν ἀλλαχου μετα χαρας και αὐτου ἐξελθοντος ἐκειθεν τοτε εἰπον οἱ μαθηται παρρησια λεγοντες, Ἀγωμεν πανταχου και παντοτε διδασκωμεν μετα σπουδης και μηδεποτε παραδιδωμεν ἀλληλους τῳ βασιλει. εἰτα παλιν ἐξηλθον κηρυσσοντες τον λογον ἐπ᾽ ἀληθειας και διδασκοντες τους ἀνθρωπους καθ᾽ ἡμεραν ἐν ταις συναγωγαις την ἀνωθεν διδασκαλιαν.

35.6 Numbers

εἷς – one   πρωτος – first   ἁπαξ – once

You have seen that εἷς (one) has different forms for masculine, feminine, and neuter:

The one: ὁ εἷς, ἡ μια, το ἑν.

Mk 10.37 Δος ἡμιν ἱνα εἷς σου ἐκ δεξιων και εἷς ἐξ ἀριστερων καθισωμεν
Grant that we may sit **one** at your right and **one** at your left

Jn 10.16 γενησονται **μια** ποιμνη, **εἷς** ποιμην
They shall become **one** flock, **one** shepherd

Mt 5.18 ἰωτα **ἑν** ἡ **μια** κεραια
One iota or **one** stroke of a letter.

Many number words are easy to translate because there are similar English words. For example:

πρωτος – first: prototype (τυπος – form, example, mark)

δευτερος – second: Deuteronomy (νομος – Law, Torah)

τρεις – three: triad, tricycle (κυκλος – circle)

ἑξ – six: hexagon (γωνια – corner)

χιλιος – thousand: Chiliasm (belief in a thousand year
reign of Christ)

μυριοι – ten thousand: myriads.

168

Note these common number words:

Units 1; 2...	Tens 10; 20...	Hundreds 100; 200...	Thousands 1,000; 2,000...	Order first...	Times once...
1 εἱς	δεκα	ἑκατον	χιλιος	πρωτος	ἁπαξ
2 δυο	εἱκοσι	διακοσιοι	δισχιλιοι	δευτερος	δις
3 τρεις	τριακοντα		τρισχιλιοι	τριτος	τρις
4 τεσσαρες	τεσσαρακοντα	τετρακοσιοι		τεταρτος	
5 πεντε	πεντηκοντα	πεντακοσιοι			
6 ἑξ	ἑξηκοντα				
7 ἑπτα			ἑπτακισχιλιοι	ἑβδομος	ἑπτακις
8 ὀκτω					
9 ἑννεα	ἑνενηκοντα				
10 δεκα			μυριοι	δεκατος	δεκακις

Note also:

ἑνδεκα – 11   δεκατεσσαρες – 14

δωδεκα – 12   πεντε και δεκα – 15

ὁ ἑκατονταρχης – the centurion, the captain

Jn 21.11   το δικτυον...μεστον ἰχθυων μεγαλων ἑκατον πεντηκοντα τριων
The net full of large fish, one hundred and fifty-three.

Translate

1. ἑξηκοντα και τεσσαρες.

Sixty-four.

2. πεντακοσιοι εἱκοσι και ὀκτω.

Five hundred and twenty-eight.

3. ἑπτακισχιλιοι ἑκατον και δεκα.

Seven thousand, one hundred and ten.

4. ὁ πρωτος και ὁ ἑβδομος και ὁ δεκατος.

The first, the seventh, and the tenth.

5. ἑποιησεν τουτο οὐκ ἁπαξ οὐδε δις οὐδε τρις ἀλλα ἑπτακις.

He did this not once, nor twice, nor three times, but seven times.

6. τοτε προσελθων ὁ Πετρος εἰπεν αὐτῳ, Κυριε, ποσακις ἁμαρτησει εἰς ἑμε ὁ ἀδελφος μου και ἀφησω αὐτῳ; ἑως ἑπτακις; λεγει προς αὐτον ὁ Ἰησους, Οὑ λεγω σοι ἑως ἑπτακις ἀλλα ἑως ἑβδομηκοντακις ἑπτα.

Then Peter came to him and said to him, "Lord, how often shall my brother sin against me and I forgive him? Up to seven times?" Jesus said to him, "I do not say to you 'up to seven times' but 'up to seventy times seven' ".

35.7 Progress test 17

Which is the correct translation?

1. παρακαλουσιν αὐτον ἱνα ἐπιθῃ αὐτῃ την χειρα.
   (a) They beg him to lay his hands on her.
   (b) They beg him to lay his hand on her.
   (c) They ask him to give her his hand.

2. εἰτα παλιν ἐδωκεν αὐτοις τεσσαρακοντα ἀρτους.
   (a) Then again she gave them four loaves.
   (b) Then a second time she took the forty loaves from them.
   (c) Then again she gave them forty loaves.

3. ἀπηγγειλαν ταυτα παντα τοις ἐνδεκα και ἠπιστουν αὐταις.
   (a) They reported the news to the Twelve and they believed them.
   (b) The men reported all these things to the Twelve and they did not believe them.
   (c) The women reported all these things to the Eleven and they did not believe them.

Which is the best English translation?

4. Καλως, Διδασκαλε, ἐπ᾽ ἀληθειας εἰπες ὁτι εἱς ἐστιν και οὐκ ἐστιν ἀλλος πλην αὐτου.
   (a) "Well, Teacher, in truth you said that he is one and there is not another except him."
   (b) "Well said, Teacher; you said truly that he is one and there is no one else beside him."
   (c) "Well said, Teacher. You were right in saying that God is one and there is no other except him."

5. Το θυγατριον μου ἐσχατως ἐχει, ἱνα ἐλθων ἐπιθῃς τας χειρας αὐτῃ ἱνα σωθῃ και ζησῃ.
   (a) "My daughter is dying. Please come and lay your hands on her so that she may be healed and live."
   (b) "My daughter has a terminal illness. I am asking that having come you should put your hands on her so that she might be saved and live."
   (c) "My daughter is near the end. I want you to come and put your hands upon her so that she may be saved and she may live."

Study these translations of 1 Corinthians 10.23, and answer questions 6–10:

παντα ἐξεστιν, ἀλλ᾽ οὐ παντα συμφερει· παντα ἐξεστιν ἀλλ᾽ οὐ παντα οἰκοδομει.
   (a) All things are allowed, but not everything is fitting; all things are allowed, but not everything builds up.

(b) Everything is permissible, but not everything is beneficial. Everything is permissible, but it is not everything that builds people up.

(c) There are all kinds of things that are not forbidden by God's Law, but they are not all positively good. There are all kinds of things which are not forbidden by God's Law, but they are not all positively helpful.

(d) We can do all kinds of things – but not everything is good. We can do all kinds of things – but not everything is helpful.

6. Which of these translations would you choose for people whose knowledge of English is limited?

7. Which of these translations would you choose for people with a wide knowledge of English?

8. In which translation does the translator make the greatest effort to interpret the meaning?

9. Which translation follows the Greek words most literally?

10. If we wanted to translate 1 Corinthians 10.23 into some other languages, which of the English translations should we consider using as we try to decide how to express the meaning in the third language?

Check your answers on page 281.

LESSON 36

ἵνα – so that, that
ἵνα ποιήσῃ – so that he may do ·
ἵνα δῶμεν – so that we may give ·

36.1

The present subjunctive active forms of λεγω are given in 11.8, column (b). In lesson 11 you learned the most common uses of the present subjunctive. For example:

> ἵνα γραφῃς – so that you may write ⁻⁻⁻

έαν γραφωσιν – if they write ⚊⚊

ὁς ἀν γραφῃ – whoever writes ⚊⚊

γραφωμεν – let us write ⚊⚊

Now compare:

1. (a) ἠλθεν ἱνα ταυτα **ποιῃ**
    He came so that he might do these things
    (b) ἠλθεν ἱνα τουτο **ποιησῃ**
    He came so that he might do this.

In (a) **ποιῃ** indicates repeated actions. It is **present** subjunctive.
In (b) **ποιησῃ** indicates a single action. It is **aorist** subjunctive.

2. (a) προσεφερον αὐτῳ τα παιδια ἱνα αὐτων **ἁπτηται**
    They were bringing the children to him so that **he might touch them**
    (b) προσηλθον αὐτῳ πολλοι ἱνα αὐτου **ἁψωνται**
    Many people came to him so that **they might touch** him.

In (a) **ἁπτηται** indicates repeated action. He kept touching the children as people kept on bringing them. ἁπτηται is 3rd person singular **present** subjunctive middle of ἁπτομαι (I touch).
In (b) **ἁψωνται** indicates single action. Many people came to him but each needed to touch him only once. ἁψωνται is 3rd person plural **aorist** subjunctive middle of ἁπτομαι.

3. (a) Τίσιν **διδωμεν;**
    To which people should we be giving? *or* To whom should we keep giving?
    (b) Δωμεν ἡ μη δωμεν;
    Should we give or should we not give?

In (a) **διδωμεν** indicates continued or repeated action. διδωμεν is 1st person plural **present** subjunctive active of διδωμι (I give).
In (b) **δωμεν** indicates the act of giving without reference to its repetition or continuity. δωμεν is 1st person plural **aorist** subjunctive active of διδωμι.

36.2 Words

ἀποθνησκω – I die
    ἀπεθανον – I died
      τεθνηκα – I have died, I am dead
ὁ θανατος – the death
      θανατοω – I kill, I put to death, I cause to be killed

ὁ αἰων – the age
    αἰωνιος – eternal, age long
    εἰς τον αἰωνα – forever
νεκρος – dead
    ὁ νεκρος – the dead man
    νεκροω – I put to death, I mortify
ὁ δουλος – the slave
    ἡ δουλεια – the slavery
    δουλευω – I serve (as a slave)
    δουλοω – I enslave, I cause to be a slave
ὁ διακονος – the servant
    ἡ διακονια – the service, serving
    διακονεω – I serve, I look after, I care
νυν – now
ὁτε – when
    ὁταν – whenever, when
    τοτε – then
    ποτε; – when?
ἑως – until (when the time is definite)
    ἑως ἀν – until (when the time is indefinite)
δια – through, by means of
    δι᾽ αὐτου – through him

36.3 Translate

1. ἠλθεν ἱνα ὁ κοσμος σωθη· και
ἀπεθανεν ἱνα ἐν τω αἰωνι τω
ἐρχομενω ζωην αἰωνιον ἐχωμεν δι᾽
αὐτου.

He came so that the world might be saved; and he died so that in the coming age we might have eternal life through him.

2. μητι ὁ διακονος ἐρχεται ἱνα
διακονηθη; οὐχι ἐρχεται ἱνα
διακονη;

Does a servant come so that he may be served? Doesn't he come so that he may serve?

3. ὁ δουλος οὐ μειζων ἐστιν του
κυριου αὐτου οὐδε ὁ διακονος
μειζων του βασιλεως.

A slave is not greater than his master nor is a servant greater than the king.

4. μητι ὁ δουλος μειζων ἐστιν του
πεμψαντος αὐτου;

The slave is not greater than the man who sent him, is he?

5. ὁτε ἠλθεν προς τον πατερα εἰπεν
αὐτω ὁ πατηρ, Ὁ ἀδελφος σου
οὑτος νεκρος ἠν και ἐζησεν.
ἀπολωλως ἠν, νυν δε εὑρεθη.

When he came to his father, his father said to him, "Your brother here was dead and came alive. He was lost, but now he has been found".

6. ὅταν ὁ υἱος του ἀνθρωπου ἐκ
   νεκρων ἀναστῃ αἰωνιον δοξαν
   δωσει πασιν τοις πεπιστευκοσιν
   εἰς το ὀνομα αὐτου.

When the Son of Man has risen
from the dead he will give eternal
glory to all who have believed in
his name.

36.4

Read carefully:

1. Seven brothers – one wife

ἑπτα ἀδελφοι ἠσαν· και ὁ πρωτος ἐλαβεν γυναικα. και ἀποθνησκων οὐκ ἀφηκεν
τεκνον. και ὁ δευτερος ἐλαβεν αὐτην και ἀπεθανεν. και ὁ τριτος ὡσαυτως και ὁ
τεταρτος και ὁ πεμπτος και ὁ ἑκτος και ὁ ἑβδομος. και οἱ ἑπτα οὐκ ἀφηκαν
τεκνον. ἐσχατον παντων και ἡ γυνη ἀπεθανεν.

2. A girl asks the king for John's head

εἰπεν ὁ βασιλευς αὐτῃ, Αἰτησον με ὃ ἐαν θελῃς και δωσω σοι. και ἐξελθουσα
εἰπεν τῃ μητρι αὐτης, Τί αἰτησωμαι; ἡ δε ἐφη, Την κεφαλην Ἰωαννου του
βαπτιζοντος. και εἰσελθουσα εὐθυς προς τον βασιλεα εἰπεν αὐτῳ, θελω ἱνα δῳς
μοι την κεφαλην Ἰωαννου του βαπτιστου.

Και ἀποθανοντος του Ἰωαννου, ἠλθον οἱ μαθηται αὐτου και ἠραν το πτωμα
αὐτου και ἐθηκαν αὐτο ἐν μνημειῳ.

Also read John 3.13–21.

Notes:
ὑψοω -- I lift up
ὁ ὀφις – the snake
μονογενης – only begotten, only
φαυλος – worthless

πρασσω – I do
ἐλεγχω – I reprove, I convict,
    I show to be wrong
φανεροω – I reveal, I make clear

36.5 So that...; to...

Clauses of purpose or aim are expressed

1. By ἱνα followed by a verb in the subjunctive:

Mk 1.38 Ἀγωμεν ἀλλαχου...ἱνα και ἐκει κηρυξω
    Let us go somewhere else so that I may preach there also
    (κηρυξω is 1st person singular aorist subjunctive active of
    κηρυσσω)

1 Jn 1.4 ταυτα γραφομεν ἡμεις ἱνα ἡ χαρα ὑμων ᾖ πεπληρωμενη
    We write these things so that your joy may be fulfilled
    (ᾖ is 3rd person singular present subjunctive of εἰμι – I am).

2. By the infinitive (to...):

Mk 2.17   οὐκ ἦλθον **καλεσαι** δικαιους
I did not come to call righteous people
(καλεσαι is aorist infinitive active of καλεω – I call)

Jn 21.3   Ὑπαγω **ἁλιευειν**
I am going off to fish
(ἁλιευειν is present infinitive active of ἁλιευω – I fish)

Mk 10.45   οὐκ ἦλθεν **διακονηθηναι** ἀλλα **διακονησαι**
He did not come in order to be served but in order to serve
(διακονηθηναι is aorist infinitive passive of διακονεω – I serve;
διακονησαι is aorist infinitive active).

3. By **εἰς** or **προς** followed by το (the) and the infinitive:

Mk 13.22   ποιησουσιν σημεια...**προς το ἀποπλαναν**
They will do signs so as to deceive
or They will work miracles with the aim of deceiving
(ἀποπλαναν is present infinitive active of
ἀποπλαναω – I deceive, I lead astray, I cause to err)

2 Cor 1.4   ὁ παρακαλων ἡμας ἐπι παση τη θλιψει ἡμων **εἰς το δυνασθαι** ἡμας
παρακαλειν τους ἐν παση θλιψει
The one who comforts us in every kind of trouble we bear so
that we may be able to comfort those who are in any kind of
trouble
(δυνασθαι is present infinitive middle of δυναμαι – I am able).

4. By **ὁπως** followed by a verb in the subjunctive:

Mt 2.8   ἀπαγγειλατε μοι, **ὁπως** κἀγω ἐλθων **προσκυνησω** αὐτῳ
Bring back a message to me so that I also may go and worship
him
(προσκυνησω is 1st person singular aorist subjunctive active of
προσκυνεω, κἀγω is και ἐγω)

Acts 9.2   **ὁπως** ἐαν τινας εὑρη...**ἀγαγη** εἰς Ἰερουσαλημ
So that, if he should find some people...he might bring them
to Jerusalem
(ἀγαγη is 3rd person singular aorist subjunctive active of
ἀγω – I lead, I bring).

36.6

36.6 ἵνα and ὅπως – so that

ὅπως basically means "how". So while ἵνα focuses attention on the *purpose* of an action, ὅπως focuses attention also on the way it is to be carried out. So ὅπως can sometimes be translated "so that in this way...". See, for example, 2 Corinthians 8.14:

ἵνα και το ἐκεινων περισσευμα γενηται εἰς το ὑμων ὑστερημα,
ὅπως γενηται ἰσοτης

So that also their surplus may meet your lack,
so that in this way there may be equality.

36.7 ἵνα

ἵνα is a word that links clauses or parts of sentences together. Care must be taken in translating it, as the links it expresses are of several different kinds. Always read the whole sentence carefully before you decide how to translate ἵνα.

1. ἵνα is most commonly used to show purpose:

Mk 3.14 και ἐποιησεν δωδεκα ἵνα ὠσιν μετ' αὐτου
He appointed twelve so that they might be with him.

2. ἵνα is used to introduce a request:

Mk 5.18 παρεκαλει αὐτον...ἵνα μετ' αὐτου ᾖ
He begged him that he might be with him

Mk 5.23 ἵνα...ἐπιθῃς τας χειρας αὐτῃ
Please lay your hands on her

Jn 17.15 οὐκ ἐρωτω ἵνα ἀρῃς αὐτους ἐκ του κοσμου ἀλλ' ἵνα τηρησῃς αὐτους ἐκ του πονηρου
I do not ask that you should take them out of the world but that you should keep them from the evil one.

3. ἵνα is used to introduce a command or prohibition:

Jn 15.12 αὑτη ἐστιν ἡ ἐντολη ἡ ἐμη, ἵνα ἀγαπατε ἀλληλους
This is my commandment – that you should love one another
or My commandment is this: love one another

Mk 3.12 πολλα ἐπετιμα αὐτοις ἵνα μη αὐτον φανερον ποιησωσιν
He sternly ordered them not to make him known

Mk 6.8 παρηγγειλεν αὐτοις ἵνα μηδεν αἱρωσιν
He ordered them that they should take nothing
or He told them not to take anything.

4. ἱνα – "that", describing or explaining what comes before it:

Jn 4.34   Ἐμον βρωμα ἐστιν ἱνα ποιησω το θελημα του πεμψαντος με
            My food is to do the will of him who sent me
     or My food is that I should do the will of the one who sent me

Jn 17.3   αὑτη δε ἐστιν ἡ αἰωνιος ζωη ἱνα γινωσκωσιν σε τον μονον ἀληθινον
            θεον
            And this is eternal life that they should know you the only
            true God
     or Eternal life is this: to know thee who alone art truly God.

5. ἱνα may also indicate a result or consequence:

Jn 9.2   τίς ἡμαρτεν...ἱνα τυφλος γεννηθη;
            Who sinned, that he was born blind?
     or Whose sin caused him to be born blind?

Gal 5.17   ταυτα γαρ ἀλληλοις ἀντικειται, ἱνα μη ἁ ἐαν θελητε ταυτα ποιητε
            For these are opposed to each other so that you do not do
            the things which you wish to do.

36.8
Revise lessons 29 and 30.

LESSON 37

ὁ Κυριος – the Lord
τον λογον, την καρδιαν: the accusative case

37.1 Cases

In 12.7 you studied the four main cases (nominative, accusative, genitive, and dative) and their commonest functions. Here are the singular forms of ὁ Κυριος – the Lord:

ὁ Κυριος	the Lord (subject form)	nominative case
Κυριε	O Lord (person spoken to)	vocative case
τον Κυριον	the Lord (object form)	accusative case

του Κυριου   of the Lord   genitive case

τῳ Κυριῳ   to the Lord, for the Lord   dative case

Abbreviations: nom., voc., acc., gen., dat.

Number: κυριος is nom. singular (sing.)
          κυριοι is nom. plural (pl.).

Gender: λογος is masculine (masc. or m.)
          καρδια is feminine (fem. or f.)
          ἐργον is neuter (neut. or n.).

Parsing nouns, adjectives, and participles
Give the case, number, gender, and nom. sing. of nouns, pronouns, and adjectives.
Give the case, number, gender, tense, mood, and voice of participles.

So: **καρδιων** is gen. pl. fem. of καρδια (a heart)

      μοι is dat. sing. of ἐγω (I)

      ἀγαθαι is nom. pl. fem. of ἀγαθος (good)

      ποιησας is nom. sing. masc. aor. part. act. of ποιεω (I do)

      ἐρχομενα is nom. or acc. pl. neut. pres. part. middle of ἐρχομαι
      (I come, I go).

37.2 The vocative case

Κυριε (Lord! *or* O Lord) is the vocative singular of Κυριος. The vocative is the form used when a person is spoken to. Ἰησου is the vocative form of Ἰησους. In English hymns and prayers we sometimes use the form "Jesu" when we are speaking to him.

Compare these nominative and vocative singular forms:

Κυριος	– Lord	Κυριε	– "Lord!"
Ἰησους	– Jesus	Ἰησου	– "Jesu"
πατηρ	– father	Πατερ	– "Father"
γυνη	– woman	Γυναι	– "Woman"

Sixteen times in the New Testament the vocative is introduced by Ὠ:

Mt 15.28   Ὠ γυναι, μεγαλη σου ἡ πιστις
           O woman, great is your faith

Mk 9.10   Ὠ γενεα ἀπιστος
           O faithless generation!

When 'Ω is used, it usually indicates that the speaker or writer is moved by emotion, which may be of concern, respect, surprise, or of disappointment.

37.3 The accusative case

λογον, λογους; καρδιαν, καρδιας; βασιλεα, βασιλεας; γυναικα, γυναικας; σε, ἡμας; τον, την, τους, τας are all in the accusative case.

Uses of the accusative case

1. The accusative case is most often used for the object of the verb:

Mk 15.29 ὁ καταλυων **τον ναον**
The person who destroys the Temple.

2. When a verb is followed by two accusatives we sometimes add a preposition when we translate into English:

Mk 5.7 ὁρκιζω σε **τον θεον**
I adjure you by God

Mk 4.10 ἡρωτων αὐτον...**τας παραβολας**
They asked him about the parables

Jn 4.46 ὁπου ἐποιησεν το ὑδωρ **οἰνον**
Where he made the water into wine
or Where he made the water wine

Acts 13.5 εἰχον δε και Ἰωαννην **ὑπηρετην**
They also had John as their assistant

3. The accusative of a noun similar in meaning to the verb it is used with may need to be expressed in English by an adverb or adverbial phrase:

Mt 2.10 ἐχαρησαν **χαραν μεγαλην** (a great joy)
They rejoiced greatly

Mk 4.41 ἐφοβηθησαν **φοβον μεγαν** (a great fear)
They were terribly afraid
or They were overcome with awe.

4. The accusative case may be used to describe or qualify other words or ideas:

Jn 6.10 οἱ ἀνδρες **τον ἀριθμον** ὡς πεντακισχιλιοι
The men, in number about five thousand

Acts 25.10 Ἰουδαιους **οὐδεν** ἠδικησα
I wronged the Jews in no way
or I did the Jews no wrong

Heb 2.17 πιστος ἀρχιερευς **τα προς τον θεον**
A faithful high priest in his service to God
(τα is accusative plural neuter of ὁ – the).

5. When we translate some Greek verbs which are followed by an
accusative case, we need a preposition before the noun in English:

πιστευομαι – I am entrusted (with):
Gal 2.7 πεπιστευμαι **το εὐαγγελιον**
I have been entrusted with the gospel

εὐλογεω – I bless, I bless God (for), I thank God (for):
Mk 8.7 εὐλογησας **αὐτα**
Having blessed God for them
or Having given thanks for them

γονυπετεω – I kneel, I fall on my knees (before):
Mt 17.14 γονυπετων **αὐτον**
Kneeling before him.

6. The accusative often shows length of time or space:

Jn 11.6 τοτε μεν ἐμεινεν ἐν ᾧ ἠν τοπῳ **δυο ἡμερας**
Then he stayed in the place where he was for two days

Mk 1.19 προβας **ὀλιγον** εἰδεν Ἰακωβον
Having gone forward a little way he saw James

Lk 24.13 ἠσαν πορευομενοι εἰς κωμην ἀπεχουσαν **σταδιους ἑξηκοντα** ἀπο
Ἱερουσαλημ
They were on their way to a village which was sixty stades
away from Jerusalem
(60 stades is about 11 kilometres).

7. The accusative case is sometimes used with the infinitive in recording
what someone says or thinks:

Mk 8.29 Ὑμεις δε τίνα **με** λεγετε **εἰναι**;
But whom do you say that I am?
(It would be poor English to translate: But whom do you say me to be?)

Mk 1.34 ὁτι ἠδεισαν **αὐτον Χριστον εἰναι**
Because they knew him to be the Christ
or Because they knew that he was the Messiah.

8. The accusative case is used after many prepositions:

> εἰς ἄφεσιν – for forgiveness
> παρα την θαλασσαν – beside the sea.

We study these prepositions in 37.4–15. (Other prepositions are followed by a genitive or dative case. See lesson 39.2–13 and 42.2–7 respectively.)

37.4 Prepositions followed by an accusative case

προς – to, towards, up to, by, close to, with; against

εἰς – into, to, in, as far as; for, with a view to

ἀνα – up, upwards; in, at the rate of

κατα – down; according to, during, about, along

ὑπερ – above

ὑπο – under

ἐπι – on, on top of, onto; against, at

περι – round, around, about

παρα – beside, along, at the side of

μετα – after

δια – because of

The basic meaning of most of these prepositions concerns *movement towards* something, or a position reached as a result of such movement. The following diagram may help you to learn these basic meanings:

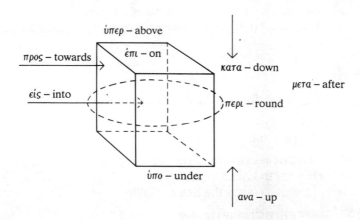

Translate

1. ἐρχεσθε εἰς την πολιν.	You are going into the town.
2. περιπατουμεν παρα την θαλασσαν.	We are walking about beside the sea.
3. ἐστιν ἐπι την γην και εἰσιν ὑπο την γην.	He is on the earth and they are under the earth.
4. ἠν ὑπερ τους οὐρανους και ἠσαν οἱ ἀγγελοι περι αὐτον κυκλῳ.	He was above the heavens and the angels were round him in a circle.
5. ἐγω ἀναβαινω εἰς Ἱεροσολυμα, ἀλλα συ καταβαινεις ἀπο Ἱεροσολυμων.	I am going up to Jerusalem, but you are going down from Jerusalem.
6. μετα δυο ἡμερας ἠλθεν ἡ γυνη λεγουσα, Νυν πιστευω δια τον λογον σου.	After two days the woman came saying, "Now I believe because of what you have said".

37.5 προς

προς – to, towards, by, close to, with, against

Mt 14.28   κελευσον με ἐλθειν προς σε
            Command me to come to you

Mk 4.1   πας ὁ ὀχλος προς την θαλασσαν...ἠσαν
            The whole crowd were beside the lake

Mk 6.3   και οὐκ εἰσιν αἱ ἀδελφαι αὐτου ὡδε προς ἡμας;
            Are not his sisters here with us?

Mk 12.12   ἐγνωσαν...ὁτι προς αὐτους την παραβολην εἰπεν
            They knew that he had spoken the parable against them.

37.6 εἰς

εἰς – into, in, as far as, for, for the purpose of, so as to

Mk 13.16   ὁ εἰς τον ἀγρον
            The person in the field

Mk 7.31   ἠλθεν...εἰς την θαλασσαν της Γαλιλαιας
            He went to Lake Galilee
    or He went as far as the Sea of Galilee

Mk 6.8   ...ἱνα μηδεν αἱρωσιν εἰς ὁδον
            ...that they should take nothing for the journey

Mk 14.55   ἐζητουν κατα του Ἰησου μαρτυριαν εἰς το θανατωσαι αὐτον
They were seeking testimony against Jesus so as to put him
to death.

37.7 παρα

παρα – beside, along, at the side of, against, contrary to, compared with,
more than

Mk 1.16   παραγων παρα την θαλασσαν
Going along beside the lake

Mk 4.4   ἐπεσεν παρα την ὁδον
It fell along the footpath

Mk 10.46   ἐκαθητο παρα την ὁδον
He was sitting at the side of the road

Acts 18.13   Παρα τον νομον ἀναπειθει οὑτος τους ἀνθρωπους σεβεσθαι τον θεον
This man is persuading men to worship God in a way that is
against the Law

Rom 1.26   αἱ τε γαρ θηλειαι αὐτων μετηλλαξαν την φυσικην χρησιν εἰς την
παρα φυσιν
For their women exchanged the natural use (of their bodies)
into that which is against what is natural

Lk 13.2   Δοκειτε ὁτι οἱ Γαλιλαιοι οὑτοι ἁμαρτωλοι παρα παντας τους
Γαλιλαιους ἐγενοντο;
Do you think that these Galileans were sinners more than all
the Galileans?
   or Do you consider that these Galileans were worse sinners
than anyone else in Galilee?

37.8 ἀνα

ἀνα – up, upwards

ἀνα occurs with the meaning "up" in many compound verbs.
For example:

   ἀναβαινω – I go up, I travel up to

   ἀνιστημι – I raise up, I rise up

   ἀναφερω – I offer up, I bear

      ἀνενεγκαι – to offer up (aorist infinitive)

   ἀναβλεπω – I look up, I see, I see again

   ἀνοιγω – I open up, I open.

37.8

ἀνα is not often used on its own in the New Testament, but note the following phrases:

ἀνα δυο – in twos
ἀνα πεντηκοντα – in groups of fifty
ἀνα δηναριον – at the rate of one denarius
ἀνα μεσον – in the middle
ἀνα εἰς ἑκαστος – each one.

37.9 κατα

κατα – down; according to

καταβαινω – I go down   κατακειμαι – I lie down
καθημαι – I am sitting down   καθιζω – I sit down
κατεσθιω – I consume, I eat   κατοικεω – I dwell, I live

το εὐαγγελιον κατα Μαρκον
The Good News, according to Mark.

Mk 7.5   κατα την παραδοσιν των πρεσβυτερων
         According to the tradition of the elders

Mk 15.6 Κατα δε ἑορτην ἀπελυεν αὐτοις ἑνα δεσμιον
         At each festival he used to release for them one prisoner

Note also: καθως – according as, as; καθως γεγραπται – as it is written.

37.10 ὑπο

ὑπο – under

Mk 4.21 Μητι ἐρχεται ὁ λυχνος ἱνα ὑπο τον μοδιον τεθῃ;
         Does a lamp come so that it may be put under the meal-tub?

Jn 1.48 ὀντα ὑπο την συκην εἰδον σε
         I saw you while you were under the fig tree

Rom 6.14 οὐ γαρ ἐστε ὑπο νομον ἀλλα ὑπο χαριν
         You are not under Law but under grace.

37.11 ὑπερ

ὑπερ – above, more than

Phil 2.9 το ὀνομα το ὑπερ παν ὀνομα
          The name which is above every name

Lk 6.40   οὐκ ἐστιν μαθητης ὑπερ τον διδασκαλον
A student is not superior to the teacher.

37.12 ἐπι

ἐπι (ἐπ', ἐφ') – onto, on, at, over, against

Mk 4.5   ἀλλο ἐπεσεν ἐπι το πετρωδες
Other (seed) fell onto the rocky ground

Mk 2.14   εἰδεν Λευιν...καθημενον ἐπι το τελωνιον
He saw Levi sitting at the customs office

Mt 27.45   σκοτος ἐγενετο ἐπι πασαν την γην
There was darkness over all the land

Mk 3.24   ἐαν βασιλεια ἐφ' ἐαυτην μερισθη...
If a kingdom should be divided against itself...

37.13 περι

περι – round, around, about

Mk 3.32   ἐκαθητο περι αὐτον ὀχλος
A crowd was sitting round him

Mk 4.10   ἡρωτων αὐτον οἱ περι αὐτον
His companions questioned him

Mk 6.48   περι τεταρτην φυλακην της νυκτος ἐρχεται
About the fourth watch of the night he comes.

37.14 μετα

μετα – after

Jn 5.1   Μετα ταυτα ἠν ἑορτη των Ἰουδαιων
After these things there was a festival of the Jews

Mk 9.31   μετα τρεις ἡμερας ἀναστησεται
After three days he will rise again.

"A week later" may be expressed either as: μεθ' ἡμερας ἑξ – after six days (counting only the six days in between – Matthew 17.1),
or as: μεθ' ἡμερας ὀκτω – after eight days (counting the first Sunday, six days in between, and the second Sunday – John 20.26).

185

37.15 δια

δια – because of, on account of, for the sake of
δια τί; – why? because of what?

Jn 4.41   πολλῳ πλειους ἐπιστευσαν δια τον λογον αὐτου
          Far more believed because of his word

Mk 2.27   Το σαββατον δια τον ἀνθρωπον ἐγενετο
          The Sabbath was made for the sake of man

Mk 4.5   δια το μη ἐχειν βαθος γης
          Because of not having any depth of earth.

37.16

Read carefully:

Your wife and another man

Καλη ἡ γυνη σου· ἀλλα πονηρα ἐστιν. δια τί οὐκ ἐστιν ἐν τη οἰκιᾳ; Ἐξηλθεν παρα την θαλασσαν και ἐβλεψεν ἀνδρα ἀλλον και εἰσηλθεν εἰς την οἰκιαν αὐτου, και νυν προς αὐτον ἐστιν. Ἐξελευση ἐπι τον ἀνδρα ἐκεινον ἀποκτειναι αὐτον; Οὐκ, ἀλλα οἰσω αὐτον προς τον κριτην και ὁ κριτης αὐτον κρινεῖ, ὁτι ὑπο νομον ἐσμεν. και κρινεῖ αὐτον κατα τον νομον. οὐ γαρ κρινεῖ αὐτον παρα τον νομον ὁ κριτης ὁτι οὐκ ἐστιν ὁ κριτης ὑπερ τον νομον. μετα δε ταυτα ἡ γυνη μου μενεῖ ἐν τη οἰκιᾳ μου οὐδε ἐλευσεται περι την πολιν οὐδε καθησει ἐπι τον θρονον τον ὑπο την συκην.

LESSON 38

ὡστε – with the result that

38.1

ὡστε – so that, with the result that, so

Note carefully the following sentences:

Mt 12.22   και ἐθεραπευσεν αὐτον, ὡστε τον κωφον λαλειν.

Translated literally this is:

And he healed him, so that the dumb to speak.

186

This is not how we express the meaning of the Greek in English. We do not use the infinitive "to speak". We need a translation more like:

He healed him so that the dumb man spoke.

Or, since λαλειν shows continuing action,

He healed him, so that the dumb man began to speak.

Mk 9.26 ἐγενετο ὡσει νεκρος, ὡστε τους πολλους λεγειν ὁτι ἀπεθανεν.

Translated literally:

He became as if dead, so that the many to be saying that he had died.

In English we need a translation like:

He became like a corpse, so that most people said, "He has died".

Note also:
οὑτως...ὡστε... – so much that...

Jn 3.16 οὑτως...ἠγαπησεν ὁ θεος τον κοσμον, ὡστε τον υἱον τον μονογενη ἐδωκεν
God loved the world so much that he gave his only Son.

38.2 Words

ὡστε – so that, with the result that, so as to; so, then, therefore
  οὑτως...ὡστε... – to such an extent that..., so much that...
ὁσος – as much, how great
  ὁσοι – all who
  ὁσα – whatever
τοιουτος – such, of such a kind, so great
ἐξισταμαι – I am amazed
κραζω – I shout
  ἀνακραζω – I shout out
ἀποκτεινω – I kill
  ἀπεκτεινα – I killed
το σαββατον or τα σαββατα – the Sabbath day, the week
ἡ ψυχη – the life, the spirit, the soul, the person
μεγας, μεγαλη, μεγα – big, large, great
  μεγαλη φωνη – in a loud voice, with a loud noise

38.3 Translate

1. ἐκραξεν φωνη μεγαλη ὡστε ἀκουειν αὑτου παντας ὁσοι ἠσαν ἐν τῃ οἰκιᾳ ἐκεινῃ.

He shouted loudly so that all who were in that house heard him.

2. ἐθεραπευσεν αὑτους τοις σαββασιν ὡστε τους Φαρισαιους ζητειν ὁπως αὑτον ἀποκτεινωσιν.

He healed them on the Sabbath day so that the Pharisees began to look for a way to kill him.

3. και λεγει αὑτοις, Ἐξεστιν τοις σαββασιν ἀγαθον ποιησαι ἠ κακοποιησαι, ψυχην σωσαι ἠ ἀποκτειναι;

He said to them, "Is it legal on the Sabbath day to do good or to do evil, to save life or to kill?"

4. οὑτως ἠγαπησεν ἡμας ὡστε δουναι την ψυχην ὑπερ ἡμων· τοιαυτη ἐστιν ἡ ἀγαπη αὑτου.

He loved us so much that he gave his life for us: his love is as great as that.

5. οἱ δε ἰδοντες αὑτον περιπατουντα ἐπι την θαλασσαν ἀνεκραξαν. και ἐλεγεν αὑτοις, Εἰρηνη ὑμιν· ἐγω εἰμι, ὡστε ἐξιστασθαι παντας.

Seeing him walking on the lake they shouted out. He said to them, "Peace be with you: it is I", so that they were all amazed.

38.4 Uses of ὡστε

1. ὡστε and the **infinitive** – clauses of result:

Mt 12.22 ἐθεραπευσεν αὑτον, ὡστε τον κωφον **λαλειν** και **βλεπειν**
He healed him, so that the dumb man could speak and see

Mk 2.12 ἐξηλθεν ἐμπροσθεν παντων, ὡστε **ἐξιστασθαι** παντας και **δοξαζειν** τον θεον
He went out before them all, so that they were all amazed and praised God

Mk 3.20 συνερχεται παλιν ὁ ὀχλος, ὡστε μη **δυνασθαι** αὑτους μηδε ἀρτον φαγειν
The crowd came together again, so that they were not able even to eat bread
or Such a crowd gathered again that they could not even eat a meal
(συνερχεται is an historic present – cf. 25.2).

2. ὡστε and the **indicative** – clauses of logical result:

Mk 2.27–8 Το σαββατον δια τον ἀνθρωπον ἐγενετο...ὡστε κυριος **ἐστιν** ὁ υἱος του ἀνθρωπου και του σαββατου
The Sabbath was made for the good of man, so the Son of Man is Lord even of the Sabbath

Gal 4.6–7 ἐξαπεστειλεν ὁ θεος το πνευμα του υἱου αὐτου εἰς τας καρδιας
ἡμων...ὡστε οὐκετι εἶ δουλος ἀλλα υἱος
God sent the Spirit of his Son into our hearts...you are
therefore no longer a slave but a son.

3. οὑτως...ὡστε..., τοσουτος...ὡστε..., πολυς...ὡστε... so great that, such
that, so much that:

Mk 2.2 και συνηχθησαν πολλοι ὡστε μηκετι χωρειν
Many people were gathered together so that there was no
longer room
or So many people came together that there was no space left

Mt 15.33 ἀρτοι τοσουτοι ὡστε χορτασαι ὀχλον τοσουτον
Enough loaves to satisfy such a large crowd.

38.5 Because... ὀτι and δια in clauses of cause or reason

Cause and reason are expressed

1. By ὀτι followed by a verb in the **indicative**:

Mk 1.34 οὐκ ἠφιεν λαλειν τα δαιμονια, ὀτι ἠδεισαν αὐτον
He was not allowing the demons to speak because they knew
him.

2. By δια followed by a verb in the **infinitive**:

Mk 4.5 εὐθυς ἐξανετειλεν δια το μη ἐχειν βαθος γης
It came up quickly because it had no depth of soil

Phil 1.7 καθως ἐστιν δικαιον ἐμοι τουτο φρονειν ὑπερ παντων ὑμων δια το
ἐχειν με ἐν τη καρδια ὑμας
As it is right for me to feel about you all because I have you
in my heart.

38.6 Grammatical terms

Clauses of purpose, aim, or intended result are called *final* clauses.
So in Mark 1.38, Ἀγωμεν ἀλλαχου εἰς τας ἐχομενας κωμοπολεις, ἱνα και
ἐκει κηρυξω (Let us go elsewhere to the neighbouring country towns so
that I may preach there also), ἱνα και ἐκει κηρυξω is a final clause.

Clauses of actual result are called *consecutive* clauses.
So in Mark 15.5, ὁ δε Ἰησους οὐκετι οὐδεν ἀπεκριθη, ὡστε θαυμαζειν τον
Πιλατον (Jesus still made no reply, so Pilate was amazed), ὡστε θαυμαζειν
τον Πιλατον is a consecutive clause.

38.7 Translating ψυχη

In the New Testament the word ψυχη covers a wide area of meaning. Like the Hebrew word "nephesh" it may refer to person, self, life, or spirit. In choosing how to translate ψυχη into English we must consider carefully the passage in which it occurs. In Mark 3.4, ψυχην σωσαι means "to save life": it is the opposite of ἀποκτειναι (to kill). Also in Mark 8.35–37, we may consider that "life" is the nearest equivalent to ψυχη, since taking up one's cross (verse 34) implies readiness to die.

But in Matthew 26.38, Περιλυπος ἐστιν ἡ ψυχη μου (my ψυχη is very sad) and John 12.27, Νυν ἡ ψυχη μου τεταρακται (now my ψυχη is disturbed), Jesus is saying that he is saddened and distressed at the very core of his being. Here "heart" may be the best equivalent English idiom: "My heart is crushed with sorrow", "Now my heart is deeply troubled".

Note also Philippians 1.27, μια ψυχη συναθλουντες τη πιστει του εὐαγγελιου (with one ψυχη, struggling side by side for the faith of the gospel). Here one might translate μια ψυχη as "in unity of spirit" or "with a single purpose".

In 1 Corinthians 15.45, ψυχη ζωσα is more or less equivalent to "a living person". But note that in 1 Corinthians 15.44–46, the adjective ψυχικος is contrasted with πνευματικος (spiritual). So perhaps the nearest English equivalent of ψυχικος is "physical".

In all our efforts to understand the New Testament in Greek and to translate it into our own languages, we must never limit ourselves to the simple question, "What is the meaning of this Greek word?" We must always be asking ourselves, "What is the meaning of the word *in this passage* and how can I express it most accurately and intelligibly in my own language?"

38.8

Read John 9.1–7.

Notes:
γενετη – birth
ὁ γονευς – the parent (γενναω – I beget, I bring to birth, I bear a child;
                              γενναομαι – I am born)
πτυω – I spit
χαμαι – on the ground
ὁ πηλος – the mud
ἡ κολυμβηθρα – the pool
νιπτω – I wash
        νιπτομαι τους ποδας – I wash my feet

38.9 Progress test 18

Which translation is correct?

1. ἀγωμεν και ἡμεις ἱνα ἀποθανωμεν μετ᾽ αὐτου.
   (a) Let us go away because we shall die with him.
   (b) Let us also go so that we may die with him.

2. προσκοπτει ὀτι το φως οὐκ ἐστιν ἐν αὐτῳ.
   (a) He stumbles because the light is not in him.
   (b) He stumbles when the light is not in him.

3. πας γαρ ὁ φαυλα πρασσων μισει το φως ὀτι οὐ ποιει την ἀληθειαν.
   (a) For everyone who does evil hates the light so that he does not do the truth.
   (b) For everyone who does evil things hates the light because he does not do what is true.

Which is the best English translation?

4. πολλα ἐπετιμα αὐτῳ ἱνα μη αὐτον φανερον ποιηϲη.
   (a) He ordered him many things so that he should not make him manifest.
   (b) He rebuked him sternly not to make him known.
   (c) He gave him strict orders not to make him known.

5. τα κυματα ἐπεβαλλεν εἰς το πλοιον, ὡστε ἠδη γεμιζεσθαι το πλοιον.
   (a) The waves began to spill over into the boat, so that it was already filling up with water.
   (b) The waves were beating against the boat and spilling into it, so that it was already getting swamped.
   (c) The waves used to beat into the boat so that already the boat was weighed down.

6. ἐγω τιθημι την ψυχην μου ἱνα παλιν λαβω αὐτην.
   (a) I place my soul in order to take it again.
   (b) I lay down my spirit so that I may take it again.
   (c) I lay down my life so that I may take it again.

7. Read carefully through the sentences in 3–6 in this test and write down all the Greek words that are in the accusative case.

Check your answers on page 281.

38.10

Revise lessons 31 and 32.

LESSON 39

του λογου, της καρδιας: the genitive case

39.1

λογου, λογων; της καρδιας, των καρδιων; τινος, τινων; ποιουντος, ποιουσης, and ποιουντων are all in the genitive case.

Uses of the genitive case

1. The genitive case is most often used to show that one thing is closely related to another, usually in some way possessed by it or belonging to it:

Jn 1.12   τεκνα θεου – children of God

Jn 1.19   ἡ μαρτυρια του Ἰωαννου
John's testimony *or* The witness given by John

Jn 1.27   οὐ οὐκ εἰμι ἐγω ἀξιος ἱνα λυσω αὐτου τον ἱμαντα του
ὑποδηματος
Of whom I am not worthy to untie the strap of his sandal

Eph 1.13   ἐσφραγισθητε τῳ πνευματι της ἐπαγγελιας
(Lit. You were sealed by the Spirit of the promise)
You were sealed by the promised Spirit.

The nature of the relationship shown by the genitive case can often only be discovered by a careful study of the passage in which it comes. For example, ἡ ἀγαπη του θεου (the love of God) may mean, "God's love" or "love for God". In 1 John 4.9, ἡ ἀγαπη του θεου means "God's love for us". In 1 John 5.3, ἡ ἀγαπη του θεου means "Our love for God". See also lesson 12.1.

In Mark 1.4, we should not translate βαπτισμα μετανοιας as "a baptism of repentance" (AV, RSV, NJB, NIV) since repentance is not something that can be baptized. We need a translation more like "a baptism in token of repentance" (NEB) or "baptism for those who repented". GNB restructures the whole sentence to express the meaning of μετανοια more clearly: "Turn away from your sins and be baptized".

2. The genitive case may be used to show time during which something is done:

Mk 5.5   δια παντος **νυκτος** και **ἡμερας**...ἡν κραζων
           Constantly, by night and by day, he was shouting

Lk 18.12   νηστευω δις **του σαββατου**
           I fast twice during each week.

3. The genitive case may be used to show separation from:

Eph 2.12   ἡτε τῳ καιρῳ ἐκεινῳ χωρις **Χριστου** ἀπηλλοτριωμενοι **της πολιτειας** του Ἰσραηλ και ξενοι **των διαθηκων** της ἐπαγγελιας
           You were at that time apart from Christ, alienated from the citizenship of Israel, and strangers from the covenants of God's promise.

4. The genitive is often used when things are compared:

Mt 27.64   ἐσται ἡ ἐσχατη πλανη χειρων **της πρωτης**
           The last deception will be worse than the first

Jn 8.53   μη συ μειζων εἶ **του πατρος** ἡμων Ἀβρααμ;
           Surely you are not greater than our forefather Abraham?

1 Cor 13.13   μειζων δε **τουτων** ἡ ἀγαπη
           But the greatest of these is love

Jn 7.31   μη πλειονα σημεια ποιησει ὡν οὑτος ἐποιησεν;
           Will he do more miracles (signs) than those which this man has done?

5. The genitive is used for price or cost:

Jn 12.5   Δια τι...οὐκ ἐπραθη **τριακοσιων δηναριων**;
           Why was it not sold for three hundred denarii?

6. The genitive is used after many verbs, especially those which have to do with hearing, touching, feeling, remembering, sharing, lacking, and departing:

Mk 9.7   ἀκουετε **αὐτου**
           Hear him! (Listen to him!)

Mk 1.31   ἠγειρεν αὐτην κρατησας **της χειρος**
           He raised her up having taken hold of her hand

Mt 26.75   ἐμνησθη ὁ Πετρος **του ῥηματος** Ἰησου εἰρηκοτος
           Peter remembered the word Jesus had said

39.1

Rom 3.23   ὑστεροῦνται **τῆς δόξης** τοῦ θεοῦ
They fall short of the glory of God

Lk 22.35   μὴ **τινος** ὑστερήσατε;
You didn't lack anything, did you?

7. The genitive is used after υἱός:

(a)
Mt 4.6   Εἰ υἱὸς εἶ **τοῦ θεοῦ**, βάλε σεαυτὸν κάτω
If you are the Son of God, throw yourself down

Mt 22.42   **τίνος** υἱός ἐστιν;
Whose son is he?

Gal 3.7   υἱοί εἰσιν **Ἀβραάμ**
They are descendants of Abraham.

(b)
Eph 5.6   ἔρχεται ἡ ὀργὴ τοῦ θεοῦ ἐπὶ τοὺς υἱοὺς **τῆς ἀπειθείας**
The wrath of God comes upon those who disobey him
    or The wrath of God comes upon those who are rebels

2 Thess 2.3   ὁ ἄνθρωπος τῆς ἀνομίας, ὁ υἱὸς **τῆς ἀπωλείας**
(Lit. The man of lawlessness, the son of destruction)

This has been translated in many different ways, e.g.

NEB   Wickedness in human form, the man doomed to perdition
NJB   The wicked One, the lost One
NIV   The man of lawlessness, the man doomed to destruction
GNB   The Wicked One who is destined for hell.

In the (a) examples, υἱός is used in its normal Greek sense of "son", or "descendant".
In the (b) examples, υἱός is used in a different way, following a Hebrew idiom. A son usually has a nature similar to that of his father. So υἱὸς τῆς ἀπειθείας (son of disobedience) means a person whose nature it is to disobey, a person whose true character is revealed in the way he constantly disobeys God.

It is sometimes very difficult to know the best way to translate υἱός into English – compare the different attempts to translate 2 Thessalonians 2.3 given above. We must be particularly careful in using "children" as a translation of υἱοί. In 1 Thessalonians 5.5 we might translate υἱοὶ φωτός ἐστε as "You are children of light". The knowledge that Paul says this to the readers and hearers of the letter makes it clear that he is not talking about children, but about Christian people of all ages. In Ephesians 5.6 it would be misleading to translate "The wrath of God comes upon the children of disobedience" (see AV). It might make the reader or hearer think that God's wrath comes on children who are disobedient. It does not mean this. It refers to people who persistently disobey God.

In Mark 2.19, οἱ υἱοι του νυμφωνος (the sons of the bridegroom's house) refers to the custom of the bridegroom's friends meeting at his house before going in procession to fetch the bride from her home. We do not have exactly the same custom in England. We can translate οἱ υἱοι του νυμφωνος as "the bridegroom's friends" or "the friends gathered at the bridegroom's house". It would be misleading to translate as "the wedding guests", since Mark 2.19–20 only mentions the bridegroom (at a time when he has not yet brought the bride home), while in English "wedding guests" suggests the presence of both bride and bridegroom.

8. Genitive with a participle – genitive absolute:

Mt 9.33 ἐκβληθεντος του δαιμονιου ἐλαλησεν ὁ κωφος
When the demon had been cast out, the dumb man spoke.

For this common usage of the genitive case, see 25.1–3.

39.2 Prepositions followed by a genitive case

ἀπο – away from, from

ἐκ – out of, as a result of

*δια – through, by means of, after

*μετα – with, among

*περι – about (as in "speak about", "pray about")

*παρα – from the side of, from

*κατα – down from, against, throughout

*ἐπι – on, in, in the time of, on account of, up to

*ὑπερ – for, on behalf of

ἀντι – in the place of, instead of

ὀπισω – behind, after

προ – before

ἐμπροσθεν – in front of, before

*ὑπο – by (when something is done by a person)

χωρις – without, apart from

Those prepositions marked * are also used with the accusative case (see 37.4, 7, 9–15). Their meaning is different when they are followed by a genitive case.

39.2

The basic meaning of many of the prepositions followed by the genitive concerns movement away from something, or a position away from something else:

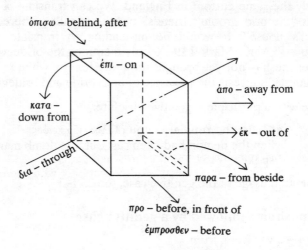

Translate

1. ὀπίσω μου.	Behind me, after me.
2. προ της οἰκιας.	In front of the house.
3. κατεβη ἐκ του οὐρανου.	He came down from heaven.
4. ἐξηλθεν παρα του θεου.	He went out from God.
5. τα ἐπι της γης.	The things on the earth.
6. ἀπηλθομεν ἀπο Ναζαρεθ.	We went away from Nazareth.
7. ἠλθετε δια της Γαλιλαιας.	You went through Galilee.
8. ὁ ὀπίσω μου ἐρχομενος.	The one coming after me.

39.3 ὀπισω

ὀπισω – behind, after

Mk 8.33 Ὕπαγε ὀπισω μου
Go away behind me

Mk 8.34 Εἰ τις θελει ὀπισω μου ἀκολουθειν...
If someone wishes to follow after me...

Jn 12.19 ὁ κοσμος ὀπισω αὑτου ἀπηλθεν
The world has gone off after him

Note: εἰς τα ὀπισω – backwards, back.

39.4 προ

προ – before

Mt 5.12 οὑτως γαρ ἐδιωξαν τους προφητας τους προ ὑμων
For thus they persecuted the prophets who were before you

Mk 1.2 Ἰδου ἀποστελλω τον ἀγγελον μου προ προσωπου σου
See, I am sending my messenger before your face

Gal 2.12 προ του γαρ ἐλθειν τινας ἀπο Ἰακωβου...
For before some people came from James...

39.5 κατα

κατα – down, down from; against

Mk 5.13 ὡρμησεν ἡ ἀγελη κατα του κρημνου εἰς την θαλασσαν
The herd rushed down the cliff into the lake

Mk 11.25 ἀφιετε εἰ τι ἐχετε κατα τινος
Forgive if you have something against someone
or Forgive if you have anything against anyone.

39.6 παρα

παρα – from (from or beside a person)

Mk 8.11 ζητουντες παρ' αὑτου σημειον ἀπο του οὐρανου
Seeking from him a sign from heaven

Mk 3.21 οἱ παρ' αὑτου ἐξηλθον
His relatives went out

39.6

Mk 5.26   δαπανησασα τα παρ' αὐτης παντα
Having spent all her wealth
(τα παρ' αὐτης – the things from beside her,
                        her possessions, her money)

Jn 9.16   Οὐκ ἐστιν οὑτος παρα θεου ὁ ἀνθρωπος
This man is not from God.

39.7 δια

δια – through, by means of, after

Mk 9.30   παρεπορευοντο δια της Γαλιλαιας
They were travelling through Galilee

Mk 14.21   οὐαι δε τῳ ἀνθρωπῳ ἐκεινῳ δι' οὑ ὁ υἱος του ἀνθρωπου
παραδιδοται
But alas for that man through whom the Son of Man is
betrayed

Heb 9.12   δια δε του ἰδιου αἱματος εἰσηλθεν ἐφαπαξ
He entered in once for all by means of his own blood
(ἐφαπαξ means "once for all", i.e. once without need for
repetition. It does not mean "once and for all people")

Mk 14.58   δια τριων ἡμερων ἀλλον ἀχειροποιητον οἰκοδομησω
After three days I will build another not made by hand
  or In three days I will build another not made by human
hands
(δια, when it refers to a period of time, often means
"after", but sometimes means "through", "throughout",
"in", "during a period of time")

Note: δια παντος – all the time, continually.

39.8 ἐπι

ἐπι – on, in, in the time of, over...

Mk 2.10   ἀφιεναι ἁμαρτιας ἐπι της γης
To forgive sins on earth

Mk 8.4   Ποθεν τουτους δυνησεται τις ὡδε χορτασαι ἀρτων ἐπ' ἐρημιας;
How will anyone be able to satisfy these people with bread
here in the wilderness?

Mk 12.14   ἐπ' ἀληθειας την ὁδον του θεου διδασκεις
You teach the way of God truly

Acts 11.28   ἥτις ἐγενετο ἐπι Κλαυδιου
                Which happened in the time of Claudius

Acts 7.27   Τίς σε κατεστησεν ἀρχοντα...ἐφ' ἡμων;
                Who appointed you as ruler over us?

Mk 12.26   οὐκ ἀνεγνωτε ἐν τη βιβλῳ Μωυσεως ἐπι του βατου;
                Have you not read in the book of Moses in the passage
                about the bush?

Rev 21.16   ἐμετρησεν την πολιν τῳ καλαμῳ ἐπι σταδιων δωδεκα χιλιαδων
                He measured the city with a reed, reaching a total of
                twelve thousand furlongs
                (Note: "furlong" is the nearest English equivalent to the
                Greek "stade". It is a term not often used today, so GNB
                converts to a more modern system of measurement – 2,400
                kilometres. But as 12 and 1,000 are symbolic numbers in
                Revelation, it seems better to retain the original figure).

39.9 μετα

μετα – with, among (nearly always with a person)

Mk 1.13   ἠν μετα των θηριων
              He was with the wild animals

Mk 1.36   Σιμων και οἱ μετ' αὐτου
              Simon and his companions

Mk 2.16   Ὁτι μετα των τελωνων και ἁμαρτωλων ἐσθιει;
              Why does he eat with the tax-collectors and sinners?

Mk 6.25   εἰσελθουσα...μετα σπουδης προς τον βασιλεα ἡτησατο...
              Coming in with haste to the king she asked...
         or She hurried in to the king and asked...

39.10 περι

περι – about, concerning

Mk 1.30   και εὐθυς λεγουσιν αὐτῳ περι αὐτης
              At once they told him about her

Mk 10.41   ἠρξαντο ἀγανακτειν περι Ἰακωβου και Ἰωαννου
              They began to be annoyed about James and John

Phil 2.20   τα περι ὑμων μεριμνησει
              He will be concerned for your affairs
              (τα περι ὑμων – the things concerning you, your affairs, your
              welfare).

39.11 ὑπερ

ὑπερ – for, on the side of, on behalf of, about

Mk 9.40   ὃς γαρ οὐκ ἐστιν καθ' ἡμων ὑπερ ἡμων ἐστιν
For the person who is not against us is on our side

Mk 14.24 Τουτο ἐστιν το αἱμα μου της διαθηκης το ἐκχυννομενον ὑπερ πολλων
This is my blood of the covenant which is poured out on behalf of many

Jas 5.16   εὐχεσθε ὑπερ ἀλληλων
Keep praying for each other
or Pray for one another

Jn 1.30   οὑτος ἐστιν ὑπερ οὑ ἐγω εἰπον...
This is the man about whom I said...

39.12 ἀντι

ἀντι – instead of, in place of, as a substitute for, for

Mt 2.22   'Αρχελαος βασιλευει...ἀντι του πατρος αὐτου Ἡρῳδου
Archelaus reigns in place of his father Herod

Mk 10.45 δουναι την ψυχην αὐτου λυτρον ἀντι πολλων
To give his life as a ransom for many

Lk 11.11   και ἀντι ἰχθυος ὀφιν αὐτῳ ἐπιδωσει;
And instead of a fish will he give him a snake?

Note: ἀνθ' ὡν – therefore, wherefore, because

Lk 1.20   ἀνθ' ὡν οὐκ ἐπιστευσας τοις λογοις μου
Because you did not believe my words.

39.13 ὑπο

ὑπο – by (by a person)

Mk 1.5   ἐβαπτιζοντο ὑπ' αὐτου
They were being baptized by him

Rom 15.24 ἐλπιζω...θεασασθαι ὑμας και ὑφ' ὑμων προπεμφθηναι ἐκει
I hope to see you and by you to be sent on there.

LESSON 40

τουτο ποιησον – do this!

40.1

Compare:

(a) εἶπεν αὐτῷ, Τουτο ποιει.
He said to him, "Do this!"

εἶπεν αὐτοις, Τουτο ποιειτε.
He said to them, "Do this!"

εἶπεν αὐτη, Αἰρε τους λιθους.
He said to her, "Pick up the stones!"

εἶπεν αὐταις, Αἰρετε τους λιθους.
He said to them, "Pick up the stones!"

(b) εἶπεν αὐτῷ, Τουτο ποιησον.
He said to him, "Do this!"

εἶπεν αὐτοις, Τουτο ποιησατε.
He said to them, "Do this!"

εἶπεν αὐτη, Ἀρον τον λιθον.
He said to her, "Pick up the stone!"

εἶπεν αὐταις, Ἀρατε τον λιθον.
He said to them, "Pick up the stone!"

In (a) the commands expressed by ποιει, ποιειτε, αἰρε, and αἰρετε are commands to do actions that are repeated (done more than once). ποιει, ποιειτε, αἰρε, and αἰρετε are *present imperative*.

In (b) the commands expressed by ποιησον, ποιησατε, ἀρον, and ἀρατε are commands to do a single action. ποιησον, ποιησατε, ἀρον, and ἀρατε are *aorist imperative*.

So (a) in Luke 22.19:

τουτο ποιειτε εἰς την ἐμην ἀναμνησιν
Do this in remembrance of me

ποιειτε is a command to do it often, to keep on doing the action. We might translate it as, "Keep doing...".

But (b) in John 2.5:

ὅ τι ἀν λεγη ὑμιν ποιησατε
Whatever he says to you, do it

ποιησατε is a command to do the action, without reference to its repetition.

Compare also:

Lk 11.3   τον ἀρτον ἡμων τον ἐπιουσιον διδου ἡμιν το καθ᾽ ἡμεραν
Keep giving us our daily bread each day

40.1

Mt 6.11   *τον άρτον ήμων τον έπιουσιον* **δος** *ήμιν σημερον*
          Give us our daily bread today.

διδου – give, keep giving, is present imperative ┄┄
δος – give, is aorist imperative ·

Notice that in Greek the imperative is used both for commands and for requests.

So in John 4.16:
    φωνησον *τον άνδρα σου και* **έλθε** *ένθαδε*
    Call your husband and **come** here.

But in John 4.15:
    Κυριε, **δος** *μοι τουτο το ύδωρ*
    Sir, **please give** me this water

and John 4.7:
    Δος *μοι πειν* (lit. give me to drink)
    Please give me a drink.

40.2 Words

ώδε – here
έκει – there
    έκειθεν – from there
όραω – I see
    όρατε μη... or *βλεπετε μη...* – see that you do not, beware lest
ίδε – look! (used to attract or direct attention: "Look here",
        "Excuse me", "Look!")
έαυτον – himself
    έμαυτον – myself, *σεαυτον* – yourself,
    έαυτους – themselves, ourselves, yourselves
άλληλους – each other, one another
    άλλος – other, another
χαιρω – I rejoice, I greet
    λιαν έχαρην – I rejoiced greatly
    χαιρε, χαιρετε – hail, hello, greetings! rejoice!
ή χαρα – the joy (distinguish from *χαρις* – grace, undeserved love)
φερω – I bear, I carry, I bring
    ένεγκαι – to bring (aorist infinitive)
    προσφερω – I carry to, I offer
    προσηνεγκεν – he offered
ή μετανοια – repentance, turning from sin to God
    μετανοεω – I repent, I change my attitude

μετα indicates change. νοια indicates attitude of mind. So in μετανοια and μετανοεω the emphasis is on change of attitude and action, on turning from a life centred on self to a life centred on God. In the English word "repentance" there is more of an emphasis on sorrow for past wrong, and in the Latin "penitentia" there is more emphasis on punishment for wrongdoing. So, while μετανοια and repentance both suggest the combination of sorrow for sin and turning from it, the emphasis in μετανοια is more on the change or turning.

40.3 Translate

1. λεγω τουτῳ, Ἐλθε ὡδε και ἐρχεται, και ἀλλῳ Πορευθητι ἐκει και πορευεται, και ἀλλῳ, Ἐνεγκε τουτο και φερει και τῳ δουλῳ μου Ποιησον τουτο και ποιει.

   I say to this man, "Come here" and he comes, to another, "Go there" and he goes, to another "Bring this" and he brings it, and to my slave, "Do this" and he does it.

2. χαιρετε ἐν Κυριῳ και ἀγαπατε ἀλληλους, καθως εἰπεν ἡμιν, Ἀγαπατε ἀλληλους· καθως ἐγω ἡγαπησα ὑμας. και ἀγαπωμεν τους ἐχθρους ἡμων, γεγραπται γαρ, Ὁρατε μη τις κακον ἀντι κακου τινι ἀποδῳ.

   Rejoice in the Lord and love each other, as he said to us: "Love each other, as I have loved you". And let us love our enemies, for it is written: See that no one gives back evil to anyone in return for evil.

3. εἰπεν Σιμωνι, Ὑπαγε ἁλιευειν και τον ἀναβαντα πρωτον ἰχθυν ἐνεγκε ὡδε, ἱνα φαγωμεν.

   He said to Simon, "Go to fish, and bring here the first fish that comes up, so that we may eat".

4. ἐαν τινες ὑμιν εἰπωσιν, Ἰδε, ὡδε ὁ Χριστος ἡ Ἰδε ἐκει, μη πιστευετε, ἀλλα εἰπατε αὐτοις, Μετανοειτε και πιστευετε ἐν τῳ εὐαγγελιῳ.

   If any people say to you, "Look! Here is the Messiah" or "Look! He is there", do not believe but say to them, "Repent and believe the Good News".

40.4

ἀκολουθειτω – he must follow
ἀκολουθειτωσαν – they must follow

ἀρατω – he must pick up
ἐλθατω – he must come, let him come

Compare:

1. (a) εἰπεν αὐτῳ, Ἀκολουθει μοι – he said to him, "Follow me!"

   (b) εἰπεν αὐτοις, Ἀκολουθειτω μοι – he said to them, "He must follow me"

40.4

2. (a) εἰ θελεις ὀπισω μου ἐλθειν ἀρον τον σταυρον σου
      If you want to follow me, take up your cross

   (b) εἰ τις θελει ὀπισω μου ἐλθειν ἀρατω τον σταυρον αὐτου
      If anyone wishes to follow me, he must take up his cross
   or If someone wishes to come after me, let him take up his cross.

In 1(a) and 2(a) the speaker addresses a command directly to the person he wishes to obey it.
In 1(b) and 2(b) the same action is required, but the person who is to do it is not spoken to directly.

Note also the different types of action:
    In 1(b) ἀκολουθειτω is in the present tense because the action of following is an action that is to be continued —
    In 2(b) ἀρατω is in the aorist tense because the action of picking up is a single action ·

In English we do not have a verbal form exactly similar to ἀκολουθειτω, so in translating we use "**he must** follow" or "**let him** follow".
So in Mark 13.15:

> ὁ ἐπι του δωματος μη καταβατω μηδε εἰσελθατω ἀραι τι ἐκ της οἰκιας αὐτου
> The man on the roof must not go down nor must he go in to take anything out of his house.

But in Mark 15.32:

> ὁ Χριστος ὁ Βασιλευς Ἰσραηλ καταβατω νυν ἀπο του σταυρου
> Let the Messiah, the King of Israel, come down now from the cross.

When we use "let" in this way it does not mean "allow". Because "let" has several meanings in English a translator must often avoid it, so that the meaning is not ambiguous.
Compare:

ἐπιτρεψον αὐτῳ ἀπελθειν
Let him go away. **Give him permission** to go away

ἀφες αὐτον ἀπελθειν
Let him go away. **Allow him** to go away

ἀπελθατω
Let him go away. **He must** go away.

In each case the second translation makes the meaning clear.

40.5 Translate

1. εἰ τις θελει ἀκολουθειν μοι,
μετανοειτω και ἐλθατω προς με και
ἀπαρνησασθω (deny) ἑαυτον και
ἀρατω τον σταυρον και φερετω
αὐτον ὀπισω μου.

If anyone wishes to follow me he must repent and come to me, he must deny himself and take up his cross and carry it after me.

2. εἰπεν μοι, Ἐλθε προς με. λιαν
ἐχαρην ὁτε τουτους τους λογους
ἠκουσα και ἠλθον προς αὐτον και
ἐλθων εὑρον χαραν μεγαλην ἐν
αὐτῳ.

He said to me, "Come to me". I was very glad when I heard these words and I came to him. When I had come I found great joy in him.

3. εἰπεν τῳ λεπρῳ, Ὑπαγε εἰς τον
οἰκον σου και ὁρα μηδενι μηδεν
εἰπῃς.

He said to the leper, "Go home and see that you say nothing to anybody".

4. προσηνεγκεν ἑαυτον τῳ θεῳ ἱνα
ἡμας σωσῃ ἐκ της ἁμαρτιας και ἱνα
ἡμεις ἁγιοι ὡμεν και ἀγαπωμεν
ἀλληλους.

He offered himself to God so that he might save us from sin and so that we might be holy and might love each other.

5. Ὁπου ἐγω ὑπαγω οἰδατε την ὁδον.
λεγει αὐτῳ Θωμας, Κυριε, οὐκ
οἰδαμεν που ὑπαγεις· πως οἰδαμεν
την ὁδον; λεγει αὐτῳ ὁ Ἰησους,
Ἐγω εἰμι ἡ ὁδος και ἡ ἀληθεια και ἡ
ζωη· οὐδεις ἐρχεται προς τον
Πατερα εἰ μη δι᾿ ἐμου.

"You know the way where I am going." Thomas said to him, "Lord, we do not know where you are going: how can we know the way?" Jesus said to him, "I am the way and the truth and the life: no one comes to the Father except through me".

40.6
Read carefully John 9.8–16.

Notes:
ὁ γειτων – the neighbour
θεωρεω – I look at, I see
προτερον – before
(πρωτος – first)
προσαιτης – beggar
καθημαι – I sit
ὁμοιος – like, similar
ἀνοιγω – I open

ἐπιχριω – I smear on
(Χριστος – Anointed)
ἀγω – I lead, I bring
ἀναβλεπω – I look up, I see again,
I recover my sight
το σημειον – the sign, the miracle
το σχισμα – the division

40.6

Now read Revelation 22.8–11, 17.

Notes:
ἐπεσα – I fell, I fell down
δεικνυμι – I show, I reveal
σφραγιζω – I seal, I seal up
καιρος – time
ἐγγυς – near
ῥυπαρος – dirty, filthy

ἡ νυμφη – the bride
διψαω – I thirst, I am thirsty
δωρεαν – freely, as a gift,
      without payment
ἀδικεω – I do wrong

40.7

Revise lessons 33 and 34.

LESSON 41

μη κλεψης – do not steal ·
μη κλαιε – do not weep, stop crying ⁼⁼⁼

41.1 Prohibitions

A prohibition is a negative command, "Do not...". In Greek, prohibitions can be expressed in two ways:

1. **μη** followed by a verb in the **aorist subjunctive**:

Mk 10.19 μη φονευσης, μη μοιχευσης, μη κλεψης, μη ψευδομαρτυρησης
      Do not murder, do not commit adultery, do not steal, do not give false evidence.

The verbs **φονευσης, μοιχευσης, κλεψης**, and **ψευδομαρτυρησης** are all 2nd person singular **aorist** subjunctive active. The aorist is used because each forbids a single or definite act, or an activity that has not yet started.

2. **μη** followed by a verb in the **present imperative**:

Mt 6.19 Μη θησαυριζετε ὑμιν θησαυρους
      Do not keep storing up treasures for yourselves
   or Do not go on storing up treasures for yourselves

Mt 6.25   μη μεριμνατε τη ψυχη ὑμων
Do not be worried in your mind
or Don't keep worrying

Mt 7.1   Μη κρινετε, ἱνα μη κριθητε
Do not judge, so that you may not be judged
or Do not keep judging other people, so that you will not be judged

Lk 8.52   Μη κλαιετε
Do not weep *or* Stop crying

Mk 9.39   Μη κωλυετε αὑτον
Do not stop him
or Do not try to prevent him.

The verbs **θησαυριζετε, μεριμνατε, κρινετε, κλαιετε**, and **κωλυετε** are all 2nd person plural **present** imperative active. The present is used because each concerns an action that is, or has been, going on.

So to a person who is already in the habit of stealing, one might say:

μη κλεπτε – do not steal, give up stealing

but to a person one hopes will not steal:

μη κλεψῃς – do not steal.

41.2 Indirect commands and prohibitions

"Do this!" is a *direct* command.
In "He told me to do this", "to do this" is an *indirect* command.

Here are three verbs often used to introduce commands.

1. **ἐπιτασσω – I command** is followed by a dative case for the person commanded, and a verb in the infinitive for the action to be done:

Mk 6.27   ἐπεταξεν ἐνεγκαι την κεφαλην αὑτου
He commanded (him) to bring his head

Lk 8.31   παρεκαλουν αὑτον ἱνα μη ἐπιταξῃ αὑτοις...ἀπελθειν
They begged him not to command them to go away.

2. **διαστελλομαι – I give instruction to**, I command, is followed by a dative case for the person instructed and ἱνα with a verb in the subjunctive for the state or action required:

Mk 5.43   διεστειλατο αὑτοις πολλα ἱνα μηδεις γνοι τουτο
He gave them strict instructions that no one should know this.

3. ἐπιτιμαω – I rebuke, I tell not to, is followed by a dative case for the one rebuked and ἱνα with a verb in the subjunctive for the action that is forbidden:

Mk 4.39   ἐπετιμησεν **τῳ ἀνεμῳ**
           He rebuked the wind

Mk 8.30   ἐπετιμησεν **αὐτοις ἱνα μηδενι λεγωσιν**
           He told them that they should speak to nobody
       or He told them not to speak to anyone.

41.3 Translate

1. ἐγω εἰπον αὐτῳ, Μη δῳς τους ἀρτους αὐτοις. μη διδου τον οἰνον αὐτοις ἀλλα δος μοι τον οἰνον.

I said to him, "Do not give them the loaves. Stop giving them the wine but give me the wine".

2. εἰπεν αὐτοις ὁ Ἰησους, Μη κλαιετε, το τεκνον οὐκ ἀπεθανεν. και λεγει τῃ μητρι αὐτου, Μη κλαιε.

Jesus said to them, "Stop crying – the child has not died". Then he said to his mother, "Don't cry".

3. ὁ βασιλευς εἰπεν τῃ θυγατρι της Ἡρωδιαδος, Ὁτι ἐαν με αἰτησῃς δωσω σοι. και εὐθυς ἡτησατο λεγουσα, Θελω ἱνα δῳς μοι την κεφαλην Ἰωαννου του Βαπτιστου. και ἀποστειλας στρατιωτην (soldier) ἐπεταξεν αὐτῳ ἐνεγκαι την κεφαλην αὐτου. και ἐπετιμησεν τῳ βασιλει ὁ Κυριος ὁτι το ἐργον του πονηρου ἐποιησεν.

The king said to the daughter of Herodias, "I will give you whatever you ask me for". Immediately she made this request: "I want you to give me the head of John the Baptist". So sending a soldier he ordered him to bring his head. The Lord rebuked the king because he had done the work of the Evil One.

41.4 Words

ὁ καρπος – the fruit, the crop
     καρποφορεω – I bear fruit
     καρπον διδωμι – I yield a harvest, I produce a crop
σπειρω – I sow
     ὁ σπορος or το σπερμα – the seed
ἡ δικαιοσυνη – the righteousness
     δικαιοω – I acquit, I declare to be righteous, I accept as righteous,
          I justify
ὁ τοπος – the place
ἡ ὁδος – the road, the path, the way
ἑτοιμος – ready
     ἑτοιμαζω – I make ready, I prepare

το αἱμα – the blood
  (When used metaphorically αἱμα is usually a symbol for death:
  see, for example, Matthew 23.30, Acts 5.28.)
οὐ μη – not
  (This double negative is emphatic. It is found especially in
  emphatic denials: οὐ μη εἰσελευσεται – he will **not** enter, he will
  certainly not enter.)
πινω – I drink
  πινειν – to be drinking
  ἐπιον – I drank
  πιειν or πειν – to drink
ἡ εἰρηνη – the peace
  εἰρηνικος – peaceful, peaceable
Like "shalom" in Hebrew and "salaam" in Arabic, εἰρηνη has a wider
area of meaning than the English word "peace". To wish a family εἰρηνη
(Luke 10.5) is not only to wish that they may live peacefully but also to
wish that God's blessing may be on them. But in Matthew 10.34, οὐκ
ἠλθον βαλειν εἰρηνην ἀλλα μαχαιραν – I did not come to bring peace but a
sword, εἰρηνην corresponds closely to the English word "peace".

41.5 Translate

1. μη βαλης τον σπορον σου εἰς την
θαλασσαν μηδε παρα την ὁδον
ἀλλα ἐτοιμασον την γην αὐτῳ· και
ὁταν ἐτοιμη ἡ τοτε σπειρε τον
σπορον εἰς την γην την
ἡτοιμασμενην και καρπον δωσει.
και ὁταν καρποφορῃ χαρησεις χαρᾳ
μεγαλῃ.

Do not cast your seed into the sea
nor along the road, but prepare
the soil for it; and when it is ready
then sow the seed into the soil that
has been prepared, and it will yield
a crop. And when it bears fruit you
will rejoice with great joy.

2. χαρις ὑμιν και εἰρηνη ἀπο του θεου
του Πατρος ἡμων ἐν ἀγαπῃ και
δικαιοσυνῃ. αὐτος γαρ ὁ θεος ἀγαπᾳ
ἡμας και ἐσωσεν ἡμας δια του
αἱματος του υἱου αὐτου. και
δικαιωθεντες δια πιστεως εἰρηνην
ἐχομεν προς τον θεον.

Grace to you and peace from God
our Father in love and
righteousness. For God himself
loves us and saved us through the
blood of his Son. So having been
accepted as righteous through
faith, we have peace with God.

41.6

Read carefully:

Instructions, warning and promise
διεστειλατο αὐτοις ἱνα μηδενι μηδεν λεγωσιν, και ἑστηκως παρα την ὁδον εἰπεν

41.6

αὐτοις, Ἐαν μη πιητε το αἱμα μου οὐκ ἐχετε ζωην μενουσαν ἐν ὑμιν και οὐ μη εἰσελευσεσθε εἰς την βασιλειαν των οὐρανων. ἀλλα τον πιστευοντα ἐν ἐμοι και πινοντα το αἱμα μου οὐ μη ἐκβαλω ἐξω· ὁτι καταβεβηκα ἐκ του οὐρανου οὐχ ἱνα δικαιους καλεσω ἀλλα ἁμαρτωλους, ὁπως εἰσελθωσιν εἰς τον τοπον ὁν ἀπερχομαι ἑτοιμασαι αὐτοις.

41.7
Read carefully John 9.17–34.

Notes:
ἑως – as far as, until
ἑως ὁτου – until
γονευς – parent
ἀρτι – now, just now
ἠδη – already
ἠλικια – age, maturity
φοβεομαι – I fear

συντιθημι – I agree
Δος δοξαν τῳ θεῳ – Give glory to
God: an idiom meaning
"Speak the truth"
λοιδορεω – I revile, I abuse
θαυμαστος – surprising, amazing
θεοσεβης – pious, religious, devout

41.8
Revise lessons 35 and 36.

LESSON 42

τῳ λογῳ, τῃ καρδιᾳ: the dative case

42.1

λογῳ, λογοις; καρδιᾳ, καρδιαις; σοι, ὑμιν; τῳ παραπτωματι, τοις παραπτωμασιν are all in the dative case.

Uses of the dative case

1. The dative case is used to show the person to whom something is given, or for whom something is done:

Mk 5.19   ὁσα ὁ Κυριος **σοι** πεποιηκεν
           What great things the Lord has done **for you**

Mk 1.30   λεγουσιν **αὐτῳ** περι αὐτης
           They speak **to him** about her

Rom 16.27 ᾧ ἡ δόξα εἰς τοὺς αἰῶνας
To whom be glory for ever

Mk 9.5 καὶ ποιησωμεν τρεις σκηνας, **σοι** μιαν καὶ **Μωυσει** μιαν καὶ **Ἠλιᾳ**
μιαν
Let us make three shelters, one for you and one for Moses
and one for Elijah

Mt 23.31 ὡστε μαρτυρειτε **ἑαυτοις**
Thus you witness against yourselves.

2. The dative case is used to show the thing with which something is
done:

Mk 1.8 ἐγω ἐβαπτισα ὑμας **ὑδατι**
I baptized you with water

Mk 15.19 ἐτυπτον αὐτου την κεφαλην **καλαμῳ**
They kept hitting his head with a stick

Mk 15.46 καθελων αὐτον ἐνειλησεν **τῃ σινδονι**
Having taken him down he wrapped him in (with) the linen
sheet

Mk 12.13 ἱνα αὐτον ἀγρευσωσιν **λογῳ**
So that they might trap him in a discussion

Rom 5.15 **τῳ του ἑνος παραπτωματι** οἱ πολλοι ἀπεθανον
By the wrongdoing of the one man the many died.

3. The dative case is used to show the time at which something
happened:

Mk 2.24 τί ποιουσιν **τοις σαββασιν** ὃ οὐκ ἐξεστιν;
Why are they doing on the Sabbath what is not allowed?

Mk 14.12 **τῃ πρωτῃ ἡμερᾳ** των ἀζυμων
On the first day of the unleavened bread

Mk 16.2 **τῃ μιᾳ** των σαββατων
On the first day of the week

Mk 12.2 ἀπεστειλεν προς τους γεωργους **τῳ καιρῳ** δουλον
At the (harvest) time he sent a slave to the farmers.

4. The dative may be used to show the person to whom something
belongs:

Jn 3.1 Νικοδημος ὀνομα **αὐτῳ**
His name was Nicodemus

42.1

Mk 2.18   οἱ δε **σοι** μαθηται οὐ νηστευουσιν
But your disciples are not fasting

Jn 17.6   **σοι** ἠσαν κἀμοι αὐτους ἐδωκας
They were yours and you gave them to me
(κἀμοι is a short form of και ἐμοι).

5. The dative is used after many verbs, for example after:

λεγω – I speak	ἐπιτιμαω – I rebuke, I tell not to
διδωμι – I give	παραγγελλω – I command
ἀκολουθεω – I follow	ἐντελλομαι – I order, I command
ἀπανταω – I meet	πιστευω – I believe
ἀρεσκω – I please	προσκυνεω – I worship
ἀφιημι – I forgive	ὑπακουω – I obey
διακονεω – I serve, I minister to, I care for	μελει – it concerns, it is a matter of concern to

Examples from Mark:

Mk 10.52   ἠκολουθει **αὐτῳ** ἐν τῃ ὁδῳ
He followed him along the road

Mk 14.13   ἀπαντησει **ὑμιν** ἀνθρωπος κεραμιον ὑδατος βασταζων
A man carrying a jar of water will meet you

Mk 6.22   ἠρεσεν **τῳ Ἡρῳδῃ** και **τοις συνανακειμενοις**
She pleased Herod and the people sitting with him (his guests)

Mk 11.25   ἱνα...ἀφῃ **ὑμιν** τα παραπτωματα ὑμων
So that he may forgive you your sins

Mk 1.13   οἱ ἀγγελοι διηκονουν **αὐτῳ**
The angels ministered to him

Mk 8.32   προσλαβομενος ὁ Πετρος αὐτον ἠρξατο ἐπιτιμαν **αὐτῳ**
Taking him aside Peter began to rebuke him

Mk 8.6   και παραγγελλει **τῳ ὀχλῳ** ἀναπεσειν ἐπι της γης
He tells the crowd to sit down on the ground

Mk 11.31   Δια τί οὐκ ἐπιστευσατε **αὐτῳ**;
Then why did you not believe him?

Mk 1.27   καὶ τοῖς πνεύμασι τοῖς ἀκαθάρτοις ἐπιτάσσει, καὶ
           ὑπακουουσιν αὐτῷ
           He even gives orders to the unclean spirits and they obey
           him

Mk 4.38   οὐ μέλει σοι ὅτι ἀπολλύμεθα;
           Doesn't it bother you that we are perishing?
        or Don't you care that we are about to die?

Mk 12.14   οὐ μέλει σοι περι οὐδενος
           You do not pay attention to anybody's status
        or A man's rank means nothing to you
           (Lit. It is not a matter of concern to you about no one).

42.2 Prepositions followed by a dative case

ἐν – in, among, by, with, towards

συν – with, together with (with a person)

παρα – beside, with, at the house of, near, in the sight of

προς – at, near to

ἐπι – on, upon (resting on), in, by, at, on account of, with a view to

Note that:
when a preposition is followed by the accusative case, the basic idea is
often movement *towards* something;
when a preposition is followed by the genitive case, the basic idea is
often movement *away from* something;
when a preposition is followed by the dative case, the basic idea is often
of position or rest *at* a place.

42.3 ἐν

ἐν – in, among, by, with, under the influence of

1. ἐν – in, inside (of time or place):

Mk 1.9   ἐν ἐκειναις ταις ἡμεραις
           In those days

Mk 1.13   ἦν ἐν τῃ ἐρημῳ
           He was in the wilderness

Mk 2.23   ἐν τοις σαββασιν
           On the Sabbath day.

2. ἐν – into:

Rom 1.25   οἵτινες μετηλλαξαν την ἀληθειαν του θεου ἐν τῳ ψευδει
Who changed the truth of God into a lie.

3. ἐν – among:

Mk 15.40   Ἠσαν δε και γυναικες...ἐν αἱς και Μαρια
There were also women...among whom was Mary.

4. ἐν – while:
ἐν with the infinitive must usually be translated "while..." or "as...".

Mk 4.4   ἐγενετο ἐν τῳ σπειρειν...
It happened while he was sowing...
or As he was sowing...

Lk 1.8   ἐν τῳ ἱερατευειν αὐτον
In the course of his priestly duties
or While he was doing his work as a priest.

Note also ἐν ᾧ – while, in the time during which

5. ἐν – by means of, with:

Lk 22.49   εἰ παταξομεν ἐν μαχαιρῃ;
Shall we strike with the sword?

Mk 4.2   ἐδιδασκεν αὐτους ἐν παραβολαις
He was teaching them by means of parables

Acts 1.3   παρεστησεν ἑαυτον ζωντα...ἐν πολλοις τεκμηριοις
He showed himself alive by means of many proofs

Jn 1.26   Ἐγω βαπτιζω ἐν ὑδατι
I baptize with water.

6. ἐν – under the influence of, under the control of:

Mk 1.23   ἀνθρωπος ἐν πνευματι ἀκαθαρτῳ
A man under the influence of an unclean spirit
or A man possessed by an unclean spirit

Mk 12.36 αὐτος Δαυιδ εἰπεν ἐν τῳ πνευματι τῳ ἁγιῳ...
Under the influence of the Holy Spirit David himself said...
or David himself, inspired by the Holy Spirit, said...

Mk 5.25   γυνη οὐσα ἐν ῥυσει αἱματος δωδεκα ἐτη
A woman being affected by a flow of blood for twelve years
or A woman who had suffered from bleeding for twelve years.

7. ἐν – for, to:

1 Jn 4.9 ἐν τουτῳ ἐφανερωθη ἡ ἀγαπη του θεου ἐν ἡμιν
In this way the love of God for us has been revealed

Mk 14.6 καλον ἐργον ἠργασατο ἐν ἐμοι
She has done a fine thing for me
or She did a beautiful thing to me.

The preposition ἐν is used in a great variety of ways. We can only tell the best way to translate it by considering the context in which it is used and the meaning of similar or parallel passages.

42.4 συν

συν – with, together with (usually with a person)

Mk 9.4 και ὠφθη αὐτοις Ἡλιας συν Μωυσει
There appeared to them Elijah with Moses

Mk 2.26 και ἐδωκεν και τοις συν αὐτῳ οὐσιν
And he even gave to those who were with him

Mk 4.10 ἠρωτων αὐτον οἱ περι αὐτον συν τοις δωδεκα τας παραβολας
Those who were round him with the Twelve asked him about the parables.

Note also Luke 24.21: συν πασιν τουτοις – in addition to all these things.

42.5 παρα

παρα – beside, with, at the house of, near, in the sight of

1. παρα – beside, near to:

Jn 19.25 εἰστηκεισαν δε παρα τῳ σταυρῳ
They stood near the cross.

2. παρα – with, among, at the house of:

Jn 1.39 παρ᾽ αὐτῳ ἐμειναν την ἡμεραν ἐκεινην
They stayed with him that day

Lk 11.37 ἐρωτα αὐτον Φαρισαιος ὁπως ἀριστηση παρ᾽ αὐτῳ
A Pharisee asks him to have a meal at his house
or A Pharisee invited him to dine with him

Rom 9.14 μη ἀδικια παρα τῳ θεῳ;
Is there unrighteousness with God?
or Can unrighteousness exist in God?

42.5

3. παρα – in the opinion of, in the sight of, before:

Rom 12.16 μη γινεσθε φρονιμοι παρ' ἑαυτοις
Do not be wise in your own eyes
or Do not keep thinking how wise you are

1 Cor 3.19 ἡ γαρ σοφια του κοσμου τουτου μωρια παρα τῳ θεῳ ἐστιν
For the wisdom of this world is foolishness in God's sight
or For when God looks at this world's wisdom he considers it foolishness

Gal 3.11 ἐν νομῳ οὐδεις δικαιουται παρα τῳ θεῳ
By means of the Law no one is justified before God.

4. παρα – from, from beside:

Mt 6.1 μισθον οὐκ ἐχετε παρα τῳ πατρι ὑμων τῳ ἐν τοις οὐρανοις
You do not have a reward from your heavenly Father
(NEB here takes παρα in sense (2) and translates, "No reward awaits you in your Father's house in heaven", but τῳ ἐν τοις οὐρανοις describes the Father, and does not refer to his home).

42.6 προς

προς – at, near, on

Mk 5.11 Ἦν δε ἐκει προς τῳ ὀρει ἀγελη χοιρων
There was there on the mountain a herd of pigs

Jn 18.16 ὁ δε Πετρος εἱστηκει προς τῃ θυρᾳ ἐξω
But Peter stood at the door outside.

42.7 ἐπι

ἐπι – on, upon (resting on), in, by, at, on account of, with a view to, in addition to

1. ἐπι – on:

Mk 6.25 ἐπι πινακι
On a dish

Mk 6.55 ἠρξαντο ἐπι τοις κραβαττοις τους κακως ἐχοντας περιφερειν
They began to carry round the sick on mats.

2. ἐπι – at, because of:

Mk 1.22   ἐξεπλησσοντο ἐπι τη διδαχη αὐτου
They were amazed at his teaching

Mk 10.22   ὁ δε στυγνασας ἐπι τῳ λογῳ ἀπηλθεν
Looking sad because of what was said, he went off
or When he heard what Jesus said his face fell, and he went away.

3. ἐπι – in:

Mk 9.39   οὐδεις γαρ ἐστιν ὁς ποιησει δυναμιν ἐπι τῳ ὀνοματι μου
For there is no one who will do a mighty work in my name.

4. ἐπι – close to, at:

Mk 13.29   γινωσκετε ὁτι ἐγγυς ἐστιν ἐπι θυραις
You know that he is near, at the gates
or Know that he is near, at the doors.

5. ἐπι – about:

Mk 6.52   οὐ γαρ συνηκαν ἐπι τοις ἀρτοις
For they did not understand about the loaves
or For they had not taken in the meaning of the loaves.

ἐπι has an extremely wide range of meanings. A translator must always take care to express its correct meaning in each context.

42.8

Summary of the common meanings of prepositions used with more than one case (see also lessons 37 and 39).

παρα – beside
    with accusative: beside, along, along beside, at the side of
    with genitive: from beside, from the side of, from
    with dative: beside, with, at the house of, in the sight of

ἐπι – on
    with accusative: on, on top of, against, at, onto
    with genitive: on, in, on account of, in the time of
    with dative: on, in, by, at

δια
    with accusative: because of, on account of, for the sake of
    with genitive: through, by means of, after

μετα
>with accusative: after
>with genitive: with

ὑπερ
>with accusative: above, more important than, superior to
>with genitive: for, on behalf of, for the sake of, about

ὑπο
>with accusative: under, underneath, subject to
>with genitive: by (by a person)

κατα
>with accusative: down, according to, during, about, along
>with genitive: down from, against

περι
>with accusative: round, around, about
>with genitive: concerning, about, on account of

προς
>with accusative: towards, up to, by, close to, with, against
>with dative: at, near to

42.9

Read John 1.35–51.

Notes:
τη ἐπαυριον – on the next day
στραφεις – having turned round (στρεφω – I turn)
μεθερμηνευω – I interpret, I translate
πετρος – a stone
δολος – guile, deceit
φωνεω – I make a noise, I call, I speak to
μειζω – greater things
ὀψη – you will see
ἀνοιγω – I open

42.10 Progress test 19

Read John 1.1–14 and answer the following questions:

1. In verses 1–5, which words are in the nominative case?
2. In verses 9–12, which words are in the accusative case?
3. In verses 3–8 and 12–14, which words are in the genitive case?
4. In verses 2–5 and 10–14, which words are in the dative case?

5. Translate these phrases in John 1.1–14:

(a) ἐν ἀρχη

(b) πρὸς τον θεον

(c) δι' αὐτου

(d) χωρις αὐτου

(e) ἐν τῃ σκοτιᾳ

(f) περι του φωτος

(g) εἰς τον κοσμον

(h) ἐν τῳ κοσμῳ

(i) εἰς το ὀνομα

(j) ἐκ θεληματος

(k) ἐν ἡμιν

Check your answers on page 281.

LESSON 43

εἰ ἐμερισθη – if it has been divided
ἐαν μερισθη – if it should be divided

43.1 εἰ, ἐαν – if

Study carefully:

1. (a) εἰ υἱος ἐστιν του θεου
   If he is the Son of God
   or If he is in fact the Son of
   God

   (b) ἐαν τις πονηρος ᾖ
   If anyone is evil
   or If anyone should be evil

2. (a) εἰ τουτο ἐποιησαμεν
   If we did this
   or If we had really done this

   (b) ἐαν τουτο ποιησωμεν
   If we do this
   or If we did this
   or If we were to do this

The clauses 1(a) and 2(a) are **definite**: they have verbs in the **indicative**. The clauses 1(b) and 2(b) are **indefinite**: they have verbs in the **subjunctive**.

εἰ means "if". It is used chiefly in statements or clauses referring to the past, and in some that refer to the present. It is used when the thought in the speaker's mind is definite, or the statement clearly either true or untrue. Its force can often best be expressed in English by the use of "in fact" or "really".

εἰ is followed by a verb in the indicative mood.

43.1

ἄν makes a statement indefinite:

Jn 14.7   εἰ ἐγνώκειτε με, και τον πατερα μου ἄν ἤδειτε
If you had in fact known me **you would** also **have known** my
Father.

ἐάν (εἰ + ἄν) is used when the idea in the mind is indefinite or
uncertain:

1 Jn 1.10   ἐάν εἰπωμεν ὅτι οὐχ ἡμαρτηκαμεν ψευστην ποιουμεν αὐτον
If we say that we have not sinned we make him a liar.

ἐάν is followed by a verb in the subjunctive mood.

The difference between εἰ and ἐάν can be seen in Mark 3.25–26:

> ἐάν οἰκια ἐφ᾽ ἑαυτην μερισθῃ...
> If a family should be divided against itself...

> εἰ ὁ Σατανας ἀνεστη ἐφ᾽ ἑαυτον και ἐμερισθη...
> If Satan has in fact risen up against himself and has been
> divided...

43.2 Translate

1. εἰ υἱος εἶ του θεου, ὑπαγε ὀπισω μου. | If you are the Son of God, go away from me.

2. εἰ ὑμεις οἰδατε δοματα ἀγαθα διδοναι τοις τεκνοις ὑμων, ποσῳ μαλλον ὁ Πατηρ ὁ ἐξ οὐρανων δωσει το Πνευμα το Ἁγιον ὑμιν. | If you know how to give good gifts to your children, how much more will the heavenly Father give the Holy Spirit to you.

3. ἐάν εἰπωμεν ὅτι ἁμαρτιαν οὐκ ἐχομεν ψευδομεθα· ἐάν δε ἐν τῳ φωτι περιπατωμεν κοινωνιαν ἐχομεν μετ᾽ ἀλληλων. | If we say that we have no sin we are lying; but if we walk in the light we have fellowship with one another.

43.3 εἰ with the imperfect indicative

> εἰ ἐπιστευετε Μωυσει, ἐπιστευετε ἄν ἐμοι
> (a) If you believed Moses (now), you would believe me.
> or (b) If you had believed Moses, you would have believed me.

Clauses with εἰ and the imperfect indicative refer "to present time or to
continued or repeated action in past time" (Liddell and Scott).

So in Galatians 1.10, with reference to the time that is present to the
writer as he writes:

εἰ ἔτι ἀνθρωποις ἤρεσκον, Χριστου δουλος οὐκ ἂν ἤμην
If I were still pleasing men, I would not be the servant of Christ.

But in 1 Corinthians 11.31, with reference primarily to past time:

εἰ δε ἑαυτους διεκρινομεν οὐκ ἂν ἐκρινομεθα
If we had judged ourselves, we would not be being judged.

In John 18.36,

εἰ ἐκ του κοσμου τουτου ἦν ἡ βασιλεια ἡ ἐμη, οἱ ὑπηρεται οἱ ἐμοι ἠγωνιζοντο ἂν

the translator has to choose between:

(a) If my kingdom were of this world my servants **would now be fighting** (compare RSV, NEB, GNB)

and (b) If my kingdom were of this world my servants **would have fought** (compare NJB, Moffatt, Phillips).

Since the verb παραδιδωμι is used both of Judas betraying Jesus to the Jews (John 18.2) and of Pilate handing him over to the Jews to be crucified (John 19.16), it is not easy to decide which way to translate John 18.36.

Note that some writers on New Testament Greek say that εἰ with the imperfect refers to present time. This is misleading. It would be better to add that in such cases it often refers to a present situation that arises out of a past situation. And it is necessary also to say that it can refer to continued action or attitude in past time.

43.4 Words

αἰτεω – I ask for
ὁ προσαιτης – the beggar
ἀνοιγω – I open
     ἤνοιξεν or ἀνεῳξεν – he opened
     ἀνοιξας – having opened
     ἠνοιγησαν or ἠνεῳχθησαν – they were opened, they opened
ἑκαστος – each
     εἱς ἑκαστος – each one
ἐμος – my
     σος – your
     ἡμετερος – our
     ὑμετερος – your (pl.)
μαλλον – more (in importance or degree)
     μαλλον...ἤ... – rather than

πλειων – more (in number or quantity)
    πλειων ἐκεινου – more than that
    πλειονα σημεια – more signs, more miracles
ὃ ἐαν – whatever
εἰ και – even if

43.5 Translate

1. ἐαν πλειονα τουτων αἰτησῃς δωσει σοι ὁ Πατηρ ὁ ἐμος.	If you ask for more than these, my Father will give (them) to you.
2. ὃ ἐαν αἰτησητε δωσω ἑνι ἑκαστῳ ὑμων.	Whatever you ask for I will give to each one of you.
3. εἰ ταυτα ᾐτησαν, ἡ μητηρ ἡ ἡμετερα ἐδωκεν ἀν αὐτοις.	If they had asked for these things, our mother would have given (them) to them.
4. εἰ γαρ πλειονα σημεια ἐποιησα ἐπιστευσαν ἀν ἐμοι.	For if I had done more miracles they would have believed in me.
5. εἰ και μειζονα σημεια ἐποιησα οὐκ ἀν ἐπιστευσαν ἐμοι.	Even if I had done greater miracles they would not have believed in me.
6. ἠγαπησαν την ἰδιαν δοξαν μαλλον ἠ την δοξαν του θεου.	They loved their own glory rather than the glory of God.
7. εἰ οὑτος ἠν ὁ Χριστος ἠνοιξεν ἀν τους ὀφθαλμους των τυφλων και ἠνεῳχθησαν ἀν τα στοματα των κωφων.	If this man was the Messiah he would have opened the eyes of the blind, and the mouths of the dumb would have been opened.
8. οἱ προσαιται οἱ ἐν Ἰερουσαλημ πλειονες εἰσιν των ἐν Ναζαρεθ.	The beggars in Jerusalem are more numerous than those in Nazareth.

43.6

Read John 9.39–41.

Note:
το κριμα – the judgement

Read John 15.18–27.

Notes:
μισεω – I hate
διωκω – I persecute
μνημονευω – I remember

ἡ προφασις – the excuse
δωρεαν – freely, without cause

43.7 Progress test 20

Which of the following could be correct translations of the Greek?

1. και είπαν αὐτῷ, Μη και ἡμεις τυφλοι ἐσμεν;
(a) They said to him, "Are we also blind?"
(b) And they said to him, "We are also blind, aren't we?"
(c) They said to him, "We are not also blind, are we?"

2. Εἰ τυφλοι ἦτε, οὐκ ἀν εἰχετε ἁμαρτιαν.
(a) If you were blind, you would not be guilty of sin.
(b) If you had been blind, you would not have been guilty of sin.
(c) If you are blind, you are not guilty of sin.

3. εἰ ἐκ του κοσμου ἦτε, ὁ κοσμος ἀν το ἰδιον ἐφιλει.
(a) If you had been of the world, the world would have loved its own.
(b) If you really belong to the world, the world will love its own.
(c) If you were of the world, the world would love its own.

4. εἰ μη ἠλθον και ἐλαλησα αὐτοις, ἁμαρτιαν οὐκ εἰχοσαν.
(a) If I did not come and speak to them, they would not be guilty of sin.
(b) If I had not come and spoken to them, they would not be guilty of sin.
(c) If I had not come and spoken to them, they would not have been guilty of sin.

Check your answers on page 281.

LESSON 44

δικαιος – righteous
δικαιοσυνη – righteousness
ἀδικια – injustice, wrong

44.1 Word stems

Study the following groups of words. Notice how the endings (suffixes) and parts added at the beginning (prefixes) determine the meaning of each word within the general area of meaning indicated by the stem.

1. **δικ** – Words to do with justice, rightness, law, and courts

        δικαιος – righteous, just, upright
        δικαιοτερος – more righteous, rather righteous
        δικαιοτατος – most righteous, very righteous
(ἡ) δικαιοσυνη – righteousness, justice, uprightness, what is right
        δικαιως – justly, righteously
(ἡ) δικαιωσις – justification, acceptance as righteous
(το) δικαιωμα – righteous act, righteousness, law, statute
        δικαιοω – I acquit, I declare to be righteous, I treat as righteous,
              I justify
(ἡ) δικη – justice, penalty, punishment
(ὁ) δικαστης – judge
(ἡ) δικαιοκρισια – righteous judgement
(ἡ) ἀδικια – injustice, unrighteousness, wrong
(το) ἀδικημα – unrighteous act, wrong
        ἀδικεω – I wrong, I do wrong to, I harm
        ἀδικως – unjustly, unfairly
        ἀδικος – unjust

2. **ἀγ** – Words to do with holiness, reverence, purity

        ἁγιος – holy
        ἁγιαζω – I make holy, I sanctify
(ὁ) ἁγιασμος – sanctification, making holy
(ἡ) ἁγιοτης – holiness
        ἁγνος – pure, chaste
        ἁγνως – purely, with a pure motive
(ἡ) ἁγνεια – purity
(ὁ) ἁγνισμος – purification
        ἁγνιζω – I purify

3. **γνο** – Words to do with knowing

    γινωσκω – I know
    ἀναγινωσκω – I read
    ἐπιγινωσκω – I come to know, I recognize
    προγινωσκω – I know beforehand
    γνωριζω – I make known
(ἡ) γνωσις – knowledge, wisdom
(ἡ) ἐπιγνωσις – knowledge
    γνωστος – known
    ἀγνωστος – unknown
    ἀγνοεω – I do not know, I am ignorant, I do not understand
(ἡ) ἀγνωσια – ignorance, misunderstanding
(ἡ) ἀγνοια – ignorance, lack of knowledge
(το) ἀγνοημα – act done in ignorance

Notice that **α** before a stem often, but not always, makes it negative. Grammarians call this **α** "alpha privative".

In 44.2–6 we study common word forms, suffixes, and prefixes. These are given as guidelines, not as rules. They indicate what is generally the case, not what is always so. If you are in any doubt over the meaning of a word, study it in its context with the aid of a lexicon and concordance.

44.2 Nouns and their endings (suffixes)

1. To show actions:

    -σις f.   ἀπολυτρωσις – redemption, βρωσις – eating, καυχησις – boasting
    -σια f.   ἐργασια – work, παρουσια – coming
    -μος m.   ἀσπασμος – greeting, βασανισμος – torture, διωγμος – persecution

2. To show the result of an action:

    -μα n.   δικαιωμα – just act, law, ὁραμα – vision, πραγμα – action, thing done

3. To show the doer of an action:

    -τηρ m.   σωτηρ – saviour
    -τωρ m.   παντοκρατωρ – ruler of all, almighty, ῥητωρ – orator
    -της m.   κλεπτης – thief, οἰκοδεσποτης – house holder, master

4. To show the means or instrument by which an action is done:

    -τρον n.   ἀροτρον – plough, λυτρον – ransom price

5. To show the profession, position or class of person:

-ευς m.   βασιλευς – king, γραμματευς – scribe, ἱερευς – priest
-ισσα f.   βασιλισσα – queen
-της m.   πολιτης – citizen, στρατιωτης – soldier

6. To show quality:

-της f.   ἁγιοτης – holiness, ἰσοτης – equality,
            χρηστοτης – goodness
-συνη f.   ἐλεημοσυνη – deed of mercy, alms,
            σωφροσυνη – moderation
-ια f.   ἀκαθαρσια – uncleanness, ἐλευθερια – liberty,
            πλεονεξια – greed

7. To show the place where something is done:

-τηριον n.   δικαστηριον – law court,
              θυσιαστηριον – altar, place of sacrifice
-ειον n.   μνημειον – tomb,
            ταμειον – treasury, store, inner room

8. To show a smaller or younger type:

-ιον n.   παιδιον – a little boy, child, τεκνιον – little child
-ισκος m.   νεανισκος – youth (νεανιας – young man)
-ισκη f.   παιδισκη – young girl, maid, female servant

44.3 Adjectives: prefixes and suffixes

A. Prefixes

1. Adjectives beginning with **α** – not:

ἀγαμος – unmarried   ἀγναφος – unwashed
ἀγνωστος – unknown   ἀδιαλειπτος – unremitting, continual
ἀδυνατος – impossible   ἀλαλος – dumb
ἀναξιος – unworthy   ἀνωφελης – useless
(ἀξιος – worthy)

2. Adjectives beginning with **δυσ** – hard, difficult:

δυσκολος – hard, difficult   δυσερμηνευτος – difficult to explain
δυσβαστακτος – hard to carry

3. Adjectives beginning with **εὐ** – good, well:

εὐγενης – well-born, noble   εὐθετος – suitable, fitting
εὐκοπωτερος – easier   εὐλογητος – blessed
εὐπροσδεκτος – acceptable   εὐχρηστος – useful

B. Suffixes

1. To show belonging or possession:

   -ιος   οὐρανιος – heavenly, ἰδιος – one's own

2. To show material:

   -ινος   λιθινος – made of stone, ξυλινος – made of wood
   -εος/ους   ἀργυρεος – silver, made of silver, χρυσεος – gold

3. To show inclination or tendency:

   -μων   δεισιδαιμων – scrupulous, reverent,
             ἐλεημων – merciful, μνημων – mindful

4. To show aptitude or nature:

   -ικος   κριτικος – able to judge, φυσικος – natural,
             χοικος – earthy
   -ιμος   χρησιμος – useful, ὠφελιμος – helpful, useful

5. To show passive force, capability, or ability:

   -τος   ἀορατος – invisible, ὁρατος – able to be seen, visible

44.4 Formation of adverbs

Most adverbs are formed with -ως or -εως:

   ἀληθως – truly   ὁμοιως – similarly
   ἡδεως – gladly, with pleasure

But note also:

   εὐ – well   εὐθυς – at once
   ἡδιστα – very gladly   ταχυ – quickly

(See also 35.1, 5.)

44.5 Verbs

Verbs are formed from nouns and adjectives by endings like:

   -αω -εω -οω -ευω -ζω -ιζω -υνω

The ending is not always a clue to the particular force or meaning, but the following are common.

1. **-αω, -εω, -ευω** – to show action or state:

ἀγαλλιαω – I exult	προσκυνεω – I worship
ἐαω – I allow	δουλευω – I serve (as a slave)
ἐρωταω – I ask	ἡγεμονευω – I govern
τιμαω – I honour	φονευω – I kill
κατοικεω – I inhabit, I dwell	φυτευω – I plant
ποιεω – I do, I make	

2. **-οω, -αινω, -υνω** – to show causation or making:

δουλοω – I enslave	θανατοω – I put to death,
πικραινω – I make bitter	I cause to be killed
(πικρος – bitter)	πληθυνω – I multiply,
ξηραινω – I shrivel up	I cause to increase
(ξηρος – dry)	παροξυνομαι – I become angry
φανεροω – I reveal	

3. **-ιζω, -αζω** – to show intensive or causative action:

ἁγνιζω – I purify	διαμεριζω – I divide
βασανιζω – I torment	λιθαζω – I stone
γνωριζω – I cause to know	ῥαντιζω – I sprinkle

44.6 Verbs formed with prepositions

Many verbs are formed using the most common meaning of the preposition:

εἰς – into
εἰσερχομαι – I go into, I enter.

But other verbs reflect less common meanings of the preposition:

ἀνα	ἀναβαινω – I go up	
(up)	withdrawal:	ἀναστρεφω – I turn back
		ἀναχωρεω – I go away
	repetition:	ἀναζαω – I live again
	thoroughness:	ἀναπαυω – I give rest to, I refresh

ἀντι	ἀντιλεγω – I speak against	
(opposite)	exchange:	ἀνταποδιδωμι – I give back in return,
		I recompense

44.6

ἀπο (from)	ἀπεχω (1) – I am away from
	ἀπολυω – I release
	ἀφοριζω – I separate
	return: ἀποδιδωμι – I give back
	ἀπολαμβανω – I take back
	completion: ἀπεχω (2) – I have fully
	ἀπολλυμι – I destroy (utterly)

δια (through)	διερχομαι – I go through, I travel through
	distribution: διαγγελλω – I proclaim (widely)
	διαδιδωμι – I distribute
	separation: διασπαω – I tear apart
	succession: διαδεχομαι – I receive in turn
	completion: διακαθαριζω – I cleanse thoroughly
	διαφυλασσω – I guard carefully

ἐκ (out of)	ἐξερχομαι – I go out, I come out
	completion: ἐκπληροω – I fill completely
	ἐξαπορεομαι – I am utterly bewildered

ἐπι (on)	ἐπιτιθημι – I put on
	ἐπερχομαι (1) – I come upon
	opposition: ἐπερχομαι (2) – I come against
	ἐπιστρεφω – I turn back
	superiority: ἐπισκοπεω – I oversee
	(ἐπισκοπος – overseer, bishop)
	upwards: ἐπαιρω – I lift up, I raise
	completion: ἐπιγινωσκω – I understand, I recognize, I realize
	ἐπιζητεω – I seek for, I enquire, I demand

κατα (down)	καταβαινω – I come down
	καταγω – I bring down (to the shore)
	opposition: καταραομαι – I curse
	κατακρινω – I condemn
	completion: καταισχυνω – I make ashamed
	κατεργαζομαι – I accomplish
	κατεσθιω – I eat up, I consume
	order: καταρτιζω – I set in order, I mend
	κατευθυνω – I make straight, I guide
	after, behind: κατακολουθεω – I follow after
	καταλειπω – I leave behind, I forsake

μετα (with)	μεταδιδωμι – I share with, I impart μετεχω – I share in, I partake of	
	change:	μεταβαινω – I go from one place to another μεταμελομαι – I change my mind, I repent μετανοεω – I change my attitude, I repent
	after, seeking:	μεταπεμπομαι – I send for, I summon

παρα (beside)	παρακαλεω – I call to my side, I entreat, I comfort παραλαμβανω – I take along (with me), I receive	
	deviation:	παρακουω – I fail to hear, I overhear παραβαινω – I overstep, I transgress

περι (about, around)	περιπατεω – I walk about, I live περιβαλλω – I put around, I clothe	
	excess, beyond:	περιλειπομαι – I am left, I survive περισσευω – I exceed, I abound

προ (in front of)	προαγω – I go in front of, I lead	
	beforehand:	προοριζω – I determine beforehand, I foreordain προφητευω – I speak beforehand, I prophesy

συν (with)		συναγω – I gather together συνεργεω – I work with
	totality:	συγκαλυπτω – I cover completely, I veil συνθρυπτω – I break in pieces, I utterly crush συντηρεω – I keep safe

ὑπερ (over)	excess:	ὑπερβαλλω – I exceed ὑπερεχω – I excel, I am in authority ὑπερνικαω – I conquer completely

ὑπο (under)	ὑποδεομαι – I bind under (ὑποδημα – sandal)	
	subjection:	ὑπακουω – I obey ὑπηρετεω – I serve, I minister to ὑπομενω – I endure
	withdrawal:	ὑπαγω – I depart ὑποστελλω – I draw back ὑποστρεφω – I turn back, I return

44.7 Useful stems in classical and New Testament Greek

ἀγ	drive, lead, go	γραφ	write
ἁγ	holiness, purity, awe	γυναικ	woman, female
ἀγαπ	love	δε	bind
ἀγορ	market, buy	δεκ/δεχ	take, receive
ἀγρ	field, country, wild	δεικ/δειξ	show, reveal
ἀγων	contest, fight, struggle	δημ	people, live, inhabit
		διατριβ	spend time, waste time
αἰσθ	feel, notice		
αἰσχρ	shame, modesty	διαφθερ	destroy, corrupt
αἰτι	cause, accuse; ask	διδα(σκ)	teach
ἀκο	hear	δικ	justice, law, penalty
ἀληθ	true, genuine	διωγ/διωκ	pursue, persecute
ἀλλ	other	δο	give
ἁμαρτ	miss, fail, sin	δοκ	seem, befit, approve; glory
ἀναγκ	compel, force, necessity	δουλ	slave
ἀνδρ	man, manliness, bravery	δρα	do, act
		δυνα	be able, possible
ἀπατ	deceive, trick	δυσ	bad, poor, hard
ἀποκριν	reply, answer	εἰδ	see, know; shape, figure
ἀπολογ	defend, excuse		
ἀπορ	want, perplexity, lack	εἰκ	reasonable; yield; twenty
ἀποστα	apartness, revolt		
ἁρπ	seize, plunder	εἰπ	say, speak
ἀρχ	begin, be first; rule	ἐλεγχ	disprove, examine, test
ἀσθεν	weak, ill		
ἀστ	city; clever	ἐλευθ	free
βα/βη	go, walk, stand	ἐλθ	come, go
βαλ/βολ	throw, strike, put	Ἑλλ	Greek, Greece
βαπ/βαφ	sprinkle, dip, wash	ἐλπ	hope
βασιλ	king, rule, reign	ἐξεταζ	question, search
βια	force, violence	ἐοικ	be like; be reasonable
βιο	life, livelihood		
βλεπ	see, look	ἐπαιν	praise
βοα/βοη	shout, demand, roar	ἐργ	work, do
βοηθ	cry for help, help, assist	ἐρχ	come, go
		ἐσ/οὐσ	be, is, being
βουλ (1)	plan, advise, resolve	ἑταιρ	companion, friend
βουλ (2)	wish	εὐ	well, good
γαμ	marry	εὐρ	broad
γεν/γιν	become, be, be born	εὑρ	find, discover
γνο/γνω	perceive, know, decide	εὐχ	pray
		ἐχ	have

231

ἐχθρ	enemy, hostile	λιπ/λοιπ	leave, abandon
ζα/ζω	live	λυ	loose, set free
ζημ	penalty, fine	μαθ	learn
ζητ	seek, search, ask	μαρτυ	witness, evidence
ἡγε	lead; think	μαχ	fight, battle
ἡδ	sweet, pleasant	μεγ	large, size
ἡσυχ	calm, rest, quiet	μελ	care, concern
θαν/θν/θνητ	die, death	μεν	remain, stay
θαυμ	wonder, amazement	μερ	part, division
θε	put, place	μηχαν	device, contrive
θεα	see, wonder	μνη	remember, mention
θεραπ	cure, look after	μισ	hate
θυ	sacrifice	ναυ	ship, nautical
θυμ	(emotion) anger,	νικ	conquer, victory
	enthusiasm, desire,	νοε/νοι	mind; plan; notice
	patience, purpose	νομ	custom, law; think
ἰατρ	cure, medicine,	νοσ	disease
	doctor	ξεν	stranger, alien, guest
ἰδ	see	οἰκ	house, inhabit, serve
ἱε/ἱη	let go, forgive,	ὀλ	destroy
	understand	ὁλ	whole
ἱερ	holy, sacred, priest	ὀμ/ὀμνυ	oath, swear
ἰσχ	strong	ὁμο	at one with
καθαρ	clean, purify	ὁμοι	similar, alike
κακο	bad, evil	ὀνομ	name
καλ/κλη	call, summon	ὀργ	anger
κατηγορ	accuse, charge, prove	ὀφελ/ὀφειλ	owe, debt, benefit
καυχα	boast	ὀψ/ὀπ/ὀφθ	sight, vision
κει	lie, recline, stretch	παθ	experience, suffering
κηρυγ	herald, announce,	παι/παιδ	child, educate, play
	preach	παν/πασ	all, every
κινδυν	danger, risk	πειθ	persuade
κλεπ/κλοπ	steal	πειρ	try, experience, test
κοιν	common, shared	πεμπ/πομπ	send
κοπ	cut, strike; toil,	πεσ/πιπτ/πτ	fall
	trouble	πιστ	trust, faith, belief
κρατ	power, sway, control	πλα/πλη/πλ	full
κριν/κρισ	judge; reply; discern	πλε/πλοι	boat, sail, voyage
κτ	kill; gain, possess	ποιε	do, make
κτισ	create, found	πολεμ	war, enemy
λαβ	take	πορ	go, travel; provide,
λαθ/ληθ	secret, conceal		wealth
λεγ/λογ (1)	speak, word, reason	πορν	fornication, harlot
λεγ/λογ (2)	gather, choose	πραγ/πραξ	act, do, accomplish

πρεσβ	old, elder, embassy	τυγχ/τυχ	happen, chance
πυθ	learn, enquire	ὑβρ	violence, insolence
σημ	sign, show, signify	ὑψ	high
σθεν	strength	φαν/φαιν	appear, seem; shine, show
σιγ	silence		
σκα/σκη/σκο	darkness, cover, tent	φερ	bear, carry, offer
σκεπ/σκοπ	see, review, consider	φιλ	friendship, love, respect
σκευ	prepare, mend, utensils	φοβ	fear, awe
σκοπ	look, see, aim	φρην/φρον	mind, thought, prudence
σοφ	wise, intelligence		
σπενδ/σπονδ	pour out	φυγ	flight, refugee
σπευδ/σπουδ	hurry, enthusiasm	φυλακ	guard, protect, prison
στα/στη	stand, set		
σταυρ	cross, crucify	φυ	nature, natural, growth
στελ	send, equip		
στρατ	army, soldier, camp, war	φων	voice, speech, noise
		χαρ	please, welcome, rejoice
στραφ/στρεφ	turn		
σω	safe, sound, saviour	χρη	need, useful; ought
ταγ/τασσ	arrange, order, command	χρι	anoint, smear
		χρον	time
ταχ	speed, hurry, quick	χρυ	gold, golden
τεκμαιρ	witness, evidence	χωρ	go, place, locality
τελ	end, completion, aim	ψευδ	false, liar, pretence
τελευτ	end, death	ψηφ	vote, decree
τεχν	art, skill, craft, trade	ψυχ	soul, life, person
τιμ/τιμα	honour, value; punish	ὠδ	song, poem
		ὠφελ	benefit, usefulness, help
τιμωρ	vengeance		
τρεφ/τροφ	rear, nurture		

Notice that a knowledge of these stems will unlock the meaning of many technical terms and complex words – for example: chronology, democrat, psychiatry, onomatopoeia, pornography, pseudonym, telescope (each comes from two Greek stems).

44.8 A comical warning

This warning is for all who wish to be astute (shrewd, carefully wise). The Greek word ἀστυ means city or town. But if you are astute that does not mean you live in a city. It is a comical warning. I live in a village (κωμη). The word comical has historical links with the feeling that village people are backward, stupid or funny. But it would be silly to say "a

233

comical warning" is one that comes from a village. So always be very careful when you find someone ready to argue about a New Testament word: "Its root meaning is...so we should understand it in this way..." You cannot tell the meaning of "comical" by looking at its root, only by seeing how it is used in the English language today.

You have been warned. Be astute.

44.9

For further study of stems, roots, and word structures see Bruce M Metzger, *Lexical Aids for Students of New Testament Greek* (Blackwell, 1980) pp. 54–118, and for classical Greek grammar and word structures, *Reading Greek, Joint Association of Classical Teachers' Greek Course, Part 1 (Grammar, Vocabulary and Exercises)* (CUP, 1978) pp. 259–334.

44.10

Read 1 John 1–2.

Notes:
ψηλαφαω – I touch
ἱλασμος – propitiation
ἑως ἀρτι – until now
ἐπιθυμια – desire
ἀλαζονεια – deception, charlatanry, bragging
ἀντιχριστος – the one opposed to Christ, the one who seeks to usurp
                    the place of Christ
ἀρνεομαι – I deny
ἐπαγγελια – promise
σχωμεν – we may have (1st person pl. aor. subj. act. of ἐχω – I have)

All the other words you either know or can deduce from the forms and stems in lesson 44.

44.11

Revise lessons 37 and 38.

LESSON 45

νιπτω – I wash (someone or something else)
νιπτομαι – I wash (part of myself)

45.1

Study carefully:

1. (a) ἐνιψα τους ποδας σου – I washed your feet
   (b) ἐνιψαμην τους ποδας – I washed my feet

2. (a) ἐκαλεσεν αὐτους – he called them
   (b) προσεκαλεσατο αὐτους – he called them to himself

3. (a) ἐνδυσατε αὐτον τα ἱματια αὐτου – put his clothes on him!
   (b) ἐνδυσασθε τα ἱματια – put the clothes on!
                   or put your clothes on!

4. (a) πεμπω αὐτον – I am sending him
   (b) ἐρχομαι προς αὐτον – I am going towards him.

In each (a) sentence the action expressed by the verb is done by the subject to someone else: ἐνιψα, ἐκαλεσεν, ἐνδυσατε, and πεμπω are all **active** voice.

In each (b) sentence the action expressed by the verb specially involves or affects the person doing it: ἐνιψαμην, προσεκαλεσατο, ἐνδυσασθε, and ἐρχομαι are all **middle** voice (31.9C).

So in 1(a) ἐνιψα is 1st person singular aorist indicative active of νιπτω (I wash), and in 1(b) ἐνιψαμην is 1st person singular aorist indicative middle of νιπτω.

ἐνιψαμην refers to a washing of part of oneself. So ἐνιψαμην τους ποδας means literally, "I washed-for-myself the feet". In English we say "I washed my feet".

Words that have to do with movement and feelings are often in the middle voice.

45.2 Words

νιπτομαι – I wash
προσκαλεομαι – I call to myself
ἀσπαζομαι – I greet
συναγονται – they come together,
   they gather together

αἰτεομαι – I request, I ask for
φοβεομαι – I fear, I reverence,
   I feel awe
ἐφοβηθη – he was afraid
ἁπτομαι – I touch

235

45.2

ἐνδυομαι – I put on (clothes)
δεχομαι – I receive
καθημαι – I sit down
ἐκπλησσομαι – I am astonished

σπλαγχνιζομαι – I feel sorry for,
I feel compassion
σπλαγχνισθεις – moved by
compassion, feeling sorry for

45.3 Translate

1. ἀσπαζονται ἡμας και ἡμεις
δεχομεθα αὐτους.

They greet us and we receive
them.

2. ἐαν μη νιψωνται τας χειρας και
τους ποδας, οὐκ ἐσθιουσι τους
ἀρτους οὐδε ἐνδυονται τα ἱματια.

Unless they wash their hands and
their feet they do not eat the
loaves nor do they put on their
clothes.

3. σπλαγχνιζεται τοις λεπροις και
λεγει αὐτοις, Μη φοβεισθε. ὀς ἀν
ὑμας δεχηται και ἐμε δεχεται.

He feels compassion for the lepers
and says to them, "Do not be
afraid. Whoever receives you also
receives me".

4. συνηχθησαν προς αὐτον παντες οἱ
Φαρισαιοι και ἐξεπλησσοντο ἐπι τῃ
διδαχῃ αὐτου· ἐλεγεν γαρ Αἰτειτε
και δοθησεται ὑμιν. και ἐλεγον
αὐτῳ, Δια τί ἡμεις οὐ δεχομεθα;
ἀποκριθεις εἰπεν αὐτοις, Διοτι
κακως αἰτεισθε ἱνα το θελημα το
ὑμετερον ποιητε.

All the Pharisees gathered round
him and they were astonished at
his teaching for he said, "Ask and
it will be given you". They said to
him, "Why do we not receive?" In
reply he said to them, "Because
you ask with a bad motive so that
you may do your own will".

45.4

λημψομαι – I will receive, I will take (λαμβανω)

Note that many verbs have a middle form in the future tense. They are
often verbs where the action concerns oneself rather than, or as well as,
someone else (verbs of perception and movement). Here are some
common examples:

ἀκουω – I hear   ἀκουσομαι – I will hear
ἀναβαινω – I go up   ἀναβησομαι – I will go up
γινωσκω – I know   γνωσομαι – I will know
εἰμι – I am   ἐσομαι – I will be
ἐσθιω – I eat   φαγομαι – I will eat
ὁραω – I see   ὀψομαι – I will see
πιπτω – I fall   πεσουμαι – I will fall

Note also:

ἐλθών – having gone   ἐλευσομαι – I will go, I will come

45.5

Read carefully:

1. A great prophet

Ἀκουσονται την φωνην του προφητου και ἐλευσονται προς αὐτον και ἀρτον φαγονται μετ' αὐτου. και ἐσται μεγας και πολλοι ὀψονται την δοξαν αὐτου και ἀναβησονται εἰς Ἱεροσολυμα, και πεσουνται προς τους ποδας αὐτου και γνωσονται ὁτι ὁ θεος ἀπεστειλεν αὐτον.

2. Jesus heals the sick and teaches the crowd

Προσκαλεσαμενος τον τυφλον και ἀσπασαμενος αὐτον εἰπεν αὐτῳ, Ὑπαγε, νιψαι τους ὀφθαλμους. ἀπηλθεν οὐν και ἐνιψατο και οἱ ὀφθαλμοι αὐτου ἠνοιγησαν. ὁ δε Ἰησους παλιν προσεκαλεσατο αὐτον και ἐκαθητο προς τους ποδας αὐτου. συναγονται οὐν προς αὐτον οἱ Φαρισαιοι και ἰδοντες τον ἀνθρωπον ἐκει καθημενον και γνοντες ὁτι νυν βλεπει, ἐξεπλησσοντο και ἐφοβουντο.

Και παλιν πολλου ὀχλου συνηγμενου προσκαλεσαμενος τους ἰδιους μαθητας λεγει αὐτοις, Σπλαγχνιζομαι ἐπι τον ὀχλον ὁτι εἰσιν ὡς προβατα μη ἐχοντα ποιμενα. και ἠρξατο διδασκειν αὐτους λεγων, Ὁς ἀν ἐμε δεχηται οὐκ ἐμε δεχεται ἀλλα τον Πατερα τον ἐμον.

Και ἐκαθητο περι αὐτον ὀχλος και ἠλθεν προς αὐτον λεπρος λεγων ὁτι Ἐαν θελῃς δυνασαι με καθαρισαι. και σπλαγχνισθεις ἐκτεινας την χειρα ἡψατο αὐτου και λεγει αὐτῳ, Θελω, καθαρισθητι. και εὐθυς ἐκαθαρισθη ὡστε ἐκπλησσεσθαι παντας τους περι αὐτον κυκλῳ καθημενους.

45.6

Read Mark 1.1–13.

Notes:

το προσωπον – the face	ἡ ζωνη – the belt
κατασκευαζω – I prepare, I fix	δερματινος – made of skin, leather
βοαω – I shout	ἀκρις – locust
ἡ τριβος – the track, the road	το μελι – the honey
εὐθυς – straight, smooth, level	ἰσχυρος – strong
ἡ χωρα – the district	κυπτω – I bend down
ἐξομολογεω – I confess	ὁ ἱμας – the strap
αἱ τριχες – the hairs	ἡ περιστερα – the dove

LESSON 46

Translating – Romans 1.1–7 and John 1

46.1

Read Romans 1.1–7.

Notes:

κλητος – called
ἀφοριζω – I set apart
κατα σαρκα – according to the flesh

ὁριζω – I mark out
ἡ ὑπακοη – the obedience
τα ἐθνη – the Gentiles, the nations

46.2 Translating long sentences: Romans 1.1–7

Romans 1.1–7 is one long sentence. In present-day English we seldom write long sentences. So when we translate a passage like Romans 1.1–7 we must divide it into shorter sentences. We shall decide how long the sentences must be, by considering:
1. the thoughts in the Greek that have to be expressed in English
2. the style of writing that is appropriate for the passage
3. the readers for whom we are translating.

Romans 1.1–7 is the beginning of a letter. Paul puts his words of greeting at the end of the first sentence (verse 7). If we divide this long sentence into several shorter sentences we may decide to put the words of greeting at the beginning, where they come in an ordinary English letter.

Study the two following translations and the notes on them.

46.3 Romans 1.1–7 – Translation A

Dear Christian friends in Rome,

You are all loved by God and called by him to be holy[1]. May you know the grace and peace which come from God our Father and the Lord Jesus Christ[2].

I, Paul, am a slave of Jesus Christ. He called me and made me an apostle[3]: I have been set apart for the preaching of the Good News of God[4]. This Good News God promised beforehand through his prophets, by means of the sacred Scriptures. It is about his Son our Lord Jesus Christ: his human descent was from David, but in divine holiness he was shown to be the Son of God by the mighty act of his resurrection from the dead.

Through him I received grace and was made an apostle so that

238

people of every race might learn to trust and obey God[5], for the sake of Jesus. You are among them, for you also[6] have been called to belong to Jesus Christ.

Notes

1. This first paragraph is from verse 7. In an English letter we usually begin with the greeting.

2. This is a passage of some importance for New Testament theology. Grace and peace come ἀπο θεου πατρος ἡμων και κυριου Ἰησου Χριστου. God our Father and the Lord Jesus Christ are so closely linked as the source of grace and peace that Paul uses ἀπο only once. He does not say ἀπο θεου... and ἀπο κυριου... as if there were two separate sources. I have avoided the GNB translation: "May God our Father and the Lord Jesus Christ give you grace and peace", for (i) it does not so clearly show the Father and the Lord Jesus as a single source of blessing, and (ii) it is a little bit more likely to be misunderstood as if the Father gives grace and Jesus gives peace.

3. κλητος ἀποστολος – It is not clear whether these words express (i) one complete idea, or (ii) two separate ideas. We might translate (i) "called to be an apostle", or (ii) "called by him and made an apostle".

4. In making a sentence end here, I have repeated the reference to the Good News in the next sentence so that the linking together of the ideas is made clear.

5. εἰς ὑπακοην πιστεως – The aim of Paul's apostleship is to produce the obedience which is the proper outcome of faith. I have attempted to express these ideas simply by "to trust and obey God".

6. και ὑμεις – "you also" – I have not translated και ὑμεις as "you too", because when read aloud it would sound the same as "you two". Our translation must be clear when it is heard as well as when it is seen. Look at John 1.33 NEB: "he who is to baptize in Holy Spirit". The translators have used capitals to indicate to the reader that John means "the Holy Spirit"; they seem to have forgotten that the hearer cannot distinguish between "Holy Spirit" and "holy spirit".

46.4 Romans 1.1–7 – Translation B

Dear Christian friends in Rome,

You are loved by God. He called you to be holy[1]. Grace and peace be yours. They come from God our Father and the Lord Jesus Christ.

I, Paul, am a slave of Jesus Christ. He called me. He made me an apostle. I have been set apart to preach the Good News of God.

God promised beforehand to send this Good News. He made his promise through the prophets. It is written in the holy writings.

The Good News is about his Son our Lord Jesus Christ. As a man he descended from King[2] David. As a holy and spiritual being[3] he has been shown to be the Son of God. This was shown by the mighty act of his resurrection from the dead.

Through him I have received grace and was made an apostle. For his sake I preach. I lead people of every race[4] to trust in God and obey him. You also are among those who have been called by Jesus Christ[5].

Notes

1. The sentences and paragraphs are shorter than in translation A. Paul's one long sentence is made into five short paragraphs. Translation B is for those who are not used to long sentences. When translating the New Testament one needs to try various kinds of translation, read them out aloud to various groups, and see which they can understand best.

2. ἐκ σπερματος Δαυιδ – "from the seed of David"; that is, descended from David. Paul and his readers knew David was a king. If our readers may not know this we may think it best to translate Δαυιδ as "King David".

3. κατα πνευμα ἁγιωσυνης – "according to the spirit of holiness". This is parallel to κατα σαρκα – "with reference to his human descent". So κατα πνευμα ἁγιωσυνης may mean "with reference to his holy and spiritual nature". But this is a difficult passage for a translator to be certain about. πνευμα ἁγιωσυνης could perhaps be a Hebrew idiom for the Holy Spirit. Paul might mean: "He was designated and shown by the Holy Spirit to be the Son of God".

4. ἐν πασιν τοις ἐθνεσιν – "among all the Gentiles, among people of every race". Paul uses τα ἐθνη most often of the Gentiles, that is of all people who are not Jewish by birth. NIV translates, "among all the Gentiles", but most recent translations use the more general sense of ἐθνη as "nations": so GNB, "people of all nations". NEB, rather strangely, has "men of all nations". Paul says nothing here about men, so it is a pity to translate τα ἐθνη in a way that might make women feel they were left out.

5. κλητοι Ἰησου Χριστου – "called of Jesus Christ". Does this mean, "called by God to belong to Jesus Christ" (translation A) or "called by Jesus Christ" (translation B)? We cannot be certain. Paul most often speaks of God the Father as the one who calls people. But in Romans 1.7, Paul uses ἀγαπητοι θεου to mean "loved by God", so here

in Romans 1.6 he may be using κλητοι Ἰησου Χριστου to mean, "called by Jesus Christ".

46.5

You will have seen that it is often very difficult to know the best way to translate a passage of New Testament Greek. We have to consider the meaning of the Greek carefully. We may need to weigh up what learned commentators say. Even so, we may have to confess that we cannot be absolutely certain.

We have also to consider carefully the people we expect to read or listen to our translation. How they use the language into which we are translating will be a guide to us in choosing the style of translation we need to make.

46.6 Translating John 1 – the NEB translation

The translation of John 1 in NEB illustrates many of the problems and pitfalls faced by translators. It also shows how important it is that, whenever possible, new translations into other languages should be done from the Greek text.

Some of the problems of translation are very difficult to solve. It is not likely that scholars will always agree on solutions. The discussion in 46.7 represents the author's considered opinions. It illustrates some of the problems and suggests ways of solving them. It is unlikely that all scholars would agree that I have always reached the right conclusion.

46.7 Notes on the translation of John 1 in NEB

1.1   Ἐν ἀρχῃ ἠν ὁ λογος – In the beginning was the Word
        NEB: When all things began, the Word already was

ἐν ἀρχῃ: these are the first words of Genesis in the Greek Septuagint (LXX). John's Gospel echoes them. We need a translation that immediately recalls Genesis 1.1. The NEB footnote, "The Word was at the creation", adds another problem. When a person is at a match or a theatre, he is a spectator. "At the creation" may suggest to the reader that the Word was a spectator at the creation – John says the Word was the agent of creation (verse 3).

1.1   ἠν προς τον θεον – was with God
        NEB: dwelt with God

ἠν does not mean "dwelt". NEB introduces an idea that is not in the Greek text.

46.7

1.1   καὶ θεος ἠν ὁ λογος – and the Word was God
         NEB: and what God was, the Word was

This is misleading. It suggests that there might be something outside of
God which the Word also is. In algebraic terms, if God is G and the
Word is W, the Greek says: W = G. NEB suggests G = X and W = X.

1.2   οὐτος ἠν ἐν ἀρχῃ προς τον θεον – He was in the beginning with
                                          God
         NEB: The Word, then, was with God at the beginning

οὐτος means "he", and there is no need to paraphrase it as "the Word".
"Then" is not in the Greek. To add it in breaks the poetic flow of John's
language. It is also confusing to have "then" in a logical sense, in a
sentence that has a reference to time. Note also that NEB has no
balance between verse 1 and verse 2 in its translation of ἐν ἀρχῃ.

1.3–4   ...οὐδε ἑν ὃ γεγονεν...
         (a) NEB text: no single thing was created without him. All that
              came to be was alive with his life
         (b) NEB footnote: no single created thing came into being
              without him. There was life in him...

The New Testament was originally written without punctuation. Should
we put a full stop after ἑν, or after γεγονεν? NEB text puts the stop after
ἑν. It then leaves the problem of translating ὃ γεγονεν ἐν αὐτῳ ζωη ἠν.
Would this mean (i) that what was created-in-him was life, or (ii) that
what was created became life-in-him? Neither suits John's theology.
NEB text tries to avoid this problem by mistranslating ἐν αὐτῳ ζωη ἠν as
"was alive with his life". It is better to put the full stop after γεγονεν, as in
the footnote.

1.6   Ἐγενετο – there was, there came into being
         NEB: There appeared

The word "appeared" often suggests surprise (as in "he suddenly
appeared") or unreality (as in "he only appeared to be rich").
     In 1.6 ἐγενετο either links John to the created order (see verse 3, παντα
δι' αὐτου ἐγενετο) or it simply introduces the next step of the story,
reflecting a Hebrew idiom. It certainly does not suggest either surprise
or unreality.

1.6   NEB: There appeared a man named John

NEB puts emphasis on the name John, bringing it near the beginning of
the sentence. The Greek says, "There was a man sent from God...",
putting the emphasis on God's sending.

1.7 ἵνα παντες πιστευσωσιν – so that all might believe
NEB: that all might become believers

πιστευσωσιν is aorist subjunctive. It gives emphasis to the act of commitment, to the trusting in God. NEB gives emphasis to the resulting state, that people become believers.

1.9 Ἦν...ἐρχομενον – was coming
NEB: was even then coming

There is nothing in the Greek text that corresponds with this "even then".

1.9 Ἦν το φως το ἀληθινον ὃ φωτιζει παντα ἀνθρωπον, ἐρχομενον εἰς τον κοσμον

There is a problem here for the translator. ἐρχομενον could be
(a) nominative singular neuter, and refer to φως: "The true light, which enlightens every man, was coming into the world" or
(b) accusative singular masculine, and refer to ἀνθρωπον: "It was the true light, which enlightens every man who comes into the world".

NEB text chooses alternative (a). This is a sensible choice, since:
   (i) verses 1–14 are all about the Word coming into the world
   (ii) John elsewhere speaks of the light, or of Jesus, coming into the world (John 3.19, 11.27, etc.), and
   (iii) John never speaks of men "coming into the world", but in John 16.21 of a man being born into the world.

1.11 εἰς τα ἰδια ἦλθεν – he came to what was his own
NEB: He entered his own realm

τα ἰδια means "what belongs to a person". GNB translates as "his own country"; but NEB as "his own realm". "Realm" is a strong word. It introduces the idea of kingship. This idea is not in τα ἰδια.

1.12 τοις πιστευουσιν – to those who believe
NEB: to those who have yielded him their allegiance

πιστευουσιν is a present participle. The emphasis is on continuing trust. NEB puts its emphasis on the initial act of commitment.

1.13 οἱ – who
NEB ignores this word

1.13 ἐγεννηθησαν – were begotten
NEB: the offspring

ἐγεννηθησαν is aorist passive of γενναω (I beget). The Greek emphasizes

243

46.7

the creating activity of God; the NEB puts the emphasis on the resulting state as offspring of God.

1.14 ἐσκήνωσεν – he dwelt
 NEB: he came to dwell

The word ἐσκήνωσεν is in the aorist tense. It emphasizes the fact: he dwelt. NEB, "he came to dwell", makes the dwelling the purpose of his coming. By putting in the idea of his coming, the NEB distorts the meaning.

1.14 δόξαν ὡς μονογενοῦς – glory as of the only-begotten

μονογενοῦς is genitive. We might translate: "such glory as belongs to the only Son". NEB, "such glory as befits the...only Son", brings in an idea of what is right or fitting. This idea does not seem to be implied by the Greek.

1.14 πλήρης χάριτος και ἀληθείας – full of grace and truth

In NEB the nearest main statement to "full of grace and truth" is, "we saw his glory". It is therefore possible to read verse 14 in NEB and think that it is the glory that is full of grace and truth. In the Greek, πλήρης is nominative and agrees with ὁ λόγος, not with δόξαν which is accusative. It would be better to put "full of grace and truth" nearer the beginning of the sentence: "...he dwelt among us, full of grace and truth...". Or if we leave it to the end of the verse we might make it a separate sentence: "He was full of grace and truth".

1.18 μονογενής υἱός – only-begotten Son, only Son

NEB is probably right to have υἱός in its text. Some early manuscripts had μονογενής θεός. This produces a contradiction in the verse: "No one has seen God...God has made him known". When we have to choose between two possible readings of a text one question we have to ask is, "Which makes better sense?" In this case, it seems clear that the answer is υἱός. For a more detailed discussion, see lesson 50.5.

1.18 ὁ ὢν εἰς τον κολπον του πατρος – the one who is against the
 Father's bosom
 NEB: who is nearest the Father's heart

We do not often use "bosom", "breast", or "chest" to indicate closeness and affection. We often use "heart" as a symbol of love. So NEB sensibly uses "heart". "Near to" might be better than "nearest".

244

1.19 ἐξ Ἱεροσολυμων – from Jerusalem

ἐξ means "from", "out of". ἐξ Ἱεροσολυμων naturally goes with ἀπεστειλαν: "They sent...from Jerusalem". NEB links it to οἱ Ἰουδαιοι, but since "the Jews from Jerusalem" makes little sense they mistranslate it as, "the Jews of Jerusalem".

1.20 ὡμολογησεν και οὐκ ἠρνησατο και ὡμολογησεν
– he admitted and he did not deny, he admitted...
NEB: he confessed without reserve and avowed...

The word "confessed" is somewhat ambiguous in English. We use it most often for confession of sin, less often for confession of faith or proclamation of truth. "Avowed" is also an unusual word. The repetition of ideas is emphatic. We might translate as "he gave them this very definite answer", or as "without hesitation he openly declared".

1.22 τί λεγεις περι σεαυτου; – What do you say about yourself?
NEB: What account do you give of yourself?

In English, to give an account either means:
(a) to tell a story or recount a narrative
or (b) to give a justification for

In this context (a) implies too long an answer, and (b) has the wrong sense. Unless a Greek text appears to be deliberately ambiguous, translators need to avoid ambiguous words and phrases.

1.23 καθως εἰπεν Ἡσαιας – as Isaiah said

These words in the Greek text are naturally to be taken as part of John's answer. NEB strangely puts "in the words of Isaiah" before John's answer.

1.23 Εὐθυνατε – make straight, make level
NEB and most translations: Make...straight

But when a desert road is prepared for an important person, what is usually done is to fill in the holes and smooth out the bumps. εὐθυς means "straight", whether in direction or across the surface. We should consider whether to translate as "make the road smooth".

1.25 Τί οὐν βαπτιζεις; – Then why are you baptizing?

NEB puts this question later in the sentence. As a result the link word οὐν (then) does not seem to fit in so well.

1.26   Ἐγω βαπτιζω ἐν ὑδατι – I baptize with water
        NEB: I baptize in water

Compare Matthew 3.11, ἐν ὑδατι and Mark 1.8, ὑδατι. Mark's use of the instrumental dative shows us that ἐν ὑδατι also means "with water". It is a Hebrew idiom. See also Luke 3.16 and Acts 1.5, where ὑδατι (with water) is parallel to ἐν πνευματι ἁγιω (with the Holy Spirit). Baptism in the New Testament is done "with water", not "in water". In Luke 3.16, NEB rightly translates ἐν πνευματι ἁγιω και πυρι as "with the Holy Spirit and with fire". But in John 1.31 and 1.33 it has the same error as in 1.26.

1.26   ὀν ὑμεις οὐκ οἰδατε – whom you do not know
        NEB: though you do not know him

"Though" is neither expressed in the Greek nor implied by it.

1.33   οὐκ ἠδειν – I did not know, I had not known
        NEB: I did not know

The past form ἠδειν covers both the simple past, "I knew" and the pluperfect, "I had known". When there is a choice between two possible translations we must consider the meaning and context carefully. If our author usually writes sensibly, we should choose the translation which makes better sense. NEB chooses, "I did not know him". It might suggest that when John had seen the sign of the Spirit he still did not know. But is it not more likely that John is saying, "I had not known him until the Spirit came upon him, but then I knew because God had told me about this sign"? He is not bearing witness to his ignorance, but to his knowledge (verse 34).

1.34   μεμαρτυρηκα ὁτι οὑτος ἐστιν ὁ υἱος του θεου
        – I bear witness that he is the Son of God
        NEB: I have borne witness. This is God's Chosen One

NEB puts a full stop unecessarily after "I have borne witness". This breaks the flow and obscures the meaning. οὑτος stands in contrast to the emphatic ἐγω (κἀγω is a short form of και ἐγω). οὑτος should be translated as "he", not as "this".

        NEB: God's Chosen One

Nearly all the old manuscripts have ὁ υἱος του θεου. A few have instead ὁ ἐκλεκτος του θεου. NEB translators considered ἐκλεκτος to be the original reading, later altered by some scribes to υἱος.

1.38   Διδασκαλε is vocative – it means "Teacher!", not as NEB, "a teacher"

1.43–45 *εὑρισκει...εὑρισκει...εὑρηκαμεν...*
   – he finds...he finds...we have found...
   NEB: he met...went to find...we have met...

In John 1.45 NEB expresses the purposefulness implied by the verb *εὑρισκει* by translating it, "he went to find". But "he met" and "we have met" do not sufficiently express the ideas of purpose and discovery expressed by the verb.

46.8

General comments on the translation of John 1 in NEB
When we translate, we must not limit our consideration to the meaning of words and sentences. We must consider also the style of writing. John 1.1–18 is repetitious and poetic in style. John 1.19–51 is a quickly moving narrative. NEB does little to help the reader to be aware of the change of style. Read John 1 in NJB or in the Penguin Classics' translation by E V Rieu, *The Four Gospels* (Penguin, 1952). Notice how the translators have shown the difference in style.

You will probably be surprised that a translation done by able scholars has, in one chapter, so many places where the translation is questionable. I have deliberately chosen a chapter with many problems. In most passages, the differences between translations concern only minor points of meaning or emphasis. However, it is important to realize that problems do exist, and that "the right answer" is not always obvious. As translators we need to learn to be very careful in our work, and not to accept someone else's translation without first examining it rigorously.

46.9

Revise lessons 39 and 40.

LESSON 47

εἶπες ὅτι ἐσθιει – you said that he was eating

47.1 Indirect statements: 1. ὅτι followed by a verb in the indicative

Compare carefully:

(a) Ἐσθιει μετα των ἁμαρτωλων
    "He is eating with the sinners"

(b) εἶπες ὅτι Ἐσθιει μετα των ἁμαρτωλων
    You said, "He is eating with the sinners"

(c) εἶπες ὅτι ἐσθιει μετα των ἁμαρτωλων
    You said that he was eating with the sinners.

Compare (a) and (c). (a) is a direct statement. In (c) there is an indirect or reported statement, "that he was eating...". Notice that in Greek the tense of ἐσθιει (present) remains the same when the sentence is reported. But in English we do not say, "you said that he is eating", but "you said that he was eating".

Now compare (b) and (c). They differ only in the capital E which indicates spoken words. The New Testament was originally written in capital letters (uncials). When written in uncials there would be no difference between sentence (b) and sentence (c). In translating, we should have to make our own choice between (b) and (c).

So in 1 John 1.6, *EAN EIΠΩMEN OTI KOINΩNIAN EXOMEN MET AYTOY*, we have to choose between using (a) direct speech, or (b) indirect speech in our translation.

(a) Direct speech:
    If we say, "We have fellowship with him..."
(b) Indirect speech:
    1. If we say that we have fellowship with him...
    or 2. If we claim to have fellowship with him...

Translate

1. θεωρουσι ὅτι προφητης εἶ συ.	They see that you are a prophet.
2. ἐθεωρουν ὅτι προφητης εἶ συ.	They saw that you were a prophet.
3. τυφλος ἦν και νυν βλεπει.	He was blind and now he sees.
4. οὐκ ἐπιστευσαν ὅτι ἦν τυφλος.	They did not believe that he had been blind.

47.2 Indirect statements: 2. Using accusative and infinitive

Compare:

(a) Σὺ εἶ ὁ Χριστός
"You are the Messiah"

(b) ἐγω σε λεγω εἶναι τον Χριστον
(Lit. I say you to be the Messiah)
I say that you are the Messiah
(σε is accusative form of συ; εἶναι is present infinitive of εἰμι).

In Mark 8.29:
Ὑμεις δε τίνα με λεγετε εἶναι;
"Whom do you say that I am?"
(τίνα is accusative of τίς; με is the accusative form of ἐγω).

Note also 3 John 14:
ἐλπιζω δε εὐθεως σε ἰδειν
I hope that I will see you soon
or I hope to see you soon
(ἰδειν – to see – is aorist infinitive).

Hebrews 3.18:
τίσιν δε ὠμοσεν μη εἰσελευσεσθαι...;
To whom did he swear that they would not enter...?

(ὠμοσεν is 3rd person sing. aor. indic. act. of ὀμνυω – I swear. εἰσελευσεσθαι is future infinitive middle of εἰσερχομαι – I enter).

47.3 Indirect requests – ἱνα followed by a verb in the subjunctive

Compare:

(a) Δος μοι τον ἀρτον (direct request)
"Please give me the loaf"

(b) θελω ἱνα δῷς μοι τον ἀρτον (indirect request)
(Lit. I wish that you would give me the loaf)
I want you to give me the loaf

(In (a) **δος** is 2nd person sing. aor. imper. active, and in (b) **δῷς** is 2nd person sing. aor. subj. active, of διδωμι).

In Mark 13.18:

προσευχεσθε δε ἱνα μη γενηται χειμωνος
But pray that it may not happen in winter.

249

47.3

Translate

1. παρεκαλουν αὐτον ἱνα αὐτου ἁψωνται.	They begged him that they might touch him.
2. παρακαλουσιν αὐτον ἱνα αὐτης ἁψηται.	They beseech him to touch her.
3. θελομεν ἱνα τουτο ποιησης ἡμιν.	We want you to do this for us.
4. δος ἡμιν ἱνα καθισωμεν μετα σου ἐν τῃ βασιλειᾳ σου.	Please grant us that we may sit with you in your kingdom.
5. προσευχεσθε ἱνα μη ἐλθητε εἰς πειρασμον.	Pray that you may not go into temptation (testing).
6. Τί σοι θελεις ποιησω; Θελω ἱνα εὐθυς δῳς μοι ἐπι πινακι τους ἁρτους ἐκεινους.	"What do you want me to do for you?" "I want you to give me at once those loaves on a dish."
7. Το θυγατριον μου ἐσχατως ἐχει, ἱνα ἐλθων ἐπιθῃς τας χειρας αὐτῃ.	My daughter is dying. Please come and lay your hands on her.

47.4 Indirect questions

Compare:

(a) ποτε ἐρχεται;
    When is he coming?

(b) οὐκ οἰδα ποτε ἐρχεται
    I do not know when he is coming.

Mk 3.2   παρετηρουν αὐτον εἰ...θεραπευσει αὐτον
          They watched him to see if he would heal him
          (Direct form: θεραπευσει αὐτον; – "Will he heal him?")

Mk 12.41 ἐθεωρει πως ὁ ὀχλος βαλλει...
          He watched how the crowd was putting...
          (Direct question: πως βαλλει; – "How is it putting...?")

Mk 13.35 οὐκ οἰδατε...ποτε ὁ κυριος της οἰκιας ἐρχεται
          You do not know when the master of the house will come
          (When he does come, you will say: ἐρχεται – "He is coming").

For indirect commands and prohibitions, see lesson 41.2.

47.5

Read John 4.1–16.

Notes:

καιτοιγε – and yet, but in fact
πλησιον – near
το χωριον – the place
πηγη – spring, well
κεκοπιακως – exhausted, tired out (perfect participle active
    of κοπιαω – I toil, I work hard)
ἡ ὁδοιπορια – the journey, the travelling
ἀντλεω – I draw (water)
ἀπεληλυθεισαν – they had gone away (3rd person plural pluperfect
    indicative active of ἀπερχομαι)
τροφη – food, provisions
ἀγοραζω – I buy (ἀγορα – market, market place)
συγχραομαι – I use in common, I associate with
ἡ δωρεα – the gift
το φρεαρ – the well
βαθυς – deep
τα θρεμματα – the flocks, the herds
διψαω – I am thirsty
ἁλλομαι – I spring up

47.6

Revise lessons 41 and 42.

LESSON 48

The influence of Hebrew and Aramaic

48.1

Imagine that there is a job I must do, which will take time and effort.
When I am in England, I might say, "I'll get it done little by little". If I
were in East Africa, I would say, "I'll get it done slowly by slowly".
"Little by little" is an English idiom. "Slowly by slowly" is not ordinary
English. It is English influenced by East African idiom.

The writers of the New Testament were all influenced by Semitic
languages, particularly Hebrew and Aramaic. Read Mark 8.22–26, for

example. You will see that και occurs ten times. Of the five sentences into which we divide the paragraph, four begin with και. Writers of classical Greek did not use και so frequently in this way. But if one reads almost any Old Testament story in Hebrew one finds that most sentences begin with the Hebrew equivalent of και. Mark's use of και indicates that he was greatly influenced by his Semitic background.

In order to assess fully the influence of Hebrew and Aramaic, one would need to know both languages well. In this lesson we can only indicate some of the ways that New Testament Greek shows Semitic influence, and consider a few of the problems this raises for us as readers and translators.

48.2 Hebrew poetry

Hebrew poetic style is full of *repetition* and *parallelism*. Almost any chapter of Proverbs or Job will illustrate this. Note the parallelism in Luke 12.48. We indicate the pattern of this parallelism by the letters ABAB:

A παντι δε ᾧ ἐδοθη πολυ,
B   πολυ ζητηθησεται παρ' αὐτου·
A και ᾧ παρεθεντο πολυ,
B   περισσοτερον αἰτησουσιν αὐτον.

Note the repetition in Matthew 6.19–20. We indicate the pattern of this repetitive parallelism by the letters ABCABC:

A Μη θησαυριζετε ὑμιν θησαυρους ἐπι της γης,
B ὁπου σης και βρωσις ἀφανιζει
C και ὁπου κλεπται διορυσσουσιν και κλεπτουσιν·
A θησαυριζετε δε ὑμιν θησαυρους ἐν οὐρανῳ,
B ὁπου οὐτε σης οὐτε βρωσις ἀφανιζει
C και ὁπου κλεπται οὐ διορυσσουσιν οὐδε κλεπτουσιν·

Notice that in this section we have used the words repetition and parallelism in this order: repetition, parallelism, parallelism, repetition. The order of the words is on the pattern ABBA. Normally in a text-book if we say, "Let us consider points (a) and (b)", we then discuss point (a) first. The order ABBA is typical of Hebrew poetry. It is called *chiasmus*. Read Matthew 7.6 and note the *chiastic* order. We might be tempted to translate this as:

> Do not give what is holy to the dogs.   (A)
>   Do not cast your pearls before pigs   (B)
> lest they trample on them with their feet   (B)
>   and lest they turn and savage you.   (A)

But once we notice the ABBA pattern we might try a more natural English order in our translation. For example:

> Do not give what is holy to the dogs
> – they may turn and savage you.
> Do not throw your pearls before pigs
> – they may trample them in the mud.

Notice also that while "trample them with their feet" is a repetitive idiom, natural in New Testament Greek, it is not so natural in English poetry. "Trample them in the mud" is not a literal translation, but it may be the best equivalent translation.

48.3 Repetition for emphasis

In Hebrew, words are often repeated to give emphasis. Note in Ecclesiastes 1.1, "Meaninglessness of meaninglessness". In English we would not naturally use such repetition for emphasis. We might perhaps use the word "utterly" to give emphasis, and translate the sentence: "Everything is utterly meaningless". Note in Revelation 1.6, εἰς τους αἰωνας των αἰωνων. "To the ages of the ages" would not be a good translation. We need something like: "to all eternity", or "for ever and ever".

A common Hebrew idiom uses the repetition of a form of the infinitive to give emphasis. This kind of verb-doubling for emphasis is found in the New Testament rarely with the infinitive, more often with the participle. For example:

Mk 4.9   Ὅς ἐχει ὡτα ἀκουειν ἀκουετω.

The infinitive ἀκουειν gives emphasis to the imperative ἀκουετω. In translating this we must find a way of emphasis that will suit the readers for whom we are translating. Consider the following possible translations:

(a) He who has ears, let him not fail to hear
(b) The person who has ears must really listen
(c) If you've got ears – *use them*.

In translations (a) and (b) we translate ἀκουω as "hear" or "listen". But ἀκουω often also includes the idea of "understand". So we might also consider:

(d) Use your minds to understand what you hear

– although this lacks the force and directness of the Greek.

Some further examples of verb repetition in the New Testament:

Mk 4.12   βλεποντες βλεπωσιν και μη ιδωσιν
(Lit. Looking they may look yet they may not see)
They certainly look, but they do not see

Acts 7.34   ιδων ειδον την κακωσιν του λαου μου
I have surely seen the persecution of my people
or I have indeed seen how my people are oppressed

Heb 6.13–14   ωμοσεν καθ᾽ εαυτου λεγων, Εἰ μην **εὐλογων εὐλογησω** σε και **πληθυνων πληθυνω** σε
He swore by himself, saying, "I will certainly bless you and I will certainly multiply you"
or He made himself the witness of his own oath: he said, "I vow that I will bless you abundantly and multiply you greatly".

A similar noun may also be used with a verb to give emphasis:

Lk 22.15   **Ἐπιθυμια ἐπεθυμησα** τουτο το πασχα φαγειν μεθ᾽ ὑμων προ του με παθειν
I have really longed to eat this Passover with you before I suffer
(Lit. ἐπιθυμια ἐπεθυμησα is "with longing I longed" or "with desire I desired")

Jas 5.17   **προσευχη προσηυξατο** του μη βρεξαι
He prayed earnestly for it not to rain
(Lit. With prayer he prayed...).

But repetitiveness is very common in Semitic idiom and it is not always emphatic:

1 Pet 3.14   τον δε **φοβον** αὐτων μη **φοβηθητε**
Do not be afraid of them

Mk 7.7   **διδασκοντες διδασκαλιας** ενταλματα ἀνθρωπων
Teaching as doctrines the commandments of men
or While they teach people to obey the commandments men have given
or While what they teach is merely men's rules.

48.4

In Semitic idiom, ideas are often placed side by side and linked together by "and" where in English we would not use "and".

Take, for example, Mark 11.1–2:

> ἀποστελλει δυο των μαθητων αὐτου και λεγει αὐτοις, Ὑπαγετε...

At first sight we might be tempted to translate this, "He sends two of the disciples **and** says to them, 'Go...' ". But the saying does not come after the sending. So in English we must not link the two ideas by "and". We might translate: "He sent off two of the disciples with these instructions, 'Go...' ".

Similarly, in John 1.48, ἀπεκριθη Ἰησους και εἰπεν should be translated "In reply Jesus said", or "Jesus replied".

Note also Matthew 22.4, οἱ ταυροι μου και τα σιτιστα (my bulls and my fattened animals) – the animals fattened up with corn (σιτος) are probably the bulls. We should translate: "My fat bulls".

In Mark 4.24, ἐν ᾧ μετρῳ μετρειτε μετρηθησεται ὑμιν και προστεθησεται (with what measure you measure it shall be measured to you and it shall be added), the concept of measuring may not be as familiar a part of our life as it was in the everyday life in Palestine. So we might prefer a translation like: "As you treat others, so you will be treated – only more so".

The GNB translators, knowing that Jews often referred to God only indirectly, take the passive μετρηθησεται (it shall be measured) to mean "God will measure out". This might have led them to a translation like: "As you hand it out to others, so God will give it back, with something more besides". But for some reason they decided that the reference must be to judgement. So they translate: "The same rules you use to judge others will be used by God to judge you – but with greater severity".

και ἐγενετο – and it happened
Particularly in Luke's Gospel, the next stage of a story is often introduced by the words και ἐγενετο. We do not usually need to express this in English, except perhaps by beginning a new paragraph:

Lk 2.15   Και ἐγενετο ὡς ἀπηλθον ἀπ' αὐτων εἰς τον οὐρανον οἱ ἀγγελοι,
          οἱ ποιμενες ἐλαλουν προς ἀλληλους, Διελθωμεν...
          When the angels had gone away from them into heaven,
          the shepherds said to each other, "Let us go...".

But see also lesson 48.11.

48.5 Commands: two examples of Semitic influence

1. Participles used for the imperative

New Testament writers sometimes follow Semitic idiom in using participles to express commands, where classical Greek authors would

use the imperative. Note in Romans 12.9–10, ἀποστυγουντες (hating)...
κολλωμενοι (cleaving to)... προηγουμενοι (showing respect, considering
better than oneself). In our translation we might say: "Hate... Hold on
to... Show respect to...".

2. *The future indicative used for the imperative*

Lk 4.8   Κυριον τον θεον σου προσκυνησεις
             (Lit. You shall worship the Lord your God)
             Worship the Lord your God.

48.6

Note the use of **οὐ...πας...** or **πας...οὐ...** for "none, not any":

1 Jn 2.21   παν ψευδος ἐκ της ἀληθειας οὐκ ἐστιν
             (Lit. Every lie is not of the truth)
             No lie comes from the truth

Mk 13.20   οὐκ ἀν ἐσωθη πασα σαρξ
             No flesh would be saved
       or Nobody would survive

Acts 10.14   οὐδεποτε ἐφαγον παν κοινον
             · I never ate anything that was ritually unclean.

48.7

εἰ (if) is used to introduce a strong denial:

Mk 8.12   εἰ δοθησεται τη γενεᾳ ταυτη σημειον
             A sign will certainly not be given to this generation

Heb 3.11   ὡς ὠμοσα ἐν τη ὀργη μου·
             Εἰ ἐλευσονται εἰς την καταπαυσιν μου
             As I swore in my wrath,
             "They will certainly not enter into my rest".

48.8 Prepositions and prepositional phrases

Note particularly:

1. ἐν used with the dative, for the instrument with which something is
done (lessons 31.3, 42.3 (5), 46.7 on John 1.26).

In Matthew 3.11, αὐτος ὑμας βαπτισει ἐν πνευματι ἁγιῳ και πυρι, baptism
with the Holy Spirit is not something separate from the baptism with
fire (cf. lesson 48.4). A translator would have to consider whether:

(a) to translate, "He will baptize you with the Holy Spirit and with fire", leaving it to a commentator to explain the Hebrew idiom; or whether,

(b) to adopt a translation like: "He will baptize you with the fire of the Holy Spirit", or "He will baptize you with the fiery Holy Spirit".

2. ἐν χειρι (by the hand of) – by means of, through.

Gal 3.19   ἐν χειρι μεσιτου
              Through a mediator

There is no reference to the mediator's hand!

3. εἰς (into) – as

2 Cor 6.18   ἐσομαι ὑμιν εἰς πατερα
              I shall be to you as a father.

4. προ προσωπου (before the face) – before, ahead of

Lk 10.1   ἀπεστειλεν αὐτους ἀνα δυο δυο προ προσωπου αὐτου
         He sent them on ahead of him in twos
         (ἀνα δυο δυο is probably also a Hebraism).

Compare: ἀπο προσωπου – from
            κατα προσωπον – before, in the presence of.

48.9 Uses of the genitive case

Some of the uses of the genitive case we have studied in lesson 39 show Hebrew and Aramaic influence. Notice particularly:

μειζων δε τουτων (lit. greater of these)
The greatest of these

το πνευμα της ἐπαγγελιας (lit. the Spirit of promise)
The promised Spirit

ὁ κριτης της ἀδικιας (lit. the judge of unrighteousness)
The unrighteous judge

τεκνα ὀργης (lit. children of wrath)
People subject to God's wrath.

See also the examples in lesson 39.1, section 7 (b).

48.10

There are many New Testament words which can only be understood when their Old Testament and Jewish background is known. For example:

νομοδιδασκαλος – teacher of the Law of Moses and of the Jewish religious tradition based on the Law of Moses

ψευδοπροφητης – false prophet: that is, someone who claims to be a spokesman for God but isn't

γραμματευς – scribe: custodian, copier, and teacher of the Old Testament Scriptures; teacher of the Mosaic Law, interpreter of Jewish Law and tradition

είδωλολατρια – worship of idols

άκροβυστια – circumcision

θυσιαστηριον – the altar of sacrifice (in the Tabernacle, or in the Jerusalem Temple)

όλοκαυτωμα – whole burnt offering

τα έθνη – the Gentiles, all non-Jewish nations or people

Χριστος – Anointed, God's Anointed One, the Messiah

είρηνη – peace: used in the wider sense of the Hebrew word "shalom" for all the blessings of welfare and peace

Notice also various Aramaic and Hebrew words, written in Greek letters:

'Αββα – Father, Daddy   'Ελωι – my God

'Ακελδαμα – Field of blood   'Εφφαθα – be opened

'Αμην – truly   Ταλιθα κουμ – girl, get up

Βοανηργες – Sons of Thunder, Thunderers

For a fuller discussion, see C F D Moule, *An Idiom Book of New Testament Greek* (CUP, 1959) pp. 171–191.

Some Hebrew words are plural in form, but singular in meaning. For example: *shamayim* (heaven). In the New Testament, especially Matthew, notice uses of ούρανοι meaning heaven. So we translate ή βασιλεια των ούρανων as "the Kingdom of heaven" (or, the heavenly Kingdom) and not as "the Kingdom of the heavens".

48.11 Translating New Testament passages influenced by Hebrew and Aramaic

Most of the New Testament writers were Jews. Their normal use of Greek was influenced naturally by their Hebraic background. When we find a Hebraism, the writer is most often using language that is normal for him. So we must usually translate into the normal idiom of our own language.

But when New Testament writers are quoting from the Old Testament we may wish to model the style of our translation on that of a well-known Old Testament translation, if one already exists in our own language.

Consider also Luke chapters 1—2. Luke 1.1–4 is a carefully constructed sentence in stylish Greek. From verse 5 onwards the language is much coloured by the Hebraic-Aramaic background. We may want to give some indication of this in our translation. For example, in verse 5 we might translate ἐγενετο as, "it came to pass". This is not modern English. It is English of the style of the Authorized Version, which itself follows Hebrew style more closely than a modern translator would normally do.

48.12

Read Luke 1.5–7 (κατα Λουκαν 1.5–7):

Notes:
ἐφημερια – division, priestly order
θυγατηρ – daughter, female descendant
ἐναντιον – before, in the presence of
δικαιωμα – statute, law
προβαινω – I go ahead
προβεβηκοτες ἐν ταις ἡμεραις – old

Apart from the Jewish names, notice that the following words and phrases show signs of Hebrew or Aramaic influence:

ἐγενετο – it came to pass, there was...
ἐν ταις ἡμεραις – note the use of "day" to refer to time or age
γυνη αὐτῳ – a wife to him: meaning "he had a wife"
ἐναντιον του θεου – before God
ἐντολαι και δικαιωματα – commandments and ordinances: these two
    words reflect a difference in Israel's religious law between basic
    commandments and a multiplicity of lesser laws and regulations.
του Κυριου – of the Lord: that is, of Yahweh.

259

LESSON 49

γενοιτο – let it happen, may it happen
δεδωκει – he had given ⁼⁼|·|

49.1

> γενοιτο – let it happen
> μη γενοιτο – may it not happen, perish the thought!

Lk 1.38   γενοιτο μοι κατα το ῥημα σου
          Let it happen to me according to your word

Acts 5.24   διηπορουν...τί ἀν γενοιτο τουτο
           They were perplexed wondering what this could be
    or They wondered what this might mean
    or They wondered where the matter might end.

Translate

1. τουτο γενοιτο ἡμιν.	Let this happen to us.
2. μη γενοιτο μοι.	May it not happen to me.
3. μη πονηρος ἐστιν ὁ θεος; μη γενοιτο.	Is God evil? Perish the thought!
4. το ἀγαθον ἐμοι ἐγενετο θανατος; μη γενοιτο.	Did what is good become a cause of death to me? Of course not.

49.2

> ἁγιασαι – may he sanctify (ἁγιαζω – I sanctify)
> εἰη – may it be (εἰμι – I am)
> πληθυνθειη – may it be multiplied (πληθυνω – I multiply, I increase)

Translate

1. Αὐτος δε ὁ θεος ἁγιασαι ὑμας και παρακαλεσαι ὑμων τας καρδιας. χαρις ὑμιν και εἰρηνη πληθυνθειη, και ἡ ἀγαπη του θεου εἰη ἐπι πασι τοις πιστευουσιν ἐν αὐτῳ.	May God himself sanctify you and comfort your hearts. Grace and peace be multiplied to you, and may the love of God be upon all who believe in him.
2. ἠθελησεν ὁ Παυλος, εἰ δυνατον εἰη αὐτῳ, την ἡμεραν της Πεντηκοστης γενεσθαι εἰς Ἱεροσολυμα.	Paul wished, if it should be possible for him, to be in Jerusalem on the day of Pentecost.

49.3 Optative mood

Forms like

δῳη – may he give
λογισθειη – may it be reckoned
ὀναιμην – may I be profited
στηριξαι – may he strengthen

ἐπιτιμησαι – may he rebuke
φαγοι – may he eat
γενοιτο – may it happen

are called *optative*.

They do not occur very often in the New Testament. They are marked by οι, ει, or αι before or in the ending.

The optative is used

1. To express a wish:

Mk 11.14   Μηκετι εἰς τον αἰωνα ἐκ σου μηδεις καρπον **φαγοι**
            May no one ever again eat fruit from you for ever.

2. To express a condition when the outcome is considered unlikely:

1 Pet 3.17   εἰ **θελοι** το θελημα του θεου
              If the will of God should so will
         or If God should want it to be so

1 Pet 3.14   ἀλλ' εἰ και **πασχοιτε** δια δικαιοσυνην...
              But if you should suffer because of righteousness...

3. To express a hesitant question:

Acts 8.31   Πως γαρ ἀν **δυναιμην**;
             For how could I?

Lk 6.11   διελαλουν προς ἀλληλους τί ἀν **ποιησαιεν** τῳ Ἰησου
             They discussed with each other what they should do to Jesus

Lk 22.23   και αὐτοι ἠρξαντο συζητειν προς ἑαυτους το τίς ἀρα **ειη** ἐξ αὐτων ὁ τουτο μελλων πρασσειν
             They began to ask themselves which of them it could be who was about to do this.

49.4 Ways of linking words and parts of sentences together

1. **και...και...** – both...and... :

Mk 7.37   Καλως παντα πεποιηκεν, και τους κωφους ποιει ἀκουειν και τους ἀλαλους λαλειν
He has done all things well, he both makes the deaf to hear and the dumb to speak.

2. **...τε και...** – both...and... :

Mt 22.10   συνηγαγον παντας οὑς εὑρον πονηρους τε και ἀγαθους
They gathered together all whom they had found, both bad and good

Jn 2.15   παντας ἐξεβαλεν ἐκ του ἱερου τα τε προβατα και τους βοας
He drove them all out of the Temple, both the sheep and the cattle.

3. **οἱ μεν...οἱ δε...** – some...others...
   οἱ μεν...ἀλλοι δε... – some...others... :

Acts 14.4   οἱ μεν ἠσαν συν τοις Ἰουδαιοις, οἱ δε συν τοις ἀποστολοις
Some were with the Jews, others with the apostles

1 Cor 7.7   ὁ μεν οὑτως, ὁ δε οὑτως
One man in this way, another man in another way

Jn 7.12   οἱ μεν ἐλεγον ὁτι Ἀγαθος ἐστιν, ἀλλοι δε ἐλεγον, Οὑ
Some said, "He is a good man," but others said, "No!"

4. **μενουν** or **μενουνγε** – no, rather; on the contrary:

Lk 11.28   μενουν μακαριοι οἱ ἀκουοντες τον λογον του θεου
No, happy are those who hear the word of God
     or Rather, blessed are those who listen to God's word.

5. **μεν οὐν** – so, so then, however:

Heb 9.1   Εἰχε μεν οὑν και ἡ πρωτη...
So then the first also had...

Acts 25.4   ὁ μεν οὑν Φηστος ἀπεκριθη...
However Festus answered...

6. **οὐ μονον...ἀλλα και...** – not only...but also... :

Jn 5.18   ὁτι οὐ μονον ἐλυεν το σαββατον, ἀλλα και πατερα ἰδιον ἐλεγεν τον θεον
Because he was not only breaking the Sabbath but was also calling God his own father

2 Tim 4.8   ὃν ἀποδωσει μοι...οὐ μονον δε ἐμοι ἀλλα και πασι τοις
ἠγαπηκοσι την ἐπιφανειαν αὐτου
Which he will give to me...and not to me only but also to
all those who have loved his appearing.

7. μεν...δε... (see also no.3)

When two ideas or words are compared or contrasted they are often
linked by μεν... and δε.... In English we often use "but" for δε. We do not
have a word which quite corresponds to μεν. "On the one hand" and
"on the other hand" are rather too weighty for μεν and δε.

Heb 1.7–8   και προς μεν τους ἀγγελους λεγει...προς δε τον υἱον...
To the angels he says..., but to the Son...

Mt 9.37   Ὁ μεν θερισμος πολυς, οἱ δε ἐργαται ὀλιγοι
The harvest is great, but the workers are few

1 Cor 1.12   Ἐγω μεν εἰμι Παυλου, Ἐγω δε Ἀπολλω
"I am Paul's man," "But I am of Apollos".

49.5 Words

φρονεω – I think of, I have in my mind, my attitude is
ἐπιτιμαω – I rebuke (with dative); I warn (with ἱνα – that)
ὁ πρεσβυτερος – the elder, the older man
ὁ νεωτερος – the younger
φρονιμος – wise, sensible
ὑπερηφανος – proud
σοφος – wise
      ἡ σοφια – wisdom
μωρος – foolish
ὑψοω – I exalt, I make high
      ὑψιστος – highest
ταπεινοω – I humble, I make low

49.6

Read carefully:

Different attitudes: old and humble, young and proud
ἐν δε ταυταις ταις ἡμεραις ἀλλοι ἀνθρωποι ἀλλον τι φρονουσιν. οἱ μεν γαρ εἰσιν
φρονιμοι παρ' ἑαυτοις και ὑψουσιν ἑαυτους, οἱ δε ἀλλοι ταπεινουσιν ἑαυτους και
οὐχ ὑπερηφανοι εἰσιν ἐν ταις καρδιαις αὐτων. εὑρισκομεν γαρ ἐν ἡμιν ὁτι οἱ μεν
πρεσβυτεροι οὐχ ὑπερηφανοι εἰσιν οὐδε θελουσιν ἑαυτους ὑψουν, οἰδασιν γαρ
ὁτι κακα τε και πονηρα ἐργα πεποιηκασιν· οἱ δε νεωτεροι οὐ το αὐτο φρονουσιν,
ὁτι σοφοι εἰσιν παρ' ἑαυτοις, ἀλλα οὐ παρα θεῳ. μενουνγε μωροι εἰσιν παρα

49.6

θεῳ, καθως γεγραπται,

Ἡ γαρ σοφια του κοσμου μωρια παρα θεῳ,

και παλιν,

Ὁστις δε ὑψωσει ἑαυτον ταπεινωθησεται και ὁστις ταπεινωσει ἑαυτον ὑψωθησεται.

οἱ μεν οὖν νεωτεροι ὑπερηφανοι εἰσιν, ἐαν δε οἱ πρεσβυτεροι ἐπιτιμωσιν αὐτοις οὐ χαιρουσιν ἐπι τοις λογοις αὐτων οὐδε θελουσιν αὐτων ἀκουειν. μακαριοι εἰσιν οἱ νεωτεροι· μενουν μακαριοι οἱ πρεσβυτεροι.

49.7 δεδωκει – he had given

Compare:

(a) Mk 14.44   **δεδωκει** δε ὁ παραδιδους αὐτον συσσημον αὐτοις
                The man who was betraying him had given them a signal

(b) 1 Jn 3.1   ἰδετε ποταπην ἀγαπην **δεδωκεν** ἡμιν ὁ πατηρ
             See what great love the Father has given us.

In (b), **δεδωκεν** (he has given), is perfect tense. It refers to a past action which has a continuing result ⊣⊦: God showed his love, and goes on loving us.

In (a), **δεδωκει** (he had given), is *pluperfect* tense. It refers to a past action which had a result, but that result is now also in the past ⊣⊦⊦: Judas had told them the sign; the result was that they could recognize the sign. When Mark told the story, that recognition was also in the past.

The marks of the pluperfect active are:

1. ε before the stem
2. the repetition of the initial consonant before the ε
3. κ between stem and ending
4. endings -ειν, -εις, -ει, -ειμεν, -ειτε, -εισαν
5. sometimes ε before repeated initial consonant (see below, Luke 11.22, ἐπεποιθει).

Note that the first three are also marks of the perfect active.

Where a perfect form has a present meaning the pluperfect form covers all past meanings:

οἰδα – I know   ἠδειν – I knew, I had known
ἑστηκα – I stand   ἑστηκειν or εἱστηκειν – I was standing, I stood
πεποιθα – I trust   ἐπεποιθειν – I trusted, I relied, I had trusted

Lk 11.22   την πανοπλιαν αὐτου αἱρει ἐφ᾽ ᾗ **ἐπεποιθει**
        He takes from him all the weapons on which he relied.

264

Note also the pluperfect passive:

Mt 7.25   *τεθεμελιωτο γαρ ἐπι την πετραν*
For it had been founded on the rock.

49.8

Revise lessons 43 and 44.

LESSON 50

ἱνα ἡ χαρα ὑμων ἡ πεπληρωμενη ACKP...

50.1 Writing books by hand

Before the printing press was developed in the fifteenth century AD, books were written by hand. If another copy of a book was needed, someone had to copy it out by hand.

If twenty people each copied out two or three pages of this book, one can be sure that several of them would make some mistakes. If from one of those copies someone else made another copy, that second copy would be likely to contain: (a) the mistakes made by the first copier; and (b) some mistakes made by the second copier.

Each book of the New Testament was written by hand, either by the author or by a scribe who helped him as a secretary. When the person or congregation to whom it was first written wanted others to be able to read it, they had copies made. As the Church spread, more and more copies were made. We call these hand-written copies of books *manuscripts* (MSS for short).

None of the original manuscripts of the New Testament books have survived. The earliest complete MSS of the New Testament that we have date from the fourth century AD.

50.2. Early translations

As the Church spread from Palestine into Syria, Asia Minor, Europe and North Africa, Christians began to want copies of New Testament books in their own languages. So the New Testament was translated into various languages in Egypt, Syria, Italy, and other lands. These early translations we call *versions*.

50.3 Sermons, commentaries, and books

In the early centuries of the Church's growth, Church leaders and thinkers wrote many letters, sermons, commentaries on the New Testament, and other books. In them they often quoted from their text or version of the New Testament. So they can be helpful to us in our study of the text of the New Testament. We call these writers the *Fathers*.

50.4 Mistakes in MSS

All the MSS we have contain mistakes. Fortunately the mistakes seldom affect the main point of any story or doctrine. When there are differences between what one MS says and what another says, we refer to them as different *readings*. When there are different readings we want to find out, if we can, what the author originally wrote. We ask ourselves questions about the variant readings. Here are some of the questions we may want to ask:

>Which reading makes better sense?
>Which one is supported by the earliest MSS?
>Which one is found in MSS in the largest number of
>geographical areas?
>Which one seems to have been used by the early translators?
>Which ones are quoted by the early Fathers?
>Which reading shows the kind of language or thought which fits
>the rest of the author's writings?

When we have studied widely and thought deeply, we will decide what we think the author wrote.

For a list of the main MSS, versions, and Fathers, see *The Greek New Testament* (Third Corrected Edition) (United Bible Societies, 1983) pp. xii-xli.

In 50.5–8, we will look at a few textual problems where what we have already learned may help us to decide which reading to adopt.

50.5 John 1.18

θεον ουδεις εωρακεν πωποτε· μονογενης υιος (or θεος) ὁ ὢν εἰς τον κολπον του πατρος ἐκεινος ἐξηγησατο.

Some of the early MSS read μονογενης θεος or ὁ μονογενης θεος. They are supported by one or two early translations and several of the Fathers. Most of the MSS, versions, and Fathers support the reading ὁ μονογενης υἱος. Which do we think John originally wrote?

The number of MSS, etc., that support a reading helps us very little. If I make a mistake in copying something and a hundred people copy from me, it is still a mistake. If one other person has made a correct copy, that will be right, even though the numbers are 101 to 1. Nor can the age of the MSS alone tell us which is right. If a mistake was made, let us suppose, in a copy made about AD 100, it will still be a mistake if it is found in an "early" manuscript copied about AD 350. But if we find two readings which for other reasons seem equally possible, then we are likely to choose the one that has the earliest MS support.

In John 1.18 we have to ask ourselves, was John likely to write:
(a) "No one has ever seen God: the only begotten God who is close to the Father's heart has declared him" *or*
(b) "No one has ever seen God: the only begotten Son who is close to the Father's heart has declared him" (or we might translate ἐξηγήσατο as "has made him known").

(b) makes better sense (see lesson 46.7). When we study the other passages in which John uses μονογενης (John 3.16, 18) we see that he uses it with υἱος, and in John 1.14 μονογενης παρα πατρος naturally implies the idea of sonship. So the way John uses μονογενης confirms what seems the more logical reading. Why, then, did the editors of the Greek New Testament (UBS 3rd Edition) adopt the alternative reading θεος? Partly because it is found in two papyrus fragments (p⁶⁶ and p⁷⁵) which are among our earliest witnesses to the gospel text. The other reason sounds strange at first, but it illustrates a fundamental principle of textual criticism. They preferred θεος because it is the "more difficult reading", the one which fits less well with John's usual way of writing. The argument is this: if John wrote θεος, a scribe would be strongly tempted to change to υἱος, but if John wrote υἱος, it is hard to explain how the alternative reading originated.

Although this kind of reasoning is important, I think that in this particular case it leads to a false conclusion. If John wrote θεος, it is hard to see what the sentence as a whole would mean. We will prefer the reading ὁ μονογενης υἱος.

50.6 Mark 15.8

ἀναβας ὁ ὀχλος – ℵBD, Latin, and Coptic versions
ἀναβοησας ὁ ὀχλος – most MSS and versions.

Did the crowd "come up" or "shout out"? In verse 13 Mark says οἱ δε παλιν ἐκραξαν (they shouted again). Study Mark's use of παλιν. He seems to use it carefully. If we read ἀναβοησας, there is a mention of shouting for παλιν to refer back to. If we read ἀναβας, the παλιν has nothing to refer back to.

Now study the use of ἀναβαινω in the New Testament, and especially in Mark. Mark uses it of people moving, and he uses it with ἐκ, εἰς, or προς, to show the place someone goes up from, or up to. He never has any use of ἀναβαινω like the English idiom, "I went up to him and said...". In Mark 15.8 there is no mention of a place, and no ἐκ, εἰς, or προς. For the English idiom of going up to someone, Mark uses προσελθων. So when we look at the usage of ἀναβαινω, it confirms what we have seen from our study of παλιν. It does not seem likely that Mark wrote ἀναβας. In my view, it is probable that he wrote ἀναβοησας. Many recent translations, however, are based on the reading ἀναβας. The editors of the UBS 3rd Edition Greek text note that there is no other occurrence of ἀναβοαω in Mark, while ἀναβαινειν occurs nine times. This is true, but does not prove anything – Mark could have used ἀναβοαω here and nowhere else in the Gospel. And the fact that several scholars agree on a reading does not necessarily mean that they are right. In matters of textual criticism it is rarely possible to be completely certain of the original reading. In each case we should carefully weigh the evidence before making our choice, and not simply accept what others have decided.

50.7 1 John 1.4

και ταυτα γραφομεν ἡμεις, ἱνα ἡ χαρα ὑμων (or ἡμων) ᾖ πεπληρωμενη.

Did John write:

(a) "We write these things so that your joy may be full" *or*
(b) "We write these things so that our joy may be full"?

The reading (a) ὑμων (of you), is found in A and C (fifth century MSS), K and P (ninth—tenth century MSS) and most other MSS and versions. The reading (b) ἡμων (of us), is found in ℵ and B (both fourth century MSS), in L (ninth century) and one Latin version.

One learned New Testament commentator said, "A positive decision on the reading here is impossible". Most recent commentators and translators have chosen reading (b) – "our joy". They believe that "our joy" could have been changed to "your joy"; the opposite change is less likely. In my view, however, "your joy" is the best reading.

Notice first that John does not say γραφομεν (we write) but γραφομεν ἡμεις (**we** write). Look at 1 John 3.14, 16, and 1 John 4.6, 10, 14, 16, 17, and 19. John uses this emphatic ἡμεις to point a contrast with another person or group. So after the emphatic ἡμεις in 1 John 1.4, we expect mention of another person or group: ἡ χαρα ὑμων fits John's use of language; ἡ χαρα ἡμων does not.

Notice also that John here speaks of his purpose in writing. Study 1 John 2.1, 7–14, and 5.13. His purpose is expressed in terms of the people for whom he is writing. Study in the Johannine writings also John 20.30–31, 15.11, 16.24. When the purpose of writing or of Jesus in speaking is mentioned, it is always so that someone else may benefit – the readers or the hearers. This adds to the likelihood that John wrote ἡ χαρα ὑμων and not ἡ χαρα ἡμων (see J H Dobson, "Emphatic personal pronouns in the New Testament", in *The Bible Translator*, April 1971, pp. 58–60).

50.8 Mark 1.41

και σπλαγχνισθεις ἐκτεινας την χειρα αὐτου ἡψατο και λεγει αὐτῳ, Θελω, καθαρισθητι·

All the MSS except one read σπλαγχνισθεις (moved by compassion). But D (a fifth century MS) has ὀργισθεις (moved by anger). The NEB translators preferred the reading ὀργισθεις, and comment: "It appeared more probable that ὀργισθεις...would have been changed to σπλαγχνισθεις than that the alteration should have been in the other direction".

What can we say about this from our study of New Testament Greek? σπλαγχνισθεις is an aorist participle (and so is ὀργισθεις). It stands in the sentence without a noun or pronoun. If we study this kind of use of an aorist participle in the New Testament, especially where the participle expresses a feeling, we shall make certain discoveries:

(a) in a phrase like ἀποκριθεις εἰπεν the action described by the aorist participle finds its natural completion or expression in the action of the verb (εἰπεν),

(b) this is particularly noticeable where the aorist participle expresses feeling.

Study the use of ὀργισθεις in Matthew 18.34 and Luke 14.21. In Matthew 18.34, the handing over of the man to the torturers is a natural outcome of the master's anger. In Luke 14.21–24, the gathering in of people so that there would be no room for those who had refused was a natural result of the man's anger. Study the use of σπλαγχνισθεις in Matthew 18.27, 20.34, and Mark 9.22. In each case the act of forgiving, healing, or helping, is a natural outcome and expression of compassion.

So when we consider Mark 1.41, we find that the evidence of all the MSS except one is supported by the way the gospel writers use the aorist participles σπλαγχνισθεις and ὀργισθεις, for the act of healing the leper can be seen as a natural result of compassion, but not a natural outcome of anger. We should almost certainly read σπλαγχνισθεις.

What should we say about the point made by the NEB translators? As well as what we have said above, we might also ask them to consider:

1. that manuscript D contains a large number of errors,

2. that in Mark 1.43 there is an unusual word ἐμβριμησαμενος (warn sternly). It is possible that someone tried to explain this by writing ὀργισθεις in the margin of his manuscript, and that a later scribe wrongly inserted it in 1.41.

50.9 Textual criticism and the translator

When we are translating the New Testament, we shall sometimes need to study carefully what textual critics have said about the text. We will not always be able to be certain which is the correct reading. If the difference between two possible readings seems to make a real difference to the meaning of the passage, we may need to put the alternative in a footnote.

Textual criticism is a task that demands years of study and familiarity with the language of the New Testament and the manuscripts and versions. We must, in general, respect the opinions of other scholars when we see that they are mostly in agreement, unless we can find clear and compelling evidence which they appear to have overlooked. Never forget that we are trying to find out what the original author is most likely to have written. We never simply ask, "Which reading is supported by most MSS, or most editors, or most translators?"

We are fortunate that the text of the New Testament rests on far more manuscripts than the text of any other ancient Greek book. But while this gives us a general confidence, it sometimes makes the study of variant readings very complicated.

Students who wish to learn more about New Testament textual studies are advised to study:

Bruce M Metzger, *A textual commentary on the Greek New Testament* (UBS, 1971).

F G Kenyon, *The text of the Greek Bible* (Third Edition) (Duckworth, 1975).

K Aland and B Aland, *The text of the New Testament* (Eerdmans, 1987).

50.10

Revise lessons 45 and 46.

LESSON 51

Culture and translation

In this lesson we look at a few examples of passages where the translator needs to understand aspects of the culture of Palestine in New Testament times, and to think carefully about the cultures of those who will use the translation.

51.1 Matthew 20.13

οὐχι **δηναριου** συνεφωνησας μοι;
You agreed with me for a denarius, didn't you?

In Matthew 20.1–16, there is a parable about men working in a vineyard. Each one was paid a denarius. This was a Roman coin – and an adequate daily wage. The AV translated it as "a penny". Maybe in AD 1611 this was a reasonable translation. In England towards the end of the twentieth century a reasonable day's wage might be about £30. But if inflation continues, that too may become out of date as a day's wage. So in translating δηναριον we might use "a day's wage" as the nearest useful equivalent. Compare:
NEB "the usual day's wage" and "a full day's wage"
GNB "the regular wage, a silver coin" and "a silver coin".

In translating passages which refer to money, quantities, and distances, we always need to think carefully about their cultural setting. A particular problem arises when the numbers are symbolic. In Revelation 21.16, for example, the symbolic meanings of 12 and 1,000 are lost if we convert the distances simply into 2,400 kilometres (see lesson 39.8).

51.2 Mark 7.27–28

τα **κυναρια** ὑποκατω της τραπεζης.

In Greek κυων means "dog" or "cur". In Palestine, dogs were scavengers, as they still are in many parts of the world. In Revelation 22.15, they are a symbol for perverts and criminals. No one would have wanted a dog in his home.

κυναριον means "puppy" (a young, little dog). In Palestine young puppies were sometimes kept in the home as pets. In Matthew's account, when Jesus spoke to the woman he did not use the word κυων. He used the word κυναριον. GNB and NEB both translate κυναριον as "dogs". Our knowledge of Palestinian culture confirms that "little puppies" would be a much better translation.

All passages that have to do with animals demand particular care from the translator, since the cultural background against which people experience animals varies so much.

51.3 Luke 14.12

Ὅταν ποιῃς **ἀριστον** ἢ δειπνον.

The people of Palestine used to eat only two main meals: a breakfast in the early morning and an evening meal about sunset. We might therefore translate Luke 14.12: "Whenever you make a breakfast or a dinner". But Jesus is talking about meals to which visitors are invited. In England we seldom invite people to breakfast. The nearest cultural equivalent of ἀριστον here is "lunch". So the NEB translates, "Whenever you give a lunch or dinner party". But in any country where people eat only in the morning and evening we might translate, "Whenever you invite people to breakfast or dinner", or "When you make a special meal for people in the morning or the evening".

Passages which concern meals, greetings, weddings, and household customs demand special care from the translator (see also lesson 39.1, section 7, on Mark 2.19, and 51.4–6, following).

51.4 Matthew 9.2

προσεφερον αὐτῳ παραλυτικον ἐπι **κλινης** βεβλημενον
People were bringing to him a paralysed man lying on a κλινη.

How should we translate κλινη? GNB and NEB both have "bed". For English readers this may produce a picture of men struggling to carry a bedstead. Most of our beds are quite heavy. In Palestine people slept on a thin mattress, rather like a quilt. This is what Matthew means by κλινη. It would be better to translate "lying on a thin mattress" than "lying on a bed".

51.5 Mark 8.26

και ἀπεστειλεν αὐτον εἰς οἰκον αὐτου λεγων, Μηδε εἰς την κωμην εἰσελθῃς
He sent him home saying, "And do not go into the village".

Look at the Critical Apparatus at the foot of the page in your Greek New Testament. You will see the MSS contain several variations of reading.

As Mark told the story, are we to suppose that Jesus told the man not to go into the village? (See RSV and GNB, based on the text above.) Or did he tell the man not to speak to anyone in the village? (See NEB, preferring the reading Μηδενι εἰπῃς εἰς την κωμην.) Here is a problem where textual and linguistic study needs to be combined with cultural knowledge.

People in Palestine lived in walled towns (πολεις) or in villages (κωμαι) with the houses closely grouped together. So when we read a text which says, "He sent him home saying, 'Do not go into the village' ", we are aware that there is a problem. How can a man go home without going into a village?

When we read the NEB text, "He sent him home saying, 'Do not speak to anyone in the village' ", we see some arguments for it. Mark's

Gospel is full of parallelism. Here he uses the two-stage opening of the man's eyes as a parallel to the opening of the minds of the disciples (verses 27–30). That story ends with strict instructions, ἵνα μηδενι λεγωσιν περι αὐτου. This makes Μηδενι εἴπῃς εἰς την κωμην look like a suitable ending for verse 26.

But now study in the New Testament the uses of ἀπεστειλεν...λεγων and ἀποστελλει...και λεγει. See, for example, Matthew 21.1–2, ἀπεστειλεν δυο μαθητας λεγων αὐτοις Πορευεσθε εἰς την κωμην, and Mark 11.1–2, ἀποστελλει...και λεγει αὐτοις Ὑπαγετε.... It looks as if when ἀποστελλω is used with λεγει, it is followed by ·a verb telling someone to go. Commands like "Don't speak to anyone" are more likely to be introduced by forms of ἐπιτιμαω or παραγγελλω.

It looks as if Mark might have written something like: "He sent him home saying, 'Go home, but do not speak to anyone in the village' ". One MS, D, reads, ...λεγων Ὑπαγε εἰς τον οἶκον σου και μηδενι εἴπῃς εἰς την κωμην. Although D is a manuscript with many errors, it might be that in this verse it preserves the original text.

51.6 Matthew 21.16

Ἐκ στοματος νηπιων και θηλαζοντων
Out of the mouth of children and sucklings.

νηπιος means a child of any age less than adult. θηλαζω means, "I suck at the breast". In Palestine, besides receiving other food, boys were often suckled at the breast until the age of four or five. Children of such an age are well able to speak and sing. In many modern cultures children are weaned before they can express themselves much in speech or song. If we translate θηλαζοντες as "sucklings" or "babes at the breast", we shall cause a misunderstanding. We might translate the phrase: "Out of the mouth of young children".

51.7 Luke 24.30

λαβων τον ἀρτον εὐλογησεν
Having taken the loaf εὐλογησεν.

How should we translate εὐλογησεν? As "he blessed", or as "he said the blessing", or as "he gave thanks"? In English families if a prayer is said before a meal, people are more likely to thank God for the food than to bless God for the food. In a Jewish family one is more likely to bless God. So far as we can tell, Jesus would probably have said a prayer in which he blessed God as the giver of food: "Blessed art thou, O Lord God...".

We have a twofold problem when we translate εὐλογεω in the New Testament when it concerns food. If we translate it as "give thanks" we leave out the aspect of blessing. But if we translate it as "bless" or "say the blessing" we may give the impression that the speaker blessed the food. In the New Testament εὐλογεω is used of God blessing people, and of people blessing God as the giver of things, not for the blessing of things.

In Luke 24.30 we might translate λαβων τον ἀρτον εὐλογησεν as "He took the loaf and blessed God", but in doing so we should be aware that this reflects a Jewish custom and may seem strange to many readers. It is partly the difficulty of translating from one language and culture to another that encourages people to read the New Testament in Greek.

51.8 Customs, culture, and translation

If we are to translate the New Testament effectively, we need to understand not only the culture of the people of Palestine at the time the New Testament was written, but also the culture of the people for whom we translate. In one Micronesian area people consider it very funny to see a person speaking with his mouth wide open. So a literal translation of Matthew 5.2, ἀνοιξας το στομα αὐτου ἐδιδασκεν αὐτους, would make them laugh. They need, as we do in English, a translation which says, "He began to teach them".

For further study of the problems of customs, culture, and translation, see E A Nida, *Customs, Culture and Christianity* (American Edition: Harper and Brothers, 1954; British Edition: Tyndale Press, 1963).

51.9

Revise lessons 47 and 48.

LESSON 52

Ἀγωμεν ἐντευθεν – Let us go on from here

52.1

In *Learn New Testament Greek* you have laid a basic foundation for reading and studying the Greek New Testament, and for translating it. But in the study of language this saying becomes true: ὁστις γαρ ἐχει, δοθησεται αὐτῳ και περισσευθησεται· ὁστις δε οὐκ ἐχει, και ὁ ἐχει ἀρθησεται ἀπ' αὐτου.

If we are not to lose the knowledge and skills we have gained, we must use them and add to them.

Nothing can take the place of a short time each day in which we read some of the New Testament in Greek. John's Epistles, John's Gospel, and Mark's Gospel are perhaps the books to read first. In this lesson we consider some books that you may find useful in your further studies, and some ways in which your knowledge of New Testament Greek may prove stimulating or useful.

52.2 A basic library for the reader and translator of the New Testament

The following books are essential:

1. *A text of the New Testament: Η ΚΑΙΝΗ ΔΙΑΘΗΚΗ*
Two editions are widely used and recommended at the time of going to press: Nestlé-Aland 26th Edition and UBS 3rd Edition (Corrected). UBS 3 has the same text as Nestlé-Aland 26, but a different apparatus. It cites fewer variant readings but gives more detailed evidence for those cited. Both Nestlé-Aland 26 and UBS 3 are available in a variety of bindings.

2. *A lexicon or dictionary of New Testament Greek*
Lexicons range from the pocket-sized to the very large. Useful for beginners is B M Newman (Ed.), *A Concise Greek-English Dictionary of the New Testament*. It is published by UBS (1971) and available either separately or bound together with the UBS 3rd Edition New Testament. For detailed study you will probably need to refer to a large lexicon, such as *A Greek-English Lexicon of the New Testament and other early Christian literature*, edited by W Bauer (translated W F Arndt and F W Gingrich) 2nd Revised Edition, published by Zondervan, 1979; or *A Greek-English Lexicon*, edited by H C Liddell and R Scott, 9th Edition, published by OUP, 1968.

For those who are particularly concerned with translating the New Testament, the following books are specially recommended:

The Translator's New Testament (BFBS, 1973).

The Translator's Handbooks and Translator's Guides series (UBS).

E A Nida and C R Taber, *The Theory and Practice of Translation* (E J Brill for UBS, 1969).

E A Nida and Jan de Waard, *From One Language to Another* (Thomas Nelson, 1968).

For advanced study, the following books are recommended:

E G Jay, *New Testament Greek: An Introductory Grammar* (SPCK, 1974).

C F D Moule, *An Idiom-Book of New Testament Greek* (CUP, 1959).

W F Moulton and A S Geden, *A Concordance to the Greek Testament*
(T & T Clark, 1978).

J H Moulton and N Turner, *Grammar of N.T. Greek* (4 vols):
(T & T Clark, 1976).

F Blass and A Debrunner, *A Greek Grammar of the New Testament and
other early Christian literature* (translated R W Funk) (Zondervan,
1959).

R W Funk, *A Beginning – Intermediate Grammar of Hellenistic Greek*
(3 vols: SBL, 1973).

B M Metzger, *Lexical Aids for Students of N.T. Greek* (Blackwell, 1980).

B M Metzger, *A Textual Commentary on the Greek N.T.* (companion to
UBS Greek N.T., Third Edition) (UBS, 1971).

52.3 Using a lexicon – a Greek dictionary

Make sure that you have learned by heart the order of the letters in the
Greek alphabet (see 16.2). This will help you to find the words in the
lexicon.

Most words are easy to find. The problem is with verbs. If you want to
find the meaning of αἱρομεν it is fairly easy to remember that the 1st
person sing. pres. indic. is αἱρω. If we want to look up ἠραν or ἁρας we
must remember that they are forms of αἱρω. If the verbal form has an
augment, that is an ε before the stem, remember that the stem will
follow the augment. So for πεπιστευκα we look up πιστευω. For ἠκουσεν
we look up ἀκουω, and for ἠγειρεν we look up ἐγειρω. Where a verb
begins with a preposition, remember that the augment normally comes
after the preposition, and if the preposition ends in a vowel, that vowel
will probably be changed. So for προσεκυνησαν we look up προσκυνεω,
and for ἐπεθυμησαν we look up ἐπιθυμεω.

B M Newman, *A Concise Greek-English Dictionary of the New
Testament*, gives help with irregular and unusual verb forms.

52.4 Reading the New Testament in Greek

When we can read the New Testament easily in Greek without needing to stop constantly to use a dictionary, it can bring us a feeling of being drawn closer to the actual people and events. There will also be an opportunity to understand some passages better than we can do in a translation. For example, in John 3, ἀνωθεν covers an area of meaning which includes "from above" and "again". A translator usually has to choose one of these meanings and ignore the other. In John's Gospel, when we read σημειον we shall know that it is both a miraculous sign and a meaningful miracle.

52.5 Translation

The skill you have been learning will prove useful, whether or not you become directly involved in the work of Bible translation. You are now able to assess existing translations; to ask "Does this express the meaning (not necessarily the words) of the original?" or "Can this be understood clearly by those who will read it?" These critical skills will be useful whenever you are using language.

52.6 Preaching

Some of us who are readers and translators of the New Testament will also be preachers. Our efforts to learn New Testament Greek may help us in a variety of ways.

In translating we have learned to consider carefully the cultural situation of the first readers and also the cultural situation of the people who may hear or read our translation. This discipline should help us in sermon preparation to think carefully how to make the Good News we preach relevant to people in the circumstances in which they live today.

If we have found some of the strange grammatical terms in this course hard to understand (aorist, infinitive, consecutive and final clauses...), then we may understand better how hard it is for ordinary people to understand a sermon if it is full of words like justification, sanctification, Trinitarianism, or even references to the Greek text!

Our efforts to understand the Greek text clearly enough to translate it may also aid us to preach clearly from it. For example, in Ephesians 2.8–9 we will notice: (1) that Paul speaks of our salvation as being (a) οὐκ ἐξ ὑμων, and (b) οὐκ ἐξ ἐργων.

This will suggest two themes that may be developed in part of our sermon: (a) that we are not saved as a result of anything that we are (character, position in society or church, inherited nature, developed talents, faith), and (b) that we are not saved by anything we have done (kindness to people, service to God, achievements).

We will notice: (2) that Paul says we are saved χαριτι. Our understanding of χαρις as free unmerited love will help us to see that Paul means that God saves us because he loves us freely. He does *not* mean that he has first given us something that could be called "grace" and then saves us because we have grace.

So our study of New Testament Greek should help us to preach clearly from the New Testament, and hopefully will help us to avoid words that people cannot understand.

52.7 New Testament Greek and theology

There are many problems discussed by theologians and by the supporters of various sects where a knowledge of New Testament Greek may be of help to us.

Theologians have argued whether the first Christian message was: (1) God's Kingdom is now present, or (2) God's Kingdom lies in the future but will soon come.

So far as Mark 1.14 is concerned, the argument is whether ἠγγικεν means: (1) "has arrived" (J B Phillips), or (2) "is at hand" (RSV).

In fact, it is a perfect tense and means, "it has come near". A perfect tense indicates a past action with a continuing result. Because it has come near, people can already respond to it. The emphasis is on present nearness rather than on future arrival. But because "it has come near" is not precisely the same in meaning as "it has already arrived", it is possible that the completion of its arrival might yet lie in the future. Perhaps the appropriate question to ask about the Kingdom in Mark 1.14 is not a question about the time of its arrival, but about how one can respond to what is already near.

Some theologians have argued that the gospels show that Jesus expected his return to be soon. If we read Mark 13.30–32 carefully in the Greek text, we will notice a contrast between ταυτα (**these** things) and ἡ ἡμερα ἐκεινη (**that** day). The destruction of the Temple was to be within one generation, but the time of Christ's return was unknown. If we can trust the evidence of Mark 13 and some of the parables, Jesus did not expect his return to be soon. Of course, an attentive reading of a good translation will also show this, but it is sometimes the careful attention to the Greek text necessary for the task of translation that makes us more sharply aware of what it actually says.

You may hear people argue that the first Christians baptized people *in* water. If you are involved as a New Testament Greek scholar you will at least know that the evidence in the gospels points to baptism *with* or *by means of* water (ὑδατι, or ἐν ὑδατι).

You might hear a Mormon argue that Revelation 14.6 is a prophecy about the book of Mormon – you will know that εὐαγγελιον in the New Testament never refers to a book, only to a message that is proclaimed. You might hear a Jehovah's Witness argue that John 1.1 means that "the Word was a god" – you will know that θεος ἦν ὁ λογος means "the Word was God".

The more technical and detailed a discussion of points of New Testament theology becomes, the more likely it is that a theologian will refer to words or passages in the Greek text of the New Testament. Because you have worked through this study course you will be in a position to understand what is being said.

52.8 New Testament Greek, classical Greek, and modern Greek

If you wish to go on to study classical Greek or modern Greek, you will find that this course in New Testament Greek will enable you to understand most of the forms and constructions. It will also help you to use a lexicon to cope with the much greater range of vocabulary.

52.9 Read the New Testament – ἡ καινη διαθηκη

Ἀγαπητοι, πολλοι και ἀλλοι λογοι εἰσιν οἳ οὐκ εἰσιν γεγραμμενοι ἐν τῳ βιβλιῳ τουτῳ. ταυτα δε γεγραπται ἱνα ἀναγινωσκητε την καινην διαθηκην και ἀναγινωσκοντες την ἀληθειαν εὑρισκητε ἐν τῳ Κυριῳ ἡμων Ἰησου Χριστῳ.

Ἀγωμεν ἐντευθεν.

Key to Progress tests

Test 1:   1 (c)   2 (a)   3 (b)   4 (a)   5 (c).

Test 2:   1 (c)   2 (a)   3 (c)   4 (b)   5 (a).

Test 3:   1 (b)   2 (b)   3 (c)   4 (c)   5 (a).

Test 4:   1 (b)   2 (b)   3 (a)   4 (b).

In 1 (a), 2 (a), 3 (b), and 4 (a) the translation follows the Greek order of words too closely.

Test 5:   1 (a)   2 (c)   3 (b)   4 (c)   5 (c)   6 (b)   7 (c)   8 (c).

Test 6:   1. In heaven.   2. God's angel.   3. God's words.
4. She knows that they are true.   5. Luke.   6. We are.
7. The angel's words and Mary's words.
8. Because they are true.
9. He who has the word of God and trusts in Jesus.
10. Those who have the apostle's book and read it.

Test 7:   1 (c)   2 (b)   3 (a)   4 (b)   5 (b).

Test 8:   1 (c)   2 (b)   3 (b)   4 (a)   5 (b).

Test 9:   1 (c)   2 (b)   3 (c).

1 (a), 2 (a), and 3 (a) follow the Greek order of words too closely.

Test 10:   1 (c)   2 (b)   3 (b)   4 (c)   5 (c).

Test 11:   1 (c)   2 (b)   3 (b)   4 (b).

1 (a) and (b), 2 (a), 3 (a) and (c), and 4 (a) follow the Greek order of words too closely. 2 (c) and 4 (c) do not express the meaning of the Greek quite so clearly.

Test 12:   1 (b) (c) (e)   2 (a) (c) (d) (e)   3 (a) (c) (e) (f) (g)
4 (a) (b) (d).

Test 13:   1 (a)   2 (c)   3 (c)   4 (a)   5 (b)   6 (b)   7 (a)
8 (a) (c) (e)   9 (a) (c) (d) (e).

Test 14:   1 (c)   2 (c)   3 (a)   4 (b)   5 (b) (c) (e) (h)
6 (a) (d) (f) (g).

Test 15:   1 (b) (d) (e) (f) (h) (i)   2 (a) (d) (e) (f) (g) (j)
3 (a) (c) (e) (f) (h) (j)   4 (b) (c) (f) (g) (i)   5 (c)   6 (c).

Test 16: 1 (b) 2 (c) 3 (a) 4 (c) 5 (b) 6 (c) 7 (c) 8 (a).

Note on 6 (c). Should we describe ὄντα as being "active"? εἰμι is active in *form* but it has no passive. The ways people use language are so variable that strict grammatical classifications do not always cover the uses adequately. For example, ἐπορευθη (he travelled) is 3rd person singular aorist... of πορευομαι. It is *middle* in meaning and *passive* in form. If we call it aorist *passive* we may cause ourselves confusion. Compare also the use of ἠγερθη for "he rose". We often need to bear in mind this comment: "We grammarians are always trying to bind the free growth of language in a strait waistcoat of necessity, but language laughs and eludes us" (A. Platt).

Test 17: 1 (b) 2 (c) 3 (c) 4 (b) or (c) 5 (a) 6 (d) 7 (b)
8 (c) 9 (a) 10 All of them.

Test 18: 1 (b) 2 (a) 3 (b) 4 (c) 5 (b) or (a) 6 (c).

7. φαυλα, το φως, την ἀληθειαν, πολλα, αὐτον, φανερον, το πλοιον, την ψυχην, αὐτην.

Test 19: 1. ὁ λογος, θεος, οὑτος, παντα, ἐν, ὁ, ἡ ζωη, το φως, ἡ σκοτια.

2. παντα ἀνθρωπον, ἐρχομενον, τον κοσμον, αὐτον, τα ἰδια, ἐξουσιαν, το ὀνομα.

3. αὐτου, των ἀνθρωπων, θεου, του φωτος; αἱματων, θεληματος, σαρκος, ἀνδρος, μονογενους, πατρος, χαριτος, ἀληθειας.

4. ἀρχη, αὐτῳ, τη σκοτια, τῳ κοσμῳ, αὐτοις, τοις πιστευουσιν, ἡμιν.

5. (a) In the beginning. (b) With God. (c) Through him. (d) Without him. (e) In the darkness. (f) About the light (to the light). (g) Into the world. (h) In the world. (i) In the name. (j) From the will (as a result of a decision or wish). (k) Among us.

Test 20: 1 (a) or (c) 2 (a) or (b) 3 (a) or (c) 4 (b) or (c).

Accents

In printed editions of the New Testament you will find three accents, known as acute ´ (for example, τί), grave ` (ὁ) and circumflex ˆ (μενῶ). These accents were not part of the original New Testament text; they appear only in manuscripts from the ninth century onwards. The system was devised by classical Greek writers as an aid to pronunciation, with ´ indicating a high tone, ` a low tone, and ˆ a rising and falling tone.

In a few cases accents distinguish words which would otherwise look the same, e.g. εἰ means "if", but εἶ means "you are". It is possible to read the New Testament without knowing anything more about accents. The rules of accenting are complex, and most students do not need to learn them. For those with a special interest, the following summary provides a basic introduction.

Note that a long syllable is usually one which contains a long vowel (η, ω) or a diphthong. However, both -αι and -οι are regarded as short when they occur at the **end** of a word (so the final syllable is short in λογοι, long in λογοις). On a diphthong it is customary to place the accent over the second vowel (τοῦτο).

Basic rules for accentuation

1. An accent may be placed above **one** of the last **three** syllables of a word (Jn 1.3: πάντα δι᾽ αὐτοῦ ἐγένετο).

2. If the last syllable of a word is **long**, an accent may only be placed above one of the last **two** syllables (πνεύματα, but πνευμάτων).

3. A **circumflex** accent may only be placed above one of the last two syllables of a word, and only over a **long** syllable (δῶμα, δοῦ, Ῥωμαῖοι).

4. In **verbs** an acute accent is placed as far back from the end as rules 1 and 2 allow (δίδωμι, ἐδίδουν). Where a verb is **contracted** (13.1) and the acute accent would have stood on the short contracting vowel it is replaced by a circumflex on the contracted vowel (φιλέ-ω becomes φιλῶ).

5. Apart from rules 1 and 2 there is no rule to show where accents are placed on **nouns**. It is necessary to learn the accent as you learn the word. But note that most frequently a noun keeps its accent on the same syllable in other cases as it is in the nominative case (ἀρχή, ἀρχῆς), unless other rules demand a change (πνεῦμα, πνεύματος – but πνευμάτων [rule 2]).

6. When a word that naturally carries an acute accent on the **last** syllable is followed by another word **in the same clause**, the acute accent is replaced by a grave accent (τοὺς ἀδελφοὺς βλέπω, but βλέπω τοὺς ἀδελφούς.)

7. In normal circumstances a word may carry only one accent. There are, however, a number of short words (for example ἐστι, με, τις, πως) which throw the accent they would have had back onto the word before, when this is possible. For example ἄνθρωπός τις – a certain man, δοῦλός τις – a slave, ἥψατό μού τις – someone touched me (note that the accent from μου has been thrown back onto ἥψατο and the accent from τις onto μου).

Two acute accents may not stand on adjoining syllables. So τόπος τις – a certain place (τόπός is impossible so τις simply loses its accent). But where a **two-syllable** word cannot throw its accent back, it retains it: ἐν τόπῳ τινὶ ἦν – he was in a certain place.

Words that throw back their accents are called *enclitics*.

8. ὁ, ἡ, οἱ, αἱ, εἰς, ἐν, ἐκ, οὐ, ὡς have no accents.

For a more detailed treatment of accentuation, see E G Jay, *N. T. Greek: An Introductory Grammar* (SPCK, 1974) pp. 11–12 and 273–77.

Index of grammar and constructions

1. Grammar

2. Constructions and types of speech

Reference grammar

In the course, grammar is introduced and taught as you need to know it. Because it is taken in step by step, it is possible to learn it without too much stress. This reference grammar should not be used until you have been through the course.

The whole course is designed to lead you into a fruitful way of looking at and understanding Greek words. Experience has shown that to use grammatical terms and lists at an early stage can seriously hinder this process.

When you have worked through the course you will look at a word like ἐποιησαν (ἐ-ποιη-σ-αν), and understand it. You will know at once the significance of ε- and of -σ-, who is indicated by -αν, and the basic meaning of the stem ποιε. If, instead of that, you have developed a habit of thinking, "What tense is it?" you will have hindered your own progress. Also the Greek language is flexible, as most languages are, and any attempt to confine it within the rigid lines of grammatical tables can at certain points cause serious misunderstandings.

Use the reference grammar after you have completed the course, to sharpen your awareness of significant forms and endings. Lessons 5, 12, 14, 20–26, 28, 31–33, 37, 39, 40, 42, 45, and 49 introduce you progressively to the ideas and terms which will enable you to understand and make use of this section.

A summary of types of noun

After the accusative singular only the endings are given. Notice the differences and similarities. In the singular, endings with **-ν** and **-α** are usually accusative; **-ου -ης -ας -ος -ους** are common marks of a genitive. All datives have **ι** in the ending. All genitive plurals end in **-ων**.

	Singular Nom.	Acc.	Gen.	Dat.	*Plural* Nom.	Acc.	Gen.	Dat.
house	ὁ οἶκος	οἰκ-ον	-ου	-ῳ	-οι	-ους	-ων	-οις
work	τὸ ἐργον	ἐργ-ον	-ου	-ῳ	-α	-α	-ων	-οις
prophet	ὁ προφητης	προφητ-ην	-ου	-ῃ	-αι	-ας	-ων	-αις
young man	ὁ νεανιας	νεανι-αν	-ου	-ᾳ	-αι	-ας	-ων	-αις
house	ἡ οἰκια	οἰκι-αν	-ας	-ᾳ	-αι	-ας	-ων	-αις
tongue	ἡ γλωσσα	γλωσσ-αν	-ης	-ῃ	-αι	-ας	-ων	-αις
man	ὁ ἀνηρ	ἀνδρ-α	-ος	-ι	-ες	-ας	-ων	-ασιν
woman	ἡ γυνη	γυναικ-α	-ος	-ι	-ες	-ας	-ων	-(ξ)ιν
star	ὁ ἀστηρ	ἀστερ-α	-ος	-ι	-ες	-ας	-ων	-σιν
fish	ὁ ἰχθυς	ἰχθυ-ν	-ος	-ι	-ες	-ας	-ων	-σιν
guard	ὁ φυλαξ	φυλακ-α	-ος	-ι	-ες	-ας	-ων	-(ξ)ιν
hope	ἡ ἐλπις	ἐλπιδ-α	-ος	-ι				
ruler	ὁ ἀρχων	ἀρχ-οντα	-οντος	-οντι	-οντες	-οντας	-οντων	-ουσι
knee	τὸ γονυ	γον-υ	-ατος	-ατι	-ατα	-ατα	-ατων	-ασι
body	τὸ σωμα	σωμ-α	-ατος	-ατι	-ατα	-ατα	-ατων	-ασιν
nation	τὸ ἐθνος	ἐθν-ος	-ους	-ει	-η	-η	-ων	-εσιν

In books of grammar, nouns like **προφητης, οἰκια, γλωσσα** (dat. pl. **-αις**) are called "first declension".

Nouns like **οἶκος** and **ἐργον** (dat. pl. **-οις**) are called "second declension".

All other nouns are called "third declension".

Note that **ὁ ἀρχων** (the person ruling) is a participle in form.

A summary of adjectives and pronouns

	Singular Nom.	Acc.	Gen.	Dat.	Plural Nom.	Acc.	Gen.	Dat.
m.	καλος	καλ-ον	-ου	-ῳ	-οι	-ους	-ων	-οις
f.	καλη	καλ-ην	-ης	-ῃ	-αι	-ας	-ων	-αις
n.	καλον	καλ-ον	-ου	-ῳ	-α	-α	-ων	-οις
m.	πολυς	πολ-υν	-λου	-λῳ	-λοι	-λους	-λων	-λοις
f.	πολλη	πολ-λην	-λης	-λῃ	-λαι	-λας	-λων	-λαις
n.	πολυ	πολ-υ	-λου	-λῳ	-λα	-λα	-λων	-λοις
m. f.	πλειων	πλει-ονα	-ονος	-ονι	-ονες	-ονας	-ονων	-οσιν
n.	πλειον	πλει-ον	-ονος	-ονι	-ονα	-ονα	-ονων	-οσιν
m. f.	ἀληθης	ἀληθ-η	-ους	-ει	-εις	-εις	-ων	-εσιν
n.	ἀληθες	ἀληθ-ες	-ους	-ει	-η	-η	-ων	-εσιν
m.	λελυκως	λελυκ-οτα	-οτος	-οτι	-οτες	-οτας	-οτων	-οσιν
f.	λελυκυια	λελυκ-υιαν	-υιας	-υιᾳ	-υιαι	-υιας	-υιων	-υιαις
n.	λελυκος	λελυκ-ος	-οτος	-οτι	-οτα	-οτα	-οτων	-οσιν
m.	δοθεις	δοθ-εντα	-εντος	-εντι	-εντες	-εντας	-εντων	-εισιν
f.	δοθεισα	δοθ-εισαν	-εισης	-εισῃ	-εισαι	-εισας	-εισων	-εισαις
n.	δοθεν	δοθ-εν	-εντος	-εντι	-εντα	-εντα	-εντων	-εισιν
m.	οὐδεις	οὐδ-ενα	-ενος	-ενι				
f.	οὐδεμια	οὐδ-εμιαν	-εμιας	-εμιᾳ				
n.	οὐδεν	οὐδ-εν	-ενος	-ενι				
m. f.	τις	τινα	τινος	τινι	τινες	τινας	τινων	τισιν
n.	τι	τι	τινος	τινι	τινα	τινα	τινων	τισιν
m. f.	ἐγω	με	μου	μοι	ἡμεις	ἡμας	ἡμων	ἡμιν
m. f.	συ	σε	σου	σοι	ὑμεις	ὑμας	ὑμων	ὑμιν

Note:
(1) There are no case endings with which you are not already familiar.
(2) Adjectives (e.g. ἀληθης) may have the same form for masculine and feminine.
(3) Adjectives and participles (verbal adjectives) agree in case, number, and gender with the nouns they qualify – e.g. εἰδεν πολυν ὀχλον, εἰδεν την γυναικα ἐρχομενην.

Comparison of adjectives and adverbs

1. Adjectives

The comparative usually ends in **-εροs**, so:

ἰσχυρος – strong   ἰσχυροτερος – stronger, rather strong
σοφος – wise   σοφωτερος – wiser

The superlative usually ends in **-τατος** or **-ιστος**, so:

ὑψηλος – high   ὑψιστος – highest, very high
μεγας – great   μεγιστος – greatest, very great
ἁγιος – holy   ἁγιωτατος – holiest, very holy, most holy

Note particularly:

ἀγαθος – good   κρειττον (κρεισσον) – better
κακος – bad   χειρων – worse
μεγας – great   μειζων – greater   μεγιστος – greatest
πολυς – much   πλειων – more   πλειστος – most
μικρος – little μικροτερος – smaller   ἐλαχιστος – smallest, least

2. Adverbs

ταχυ, ταχεως – quickly   ταχιστα – very quickly
                μαλλον – more, rather   μαλιστα – most, especially
πολυ – much   πλειον – more
ἡδεως – gladly   ἡδιστα – very gladly
ἐυ – well   βελτιον, κρεισσον – in a better way

Note: εἰς το χειρον (ἐλθουσα) – (having become) worse.

A summary of important verbal forms

1. λυω – I untie, I loose, I break. Stem: λυ

Active Indicative	Singular 1st p.	2nd p.	3rd p.	Plural 1st p.	2nd p.	3rd p.
Present ⁓	λυ-ω	-εις	-ει	-ομεν	-ετε	-ουσιν
Future ⊦	λυσ-ω	-εις	-ει	-ομεν	-ετε	-ουσιν
Imperfect ⁓⊦	έλυ-ον	-ες	-εν	-ομεν	-ετε	-ον
Aorist ⊣⊦	έλυσ-α	-ας	-εν	-αμεν	-ατε	-αν
Perfect ⊣⊦	λελυκ-α	-ας	-εν	-αμεν	-ατε	-ασιν
Pluperfect ⊣⊦⊦	λελυκ-ειν	-εις	-ει	-ειμεν	-ειτε	-εισαν
Subjunctive						
Present ⁓	λυ-ω	-ης	-η	-ωμεν	-ητε	-ωσιν
Aorist ·	λυσ-ω	-ης	-η	-ωμεν	-ητε	-ωσιν
Imperative						
Present ⁓	—	λυ-ε	-ετω	—	-ετε	-ετωσαν
Aorist ·	—	λυσ-ον	-ατω	—	-ατε	-ατωσαν
Infinitive						
Present ⁓	λυειν					
Aorist ·	λυσαι					
Participle						
Present ⁓	λυων – λυουσα – λυον					
Aorist ⊣⊦	λυσας – λυσασα – λυσαν					

2. λυομαι – I am untied, I am loosed

Passive Indicative	Singular 1st p.	2nd p.	3rd p.	Plural 1st p.	2nd p.	3rd p.
Present ˉˉˉ	λυ-ομαι	-η	-εται	-ομεθα	-εσθε	-ονται
Future �	λυθησ-ομαι	-η	-εται	-ομεθα	-εσθε	-ονται
Imperfect ˉˉˉ|	ἐλυ-ομην	-ου	-ετο	-ομεθα	-εσθε	-οντο
Aorist ˉ|	ἐλυθ-ην	-ης	-η	-ημεν	-ητε	-ησαν
Perfect ˉ|˖	λελυ-μαι	-σαι	-ται	-μεθα	-σθε	-νται
Pluperfect ˉ|˖|	(ἐ)λελυ-μην	-σο	-το	-μεθα	-σθε	-ντο
Subjunctive						
Present ˉˉˉ	λυ-ωμαι	-η	-ηται	-ωμεθα	-ησθε	-ωνται
Aorist ·	λυθ-ω	-ης	-η	-ωμεν	-ητε	-ωσιν
Imperative						
Present ˉˉˉ	—	λυ-ου	-εσθω	—	-εσθε	-εσθωσαν
Aorist ·	|—	λυθ-ητι	-ητω	—	-ητε	-ητωσαν
Infinitive						
Present ˉˉˉ	λυεσθαι					
Aorist ·	λυθηναι					
Participle						
Present ˉˉˉ	λυομενος – λυομενη – λυομενον					
Aorist ˉ	λυθεις – λυθεισα – λυθεν					

3. νίπτομαι – I wash (part of myself) – Middle

Present, imperfect, perfect, and pluperfect, are the same in middle and passive. Future and aorist have different forms in the middle voice. Note the following:

Middle Indicative	Singular 1st p.	2nd p.	3rd p.	Plural 1st p.	2nd p.	3rd p.
Present ‒‒‒‒	νιπτ-ομαι	-η	-εται	-ομεθα	-εσθε	-ονται
Future ⊢	νιψ-ομαι	-η	-εται	-ομεθα	-εσθε	-ονται
Aorist ‒⫶	ἐνιψ-αμην	-ω	-ατο	-αμεθα	-ασθε	-αντο
Subjunctive						
Aorist ·	νιψ-ωμαι	-η	-ηται	-ωμεθα	-ησθε	-ωνται
Imperative						
Aorist ·	—	νιψ-αι	-ασθω	—	-ασθε	-ασθωσαν

Infinitive	
Present ‒‒‒‒	νιπτεσθαι
Aorist ·	νιψασθαι

Participle	
Present ‒‒‒‒	νιπτομενος – νιπτομενη – νιπτομενον
Aorist ⫶	νιψαμενος – νιψαμενη – νιψαμενον

Note that if you need to be able to parse verbal forms (see 33.11) these tables will assist you in learning. For example, if you wish to parse **λυθησομεθα** (we will be loosed), by looking at (2) **λυομαι** you will see from the column it is in that **λυθησομεθα** is in 1st person plural, and from the section and line that it is future indicative passive. Similarly **νιψαι** (wash!) is 2nd person singular aorist imperative middle.

4. καλεω → καλω; ἀγαπαεις → ἀγαπᾳς; φανεροει → φανεροι

When the stem of a verb ends in a vowel, the vowel combines with the initial vowel of the ending. These verbs have the same endings as **λυω** and **νιπτομαι**, except for the result of the contraction of the vowels. The following table shows the contractions that result from combining vowels e.g. $α + ει = ᾳ$, $ε + ει = ει$, $ο + ει = οι$.

		End of stem		
		α	ε	ο
Verb ending begins	α	α	η	ω
	ε	α	ει	ου
	ει	ᾳ	ει	οι
	ι	αι	ει	οι
	η	α	η	ω
	ῃ	ᾳ	ῃ	οι
	ο	ω	ου	ου
	ου	ω	ου	ου
	οι	ῳ	οι	οι
	ω	ω	ω	ω

5. ἱστημι – I cause to stand, I set, I establish

Note, for example:

Mk 9.36 ἐστησεν αὐτο ἐν μεσῳ αὐτων
He set him in the middle of them
Mk 7.9 ἱνα την παραδοσιν ὑμων στησητε
So that you may establish your tradition.

Active Indicative	Singular 1st p.	2nd p.	3rd p.	Plural 1st p.	2nd p.	3rd p.
Present ⁓	ἱστ-ημι	-ης	-ησι	-αμεν	-ατε	-ασιν
Future ⊢	στησ-ω	-εις	-ει	-ομεν	-ετε	-ουσιν
1st Aorist ⊣	ἐστησ-α	-ας	-εν	-αμεν	-ατε	-αν
Subjunctive 1st Aorist ·	στησ-ω	-ης	-η	-ωμεν	-ητε	-ωσιν

Infinitive
Aorist ·   στησαι (to establish – Rom 10.3)

Note also: σταθησεται – it shall be established.

6. ἑστηκα – I am standing, I stand

Note, for example, Revelation 3.20: ἑστηκα ἐπι την θυραν – I am standing at the door. In the perfect and pluperfect ἱστημι has a middle sense: I have caused myself to stand (that is, I am standing) and I had caused myself to stand (I was standing). ἱστημι also has a second form of the aorist active ἐστην (I stood). The aorist passive ἐσταθην also means "I stood". Note the following forms:

Active Indicative	Singular 1st p.	2nd p.	3rd p.	Plural 1st p.	2nd p.	3rd p.	Meaning (1st p. sing.)
Perfect (Present) ⁓	ἑστηκ-α	-ας	-εν	-αμεν	-ατε	-ασιν	I am standing
Pluperfect (Imperfect) ⁓	εἱστηκ-ειν	-εις	-ει	-ειμεν	-ειτε	-εισαν	I was standing
2nd Aorist ⁓|	ἐστ-ην	-ης	-η	-ημεν	-ητε	-ησαν	I stood

Subjunctive

| 2nd Aorist · | στ-ω | -ης | -η | -ωμεν | -ητε | -ωσιν | |

Imperative   (συ) στηθι   (ὑμεις) στητε – stand!

Infinitive

Aorist ·   στηναι – to stand

Participles

2nd Aorist	στας	στασα	σταν	standing
1st Perfect	ἑστηκως	ἑστηκυια	ἑστηκος	standing
2nd Perfect	ἑστως	ἑστωσα	ἑστος	standing
Aorist Passive	σταθεις	σταθεισα	σταθεν	standing

Note also στησονται – they will stand, ἐσταθην – I stood.

7. Principal parts

From a knowledge of the stem, the present, future, aorist and perfect indicative, and the aorist passive of a verb, it is usually possible to tell the meaning of any form of the verb that is encountered. Note the following:

Meaning	Present	Main stem	Future	Aorist	Perfect	Aorist Passive
untie	λυω	λυ	λυσω	ἐλυσα	λελυκα	ἐλυθην
do	ποιω	ποιε	ποιησω	ἐποιησα	πεποιηκα	ἐποιηθην
love	ἀγαπω	ἀγαπα	ἀγαπησω	ἠγαπησα	ἠγαπηκα	ἠγαπηθην
exalt	ὑψω	ὑψο	ὑψωσω	ὑψωσα	ὑψωκα	ὑψωθην
pick up	αἱρω	ἀρ	ἀρω	ἠρα	ἠρκα	ἠρθην
throw	βαλλω	βαλ/βλη	βαλω	ἐβαλον	βεβληκα	ἐβληθην
write	γραφω	γραψ	γραψω	ἐγραψα	γεγραφα	ἐγραφην
raise	ἐγειρω	ἐγειρ	ἐγερω	ἠγειρα	—	ἠγερθην
judge	κρινω	κριν	κρινῶ	ἐκρινα	κεκρικα	ἐκριθην
go	βαινω	βα/βη	βησομαι	ἐβην	βεβηκα	—
drink	πινω	πι	πιομαι	ἐπιον	πεπωκα	—
fall	πιπτω	πεσ	πεσουμαι	ἐπεσον	πεπτωκα	—
know	γινωσκω	γνο/γνω	γνωσομαι	ἐγνων	ἐγνωκα	ἐγνωσθην
become	γινομαι	γιν/γεν	γενησομαι	ἐγενομην	γεγονα	ἐγενηθην
come, go	ἐρχομαι	ἐρχ/ἐλθ	ἐλευσομαι	ἠλθον	ἐληλυθα	—
put	τιθημι	θε	θησω	ἐθηκα	τεθεικα	ἐτεθην
give	διδωμι	δο	δωσω	ἐδωκα	δεδωκα	ἐδοθην
forgive	ἀφιημι	(ἀπο) ἑ	ἀφησω	ἀφηκα	ἀφεωνται	ἀφεθην
cause to stand	ἱστημι	στη/στα	στησω	ἐστησα	—	—
stand	—	στη/στα	στησομαι	ἐστην	ἐστηκα	ἐσταθην
destroy	ἀπολλυμι	(ἀπο) ολεσ	ἀπολεσω	ἀπωλεσα	—	—
perish	ἀπολλυμαι	(ἀπο) ολο	ἀπολουμαι	ἀπωλομην	ἀπολωλα	—

Index of Greek words

The first entry will normally tell you the basic meaning of the word. Other entries give further developments or discussion. The index covers the words in the word lists and others that are discussed. It does not contain all the words in quoted New Testament verses, nor all the words in lesson 44.

ἀγαθος
28.1,3
ἀγαλλιαω
44.5
ἀγαμος
44.3
ἀγαπαω
11.2
13.1
15.5
30.1
ἀγαπη
11.2
39.1
ἀγγελια
10.7–10
ἀγγελος
10.7
ἁγιαζω
44.1
49.2
ἁγιος
28.2,6
44.1
ἁγιωσυνη
46.4
ἀγορα
47.5
ἀγοραζω
47.5
ἀγω
22.8
36.5
ἀδελφη
11.2

ἀδελφος
11.2
ἀδικεω
40.6
αἱμα
17.5
41.4
αἱρω
9.3
22.1
23.2,6,7
30.1
αἰτεομαι
45.2
αἰτεω
43.4
45.2
αἰων, αἰωνιος
36.2
ἀκαθαρτος
23.2
ἀκοη
32.7
ἀκολουθεω
14.7
40.4
ἀκουω
8.5
19.3
21.5
26.4,7
ἀκρις
45.6
ἀκροβυστια
48.10

ἀλαζονεια
44.10
ἀλαλος
31.4
ἁλας
28.2,9
ἀληθεια
9.7
13.8
35.4
ἀληθης, ἀληθως
3.1–4
35.1
ἁλιευω
36.5
ἀλλα
7.6
ἀλλαχοθεν,
ἀλλαχου
35.5
ἀλληλους
13.7
ἁλλομαι
47.5
ἀλλος
28.2
ἁμαρτανω
23.2
ἁμαρτια
9.7
17.5
ἀμην
14.7
ἀμνος
22.6

ἀν
11.1–3
ἀνα
37.8
44.6
ἀναβαινω
22.4
26.5
50.6
ἀναβλεπω
40.6
ἀναβοαω
50.6
ἀναγγελλομεν
17.5
ἀναγινωσκω
8.5
14.6
21.5
26.5
ἀναζαω
44.6
ἀνακραζω
38.2
ἀναξιος
44.3
ἀναπαυω
44.6
ἀναστρεφω
44.6
ἀναφερω
37.8
ἀνηρ
19.3

297

ἀνθρωπος
7.6
ἀνιστημι
34.1
ἀνοιγω
43.4
ἀνομια
39.1(7)
ἀντι
28.2
39.12
44.6
ἀντιχριστος
44.10
ἀνωθεν
35.5
52.4
ἀξιος
39.1
44.3
ἀπαγγελλω
10.7
23.7
ἀπαξ
35.6
ἀπαρνησασθω
40.5
ἀπειθεια
39.1
ἀπεκριθη
see
  ἀποκρινομαι
ἀπερχομαι
17.3
20.1
ἀπιστος
37.2
ἀπο
17.3
39.2
44.6
ἀποθνησκω
36.2

ἀποκρινομαι
22.3
23.7
27.1
29.2,4
ἀποκτεινω
38.2
ἀπολλυμι
34.1,3,6
44.6
ἀπολυτρωσις
44.2
ἀποστελλω
8.5
14.6(4)
26.5
ἀποστολος
7.6
ἁπτομαι
29.2,6
36.1
ἀπωλεια
39.1
ἀρεσκω
42.1(5)
ἀριστον
51.3
ἀρνεομαι
44.10
ἀρτι
41.7
ἀρτος
24.1
38.4
ἀρχη
3.5
ἀρχιερευς
33.8
ἀρχομαι
18.2,3
29.2
ἀσκος
34.5,6

ἀσπαζομαι
45.2
ἀστυ
44.8
αὐριον
20.4
αὐτη
9.7
αὐτη
9.7
αὐτος
7.1–6
25.1
28.8
ἀφιημι
34.1,3
42.1
βαθυς
47.5
βαινω
see ἀναβαινω,
καταβαινω
βαλλω
18.3
22.1,3
23.1–8
26.1,4
βαπτιζω
15.6
31.1,3,6,7
32.1–3
βαπτισμα
39.1
βαπτιστης
15.6
βασιλεια
9.7
48.10
βασιλευς
9.7
12.7
βιβλιον
12.5

βλασφημεω
28.5
βλεπω
14.7
βοαω
16.6
βρωμα
36.7
βρωσις
44.2
γαρ
12.5
γειτων
40.6
γενεα
37.2
γενετη
38.8
γενναω
27.5
46.7(on
Jn 1.13)
γενος
12.7
γη
9.7
γινομαι
27.5
29.1,4,8
46.7
48.4
γινωσκω
8.5
22.1
44.1
γλωσσα
13.4,8
γονευς
38.8
γραμματευς
33.8
48.10

εὐ	ζωον	θεος (cont.)	ἱμας
44.3	26.2	46.7(on	45.6
εὐαγγελιον	ζφοποιεω	Jn 1.1)	ἱνα
12.5	26.2	52.7	11.1,2,5
37.3(5)	ἡ	θεοσεβης	36.1,5,7
52.7	18.5	41.7	38.6
εὐθυνω	ἠδη	θεραπευω	47.3
46.7(on	31.8	32.4	ἱστημι
Jn 1.23)	ἠλθεν	θεωρεω	34.1,3
εὐθυς	see ἐρχομαι	40.6	ἰσχυρος
35.1	ἡλικια	θηλαζω	45.6
εὐλογεω	41.7	51.6	ἰχθυς
37.3,5	ἡμεις	θησαυρος	31.6
51.7	10.1–4	41.1	καθαπερ
εὑρισκω	ἡμερα	θνησκω	32.7
8.5	9.7	33.3,5	καθαρα
15.5	28.2	θρεμματα	9.1
22.1	ἡμετερος	47.5	καθαριζω
46.7(on	43.4	θρονος	17.5
Jn 1.43,45)	ἠν	7.6	καθημαι
ἐφαπαξ	see εἰμι	θυγατηρ	40.6
39.7	ἠρξατο	48.12	45.2
ἐφη	see ἀρχομαι	ἰατρος	καθως
see φημι	ἠψατο	35.2	22.4
ἐχω	see ἁπτομαι	ἰδε	και
8.5	θαλασσα	22.4	10.7
15.5	23.2	40.2	48.4
19.2	θανατος	ἰδιος	49.4
20.3	36.2	22.8	καινος
26.1,5	θανατοω	28.2,6	28.1,2
30.3	36.2	30.3,5	καιρος
33.3	44.5	46.7(on	33.8–10
ἑωρακα	θαυμαζω	Jn 1.11)	κακος
see ὁραω	26.7	ἰδων	28.1,2
ἑως	θαυμαστος	see ὁραω	καλεω
36.2	41.7	ἱερευς	13.4
ζαω	θελημα	17.3	14.6
26.2	18.3	ἱερον	19.5
30.1	θελω	17.3	καλος
ζητεω	18.3	ἱημι	28.2
13.4	θεος	34.1,3	καλως
ζωη	2.5	ἱλασμος	19.7
26.2	3.1	44.10	28.5

μετα (cont.)
44.6
μεταβαινω
20.9
μετανοεω
40.2
μετανοια
39.1
40.2
μετρεω
48.4
μη
11.2,6
13.8
27.3
34.5
41.1,4
49.1
μηδε
27.1
μηδεις
31.4
μηδεν
31.4
μηδεποτε
35.5
μηκετι
25.4
μητηρ
19.3
μητι
27.3
μισεω
14.6
43.6
μνημειον
26.7
μνημονευω
43.6
μονογενης
30.5
46.7
50.5

μονον
35.3
μωρος
49.4
μωρος
49.5
νεκρος
36.2
νεωτερος
49.5
νηπιος
51.6
νιπτω, νιπτομαι
38.8
45.1,2
νομος
22.8
33.8
νυμφη
28.8
νυμφιος
28.8
νυν
19.7
ὁ, ἡ, το
12.7
19.1,2,5
20.5
23.1
28.2,3,6
30.3
31.7
39.10
ὁδος
41.4
οἰδα
27.1
33.1,2
οἰκια
17.3
οἰκοδομεω
23.7
οἰκος
17.3

οἰνος
34.5,6
ὀκτω
35.6
ὀλιγος
35.3
37.3(6)
ὁλος
13.7
28.2
ὁμοιος, ὁμοιως
35.1
ὀνομα
31.4
ὀπισθεν
35.5
ὀπισω
39.3
ὁπως
36.5,6
ὁραω
22.4,8
24.2
30.1
31.11
40.2
ὀργιζω
50.8
ὀρθος, ὀρθως
35.1
ὁρος
31.4
ὁς, ἡ, ὁ
10.5
11.1–3
12.8
ὁσος
38.2
ὀσφρησις
32.7
ὁτε
27.1

ὁτι
8.4
38.5
οὐ, οὐκ, οὐχ
7.6
11.2
27.3
οὐδε
16.4
οὐδεις
27.5
31.4
οὐδεμια
17.5
οὐδεν
31.4
οὐδεποτε
35.5
οὐκ
see οὐ
οὐκετι
25.4
οὐν
16.4
οὐρανος
7.6
42.5(4)
οὐς, ὠτα
8.6
10.5
32.4
48.3
οὑτος
3.3
7.6,8,9
12.8
οὑτως
28.5
38.1
49.4(3)
οὐχ
see οὐ

303

προαγω
31.8
προβαινω
48.12
προβατον
19.2
προς
2.5,6
17.1,3
36.5(3)
37.5
42.6,8
προσαιτης
40.6
προσευχη
48.3
προσευχομαι
29.2,4,6–8
30.1
48.3
προσκαλεομαι
45.2
προσκυνεω
19.3
προσκυνητης
19.7
προστιθημι
48.4
προσφερω
40.2
προσωπον
45.6
προτερον
40.6
προφασις
43.6
προφητης
4.5
πρωτος
28.2
31.11
35.6

πτυω
38.8
πτωμα
36.4
πυρ
46.7(on
Jn 1.26)
48.8
πωποτε
31.11
πως
27.1
ραντιζω
44.5
ρηγνυμι
34.5
ρημα
49.1
ρυπαρος
40.6
σαββατον,
σαββατα
38.2
σαρξ
30.5
32.4
σεαυτον
16.6
σημειον
36.5
40.6
48.7
52.4
σιτιστος
48.4
σκηνη
28.8
σκηνοω
30.5
46.7(on
Jn 1.14)
σκοτια, σκοτος
13.4

σος
43.4
σοφια, σοφος
49.5
σπειρω
41.4
σπερμα
41.4
46.4
σπλαγχνιζομαι
45.2
50.8
σπορος
41.4
σπουδη
35.4
σταδιον
37.3(6)
39.8
σταυρος,
σταυροω
23.2
στομα
32.4
51.8
στρεφω
42.9
συ
13.4
συκη
22.8
συν
42.2,4
44.6
συναγω
44.6
45.2
συναγωγη
17.3
συντιθημι
41.7
σφραγιζω
40.6

σχισμα
40.6
σωζω
20.1
26.2
30.1
32.3
33.1
σωμα
28.2
32.4
σωτηρ
26.2
σωτηρια
19.7
26.2
ταλαντον
33.3
ταπεινοω
49.5
ταυρος
48.4
ταχιστος,
ταχιστα
35.1
ταχυς, ταχυ
35.1
τεκνιον
12.5
τεκνον
12.5
τεσσαρακοντα
35.6
τεσσαρες
35.6
τετρακοσιοι
35.6
τηρεω
15.6
τιθημι
34.1,3
τιμαω
20.9

This book